More Praise for *The Energetic Brain*

"Creative yet authoritative...Reynolds, Vannest, and Harrison have created an important new work that stands apart from the hundreds of books on this topic. *The Energetic Brain* is a must read for parents, educators, professionals, and adults living with ADHD. This book has moved to number one on my short list of recommended readings for patients and professionals on this topic."
—**Sam Goldstein, PhD,** editor-in-chief, Journal of Attention Disorders

"If you have ADHD or love someone who has ADHD, this practical, reader-friendly book is a must for your bookshelf. At last—science-based explanations of ADHD that are easy to understand and apply to life success. Hats off to Dr. Cecil Reynolds, a true Renaissance Man, and his co-authors."
—**Alan S. Kaufman, PhD,** Clinical Professor of Psychology, Yale University

"Both authoritative and accessible; the authors provide parents with practical tools that are informed by the best science available."
—**Randy Kamphaus,** dean, College of Education, Georgia State University, and Distinguished Research Professor, Counseling and Psychological Services, Georgia State University

"*The Energetic Brain* is practical, easy to understand, and applicable for parents and teachers alike. After reading this book, I feel more confident in my knowledge of ADHD and am better prepared to advocate for my students. I now know what to keep in mind throughout the IEP process, and understand how the ADHD

brain works. This is a must read for all who want a greater understanding of ADHD."
—**Lauren Williams,** parent and special education teacher, Bryan, Texas

"*The Energetic Brain* is one of the few books on ADHD that captures the interface between behavioral and academic concerns, and provides useful suggestions for both teachers and parents."
—**Cynthia A. Riccio, PhD,** professor, Texas A&M University

THE ENERGETIC BRAIN

THE ENERGETIC BRAIN

Understanding and Managing ADHD

Cecil R. Reynolds, Kimberly J. Vannest,
Judith R. Harrison

Foreword by Sally Shaywitz

JOSSEY-BASS
A Wiley Imprint
www.josseybass.com

Published by Jossey-Bass
A Wiley Imprint
One Montgomery Street, Suite 1200, San Francisco, CA 94104-4594—www.josseybass.com

Jossey-Bass books and products are available through most bookstores. To contact Jossey-Bass directly call our Customer Care Department within the U.S. at 800-956-7739, outside the U.S. at 317-572-3986, or fax 317-572-4002.

Wiley publishes in a variety of print and electronic formats and by print-on-demand. Some material included with standard print versions of this book may not be included in e-books or in print-on-demand. If this book refers to media such as a CD or DVD that is not included in the version you purchased, you may download this material at **http://booksupport.wiley.com**. For more information about Wiley products, visit **www.wiley.com**.

Library of Congress Cataloging-in-Publication Data

Reynolds, Cecil R., 1952–
    The energetic brain : understanding and managing ADHD / Cecil R. Reynolds, Kimberly J. Vannest, Judith R. Harrison ; foreword by Sally Shaywitz. – 1
        p. cm.
    Includes bibliographical references and index.
    ISBN 978-0-470-61516-4 (pbk.), ISBN 978-1-118-16514-0 (ebk.),
978-1-118-16515-7 (ebk.), 978-1-118-16516-4 (ebk.)
    1. Attention-deficit hyperactivity disorder.   I. Vannest, Kimberly J., 1967–   II. Harrison,
Judith R., 1962–   III. Title.
    RJ506.H9R49   2012
    616.85'89–dc23
2011038826

Printed in the United States of America
FIRST EDITION
PB Printing   10   9   8   7   6   5   4   3   2   1

CONTENTS

ACKNOWLEDGMENTS

We wish to thank all of our families, colleagues, and friends who have supported us endlessly throughout this process and specifically Lauren Williams, who dropped everything and worked long hours, often with short notice, pulling together a glossary and locating references. To our many mentors who taught us so much about science as well as how to be good clinicians, including Larry Hartlage, Alan Kaufman, Steven Evans, Ken Denny, Jim Kauffman, Tim Landrum, Rich Parker, Bruce Thompson (and Judith Harrison would like to note that she includes her coauthors Cecil Reynolds and Kimberly Vannest in this esteemed group): know that we never tire of expressing our gratitude for your guidance and the examples you have set for us. Additional acknowledgments are due to the friends and family who inadvertently provided us the living examples that appear throughout this book. In addition, we want to thank Marjorie McAneny for her patience, support, and guidance throughout the process as well as her acceptance of our approach to this work, along with her support staff at Jossey-Bass/Wiley. Having written so many graduate-level textbooks, we could not have succeeded in writing an intelligible book for those with ADHD and their families and friends without her commentary and advice. To Sally Shaywitz we express our sincere gratitude for taking time away from her many demanding clinical and research pursuits as well as her family to write a foreword to our book.

Cecil R. Reynolds, PhD, is currently an Emeritus Professor of Educational Psychology, Professor of Neuroscience, and Distinguished Research Scholar at Texas A&M University. A leading authority in the field of school psychology, Reynolds is the author or editor of more than fifty books, including *The Handbook of School Psychology* and the *Encyclopedia of Special Education* in addition to many textbooks in neuropsychology. He is also the author of several of the most widely used tests of personality and behavior including the BASC (*Behavior Assessment System for Children*) and the *Revised Children's Manifest Anxiety Scale*. He is also senior author of the *Test of Memory and Learning*, the *School Motivation and Learning Strategies Inventory*, and coauthor of several computerized test interpretation systems. He is senior author of the *Reynolds Intellectual Assessment Scales* (RIAS).

Dr. Reynolds maintained a clinical practice treating trauma victims and individuals with traumatic brain injury (TBI) for twenty-five years before retiring from clinical work at the end of 2003. He has served on the editorial boards of many notable scientific journals including *School Psychology Quarterly*, *Journal of Special Education*, and *Psychological Assessment*, of which he is currently editor-in-chief. Previously, he served as editor-in-chief of *Archives of Clinical Neuropsychology* and *Applied Neuropsychology*. Reynolds is the recipient of numerous national awards including the Lightner Witmer Award. In 2000, he received the National Academy of Neuropsychology's Distinguished Clinical Neuropsychologist Award, the Academy's highest award for research accomplishments. His service to the profession and to society has been recognized as well through the President's Gold Medal for Service to the National Academy of Neuropsychology as well as the Academy's Distinguished Service Award, and the University of North Carolina at Wilmington 50th Anniversary Razor Walker Award for Service to the Youth of North Carolina. In 2010, he received the Jack I. Bardon Award for Lifetime Distinguished Service Contributions to school psychology.

Kimberly J. Vannest, PhD, is a noted researcher and teacher in the area of interventions for students with and at risk of emotional and behavioral disorders, progress monitoring, and single case research design. She is the author of five books including the *BASC-2 Intervention Guide*, more than forty-five peer reviewed journal publications, and five software programs for academic and behavioral progress monitoring. A former high school teacher in North San Diego County, California, she earned her PhD at Louisiana State University and worked for the Governor's office on K–12 school reform and as a state trainer in Positive Behavioral Support. Dr. Vannest has earned the Montague Scholar Center for Excellence in Teaching Award, is a Regents Fellow for her scholarship, and was named the outstanding new faculty member at Texas A&M University where she is now an associate professor in the Special Education Program, in the Department of Educational Psychology.

Judith R. Harrison, PhD, is currently a clinical research scientist for the Center for Intervention Research in Schools (CIRS) and the Center for Adolescent Research in Schools (CARS) at Ohio University. She has published several peer-reviewed articles on behaviors demonstrated by children and adolescents, behaviors that discriminate youth with ADHD from those without, and interventions for youth with emotional and behavioral disorders (EBD) and ADHD. Dr. Harrison's research interests include effectiveness, feasibility, and teacher acceptability of school-based strategies for EBD and ADHD. Dr. Harrison is a licensed professional counselor and a certified teacher in the state of Texas. She has taught and counseled students in elementary and secondary schools for over twenty years.

From us all: To all of the families, children, adolescents, and adults with ADHD who have taught us so much as we have worked with them in so many different capacities over the years. Thank you.

CRR: To Julia always, for always

KV: To Jack, Peyton, & Owen

JH: To my children, Clint, James, Alana, and Emma, my daughter-in-law, Cassidy, my grandchildren, Campbell and Cannon, and all of those yet to come. May you flourish in your strengths and embrace your challenges.

FOREWORD

In the almost century and a half since Dr. Heinrich Hoffman described young Fidgety Phil who couldn't sit still, but rather "wriggled and giggled, and then I declare, Swung backward and forward and tilted his chair," the symptoms characterizing what we now term attention-deficit hyperactivity disorder, or ADHD, have remained rather constant. Although the behaviors described in 1865 continue to be readily recognizable in ADHD children today, our fundamental understanding of ADHD, particularly the appreciation of its neural basis, has undergone a revolution.

As a result of this remarkable scientific progress in elucidating the neural underpinnings of the core behaviors characteristic of ADHD, we can now approach the disorder with the same degree of rigor associated with other important conditions that have an impact on the health and well-being of children and adults. Most critically, this new knowledge has transformed our entire approach to those who have ADHD from one based on anecdote and myth to one that reflects exacting scientific evidence and uses data-driven interventions to manage the disorder.

Contrary to what often appears in the popular press, ADHD is not an example of children who want to behave badly or who don't want to learn, or parents who have somehow been derelict and let down their children; no, ADHD is a brain-based disorder related to the self-regulation of behavior and, in fact, a result of an "energetic brain" at that. This is the well-founded and strongly supported contention of renowned authority in school psychology and neuroscientist Cecil R. Reynolds and his noteworthy collaborators, researcher and teacher Kimberly J. Vannest and researcher and counselor Judith R. Harrison, in *The Energetic Brain*.

The Energetic Brain is a gift to parents, educators, and all those who know and care about a child or an adult with ADHD. Above all else, this trio of experts is both knowledgeable and caring—about the science and about the actual sufferer. Often articles or books about a disorder are written by scientists who study the entity and are able to share small interesting bits of minutiae about the subject, but appear never to have met an actual person who has the disorder and, as a consequence, do not understand from either a personal or practical sense what it means to the person with the disorder. Such scientific writings appear to focus on the parts but, at the same time, miss the integrated whole in the real person. In contrast, well-meaning advocates who have intimate knowledge of the actuality of a disorder will give practical advice but lack the scientific expertise and authority to back up their advice. Here, in *The Energetic Brain*, the reader is able to benefit from the authors' collective expertise in neuroscience, psychology, education, and behavior as well as their deeply grounded experience as clinician, teacher, and counselor, respectively. In addition, as they indicate in reference to ADHD, "Two of the authors of this book admittedly have it, and the third is in denial." As a consequence, the book is a compendium of guidelines and advice based on the authors' up-to-date scientific knowledge and real-life clinical experience advising children and adults who have ADHD and on their personal experience living with ADHD.

This book essentially clears the fog so often surrounding ADHD and provides a clear, scientifically based, and practical step-by-step guide to the disorder's successful management, primarily in children and adolescents but also touching on issues relevant to adults. Written in a style that is easygoing, accessible, kind, and hopeful, *The Energetic Brain* provides grounded, down-to-earth, scientifically sound advice on virtually every aspect of ADHD important to those who are affected and their families.

As a physician and neuroscientist, I was especially heartened by the focus on, description, and interpretation of the neurobiology underlying ADHD. This knowledge is empowering to parents and educators, who are often overwhelmed by a dizzying array of symptoms and frequently conflicting advice on where to begin and what is the right course of action. *The Energetic Brain* presents the scientific evidence and sensibly concludes that "ADHD is truly a disorder of the brain, the organ that controls behavior." Beginning with a clear description ("Brain 101") of brain architecture and messaging systems, and continuing with a discussion of the specific structural (right prefrontal) pathways, and the neurotransmitters (dopamine and norepinephrine) and their roles in modulating behavior, *The Energetic Brain* helps the reader to understand how ADHD is not only brain-based, but also reflects an energetic brain.

Data based on both structural and functional studies of the brain suggest that the brains of individuals with ADHD differ from those who do not have ADHD. In ADHD, there appears to be less density of neurons in the prefrontal regions responsible for initiating and organizing behavior and for inhibiting behavior that is inappropriate, essentially the "point of coordination of the executive system of the brain—the brain's coordination and decision-making system"—the system responsible for self-regulation of behavior. Furthermore, these prefrontal regions house receptor sites for the neurotransmitters that play a major role in self-regulation or control of behavior. Evidence points to "an imbalance in the levels" or perhaps the utilization of the neurotransmitters dopamine and norepinephrine. Thus, this confluence of abnormalities in both structure and function of the brain pathways and the neurotransmitters responsible for regulating behavior is at the root of the difficulties characterizing ADHD. As the authors point out, the importance of understanding the brain basis of ADHD difficulties is that this knowledge takes "the blame away," allowing the focus to be on "what to do to help the child."

Children affected by ADHD present difficulties with inattention, hyperactivity, and impulsivity because those systems in the brain responsible for regulating attention, motor behavior, and decision making are not working as they should be. The challenge: what can be done to help these brain systems function more actively and appropriately? And this, as *The Energetic Brain* explains, is precisely the role of medications, stimulants such as methylphenidate (Ritalin) or mixed amphetamine salts (Adderall), and norephinephrine reuptake inhibitors such as atomoxetine (Strattera). These medications result in more normal levels of neurotransmitters which, in turn, increase arousal of brain systems responsible for modulating behavior. In other words, through the action of these medications, the person gains more control over his or her behavior so that he or she can inhibit inappropriate speech or motor behaviors, pay better attention, and be more in tune with signals and messages emanating from the environment. To be able to do so gives a person affected by ADHD more control over his or her behavior rather than being at the mercy of a much too energetic brain that is overwhelming him or her with barrages of different messages. The fog dissipates and it becomes clear, first, that modulating the child's behavior is not just a matter of will—the child cannot will the brain to produce more of the needed neurotransmitters—and second, that just as choosing to use medicine to treat

ADHD has consequences, electing not to use medication has consequences as well. Understanding ADHD at the level of the brain clears away both the confusion and guilt, helping readers to make intelligent decisions about treatment and evaluate more clearly the issues affecting those with ADHD.

Empowering the reader with a clear understanding of the neurobiological basis of ADHD, the authors then gently guide us through the maze of treatment options such as choice of medication, including actions and side effects, and provide evidence for the lack of relationship of treatment with stimulants to later substance abuse, alcohol abuse, or smoking in adulthood.

The authors, too, stress that effective management of ADHD is not only about medication and explain the need for multimodal treatment. As they state, "Medication can create a more normal operating state for the brain but it will not teach reading or math, and medication will not undo bad habits if bad habits and ineffective or problematic coping strategies were learned, and medication will not create new social skills."

Throughout, the authors emphasize the power of knowledge and awareness to prevent problems. They stress the importance of early and accurate diagnosis, the value of informed decisions based on scientific findings rather than fears or myths, while also strongly encouraging parents and educators to take advantage of the child's strengths—the energy, passion, focus, exuberance—to help gain control of his or her energetic, highly charged brain and rein in the out-of-control negative behaviors. Families with a child with ADHD will recognize their child and themselves and, most important, find doable and effective strategies to ensure that their child's strengths will be recognized and called into play to ensure a positive outcome.

That the authors are astute and caring clinicians is evident throughout; I particularly appreciate their insightful discussion of the Continuous Performance Test (CPT), noting that this test, once considered an important measure in the diagnosis of ADHD, takes place in the isolated quiet setting of a laboratory rather than the real-world tumult of the classroom or workplace where distractions are constantly assaulting the person. As a result, they wisely caution that a person with ADHD could perform well in such an artificial setting, leading to an incorrect diagnosis.

Above all, this book is not only scientifically rigorous, it is optimistic and positive in its well-thought-out discussions of each of the different components of a multimodal treatment plan. Recognizing that ADHD affects so many areas of life— parents and family; school and classroom behavior; learning and academics; peer relations and social life; and work—there are clear explanations of options available to improve each area. Always the focus is on the positive, whether in discussing parent-child interactions or what goes on at school. The authors emphasize affection, positive attention, and affirmation, reminding parents that parenting is truly a skill, and a skill that they can learn. In the same vein, there is a heartening discussion of schoolwide programs focused on positive behavioral intervention and support (PBIS). In PBIS the goal is preventative and proactive problem solving emphasizing teaching positive, appropriate behavior rather than resorting to punishment. I was interested to learn that Zero Tolerance policies, when examined, prove to be ineffective.

Parents and educators will benefit from explanations of the different tools available to help mitigate the negative effects of ADHD. For example, in addition to the use of medications to address the neurobiological origins of the difficulties, interventions such as social skills training help the child with ADHD to learn new behaviors to replace the old problematic ones that rupture friendships. Here the focus is on changing the external antecedents and consequences. Alternatively, to help adolescents and adults cope with the impact of ADHD, cognitive behavioral strategies work to replace negative, often destructive, thought processes with new, more positive adaptive patterns.

Among the many useful classroom strategies, I was particularly impressed by the simple, step-by-step example of note taking, which without question would help virtually all students with ADHD. Reading *The Energetic Brain* is like having a knowledgeable, wise friend who understands what you are going through and, what's more, knows how to help you in an unassuming manner. At the end, you let out a sigh of relief and are so pleased that you now understand and know exactly how to cope with ADHD in order to achieve a positive outcome for your child, your student, or yourself.

Sally E. Shaywitz, M.D.
Co-Director, Yale Center for Dyslexia & Creativity
Author, *Overcoming Dyslexia*

PREFACE

Attention-deficit hyperactivity disorder, known more popularly as ADHD, is present at all levels of society. Doctors have it. Lawyers have it. Scientists, airline pilots, politicians, members of the armed services, teachers, grocery clerks, homemakers, salesmen, mechanics, cab drivers, and barbers all have it. Name an area of employment at any socioeconomic level and we can assure you, there are cases of ADHD present. Two of the authors of this book admittedly have it, and the third is in denial. It respects no vocation, no social class, and no boundaries. Most people with ADHD have thriving employment careers, some become successful celebrities and artists, some are professional athletes, and yes, as in all facets of society, some individuals with ADHD engage in criminal activity, develop substance abuse issues, experience many job changes, unemployment, and have continued difficulties with relationships. This is a book about how to understand and manage ADHD to maximize your own life success or that of someone you know who has ADHD.

This book is about the truth about energetic brains! It has been said that having ADHD is like having a Ferrari engine equipped with bicycle brakes. All brains are energetic but most have high-quality, heavy-duty brakes; in the case of the ADHD brain, the brakes are malfunctioning. Although we like this analogy, we find it incomplete. Most brains also have high-energy, power-assisted steering that directs attention and keeps us on the right track. In the ADHD brain, not only are the brakes inconsistent, but the steering is also sometimes awry. In *The Energetic Brain* we discuss how to understand and develop the proper "braking system" for the ADHD brain, knowing when to apply brakes and when to let the brain run, and, how to steer the energetic brain more effectively to maximize successful life experiences.

Controversy about ADHD is everywhere. In the popular media, throughout the Internet, and even on professional and medical listservs there are often questions as well as accusations about the existence of ADHD. Some go so far as to argue it is a made-up disorder, born of conspiracy among "big pharma," psychiatry, and other mental health professions in order to pad their executives' pockets. Some argue that we are placing our children in chemical restraints through medicinal treatment of ADHD. Some offer simple cures: if you will only buy their vitamin and supplement plan, subscribe to their diet, or simply reduce sugar intake, all will be well. In *The Energetic Brain* we address these controversies head on.

The truth is that ADHD is real. It was known and recognized long before drug companies existed, before psychiatry was a profession, albeit under different names and descriptions. ADHD exists, and it is a brain disorder. ADHD exists in varying degrees of severity as do most disorders or illnesses. However, it need not impose any permanent limitations on those who have it. It can be managed, treated, and although not "cured" in the classic sense of the term, individuals with ADHD who are correctly diagnosed and treated can be just as successful in school, work, and in social and recreational settings as they would have been without ADHD—and some even more so. They can have successful adult relationships and be good, loving, competent partners and parents.

ADHD is also overdiagnosed. We think much of the public controversy over this disorder stems largely from inadequate, briefly determined diagnoses and misdiagnoses of ADHD in people, especially children, who actually have other disorders that should be treated differently, but which on the surface look a lot like ADHD.

Among the many topics we cover in this book are: what ADHD is; what it isn't; how ADHD is best treated and managed; why it is so often incorrectly diagnosed; how diagnosis should be done; the controversies surrounding ADHD diagnosis and treatment; solving the learning and social problems of individuals with ADHD; and how ADHD is seen under the Americans with Disabilities Act (ADA) and "Section 504" of the Vocational Rehabilitation Amendments of 1973, which grant individuals with ADHD certain additional rights in educational and vocational settings.

Our aim in writing *The Energetic Brain* is to arm you with real information—not faddish approaches to ADHD, but information steeped in real science, primarily the neurosciences, the psychological and cognitive sciences, and the education sciences—all tempered and interpreted in the context of our own decades of experience as clinical practitioners, teachers, and counselors. We do not offer a cure where there is none, and we also do not pretend that any of this is easy or a "quick fix." Instead, we provide information that will lead to better understanding and decision making, whether you are the parent of a child with ADHD, an educator, a clinician, or you have an ADHD diagnosis yourself. We offer you knowledge of the legal rights associated with ADHD. We also give you proven skills to manage the energetic brain proficiently and to use its positive attributes to promote success in all aspects of life.

In the pages to follow, we address these facts and issues surrounding the energetic brains of individuals with ADHD in understandable terms from the standpoint of the sciences, of classroom and related learning environments, and of behavioral research. We hope this information will improve the quality of the journey that is life for all who have ADHD, their families, and their loved ones.

Cecil R. Reynolds
Kimberly J. Vannest
Judith R. Harrison
May 2011

THE ENERGETIC BRAIN

Getting to Know ADHD

1

What Is ADHD?

ADHD is real. It exists, and it is a brain disorder. ADHD appears in varying degrees of severity as do most disorders or illnesses. However, it need not impose any permanent limitations on anyone who has it. ADHD can be managed and treated, and although they cannot be "cured" in the classic sense of the term, individuals with ADHD who are correctly diagnosed and treated can be just as successful in school, work, and in social and recreational settings as they could be without ADHD. In fact, many people find that ADHD leads them to discover and apply personal strengths to make them even more successful in life! However, a great deal of misinformation and non-truths about the reality of ADHD as a disorder exist.

In preparing to write this work and out of curiosity about what information is available to the public, we Googled the simple term "ADHD" and received over 15,000,000 hits. (Googling just the one medicine name "Ritalin" produced another 500,000-plus hits.) That is a huge amount. We sampled several hundred of the sites located, and were not at all surprised to see extreme positions represented and great diversity in the quality and type of information available. Websites that discuss ADHD are no different from most other web-based information.

The simultaneous blessing and curse of the Internet is that anyone can put up a website professing expertise and presenting opinion as knowledge. The many websites we visited ranged from those providing clear guidance and information to the public (such as medical schools, government agencies, the National Institutes of Health, and well-known scientific or professional societies such as the American Medical Association) to others providing clear and trustworthy information for mental health professionals (such as professional clinics, private and community health providers), to other sites sponsored by organizations that appear to believe ADHD is a fraud being imposed upon unsuspecting parents. We found sites developed by individuals with a self-proclaimed diagnosis of ADHD, including blogs about the impact of ADHD on their lives and a variety of treatment approaches, some rather miraculous in their claims. Other sites profess the ability to diagnose ADHD accurately in "two minutes or less."

The controversies and complications in understanding ADHD at both the child and the adult levels are quickly recognized in such a web search; however, though it is often said the most important questions is whether ADHD is real or not, the real "hot button" issue is the use of stimulant medication with children. Many myths exist regarding ADHD (see Table 1.1). The use of medication (particularly in children) evokes emotion in many and has even led to conspiracy theories—one being that the professional organizations and the large drug companies (sometimes derisively referred to as "big pharma") have joined together to create the "myth" of the existence of ADHD as a moneymaking scheme. While a wide range of views on the topic is expected on public forums, it may surprise you to learn that some disagreement also occurs in the professional realm as well, although one might not expect to find such a range of views and representations among professional mental health practitioners and agencies.

Table 1.1: Myths and Facts.

Myth	Fact
Children are hyperactive because their parents do not make them behave.	Parenting styles do not cause hyperactivity.
Children outgrow ADHD. Adults cannot have ADHD.	ADHD lasts a lifetime for some individuals.
Teachers just want children medicated so that they do not have to do their job.	ADHD is a biological disorder with primary symptoms of inattention, hyperactivity, and impulsivity.
Hyperactivity is just "boys being boys."	
Doctors prescribe medication for ADHD just to make money.	
ADHD was created by drug companies to sell medication.	
Children and adolescents use ADHD as an excuse to not do work at school.	
Children and adolescents do not have ADHD; they are just lazy.	
Parents just want to say that their children have ADHD so that they can get accommodations at school.	
All you have to do is tell a physician that your child has ADHD to get some medication.	Physicians have an ethical and legal obligation to only prescribe medication as indicated.
Girls cannot have ADHD.	Girls are less frequently diagnosed, but can have ADHD.
Giving your child medication can cause them to use illegal drugs as adolescents.	Adolescents with ADHD are at an increased risk of illegal substance use, but this is due to impulsivity and risk-taking behavior, not because they have had prescribed medication.
Children with ADHD never grow up to be successful adults.	Many successful adults have ADHD.

Most if not every professional organization uses web-based communication forums. The authors of this text are members of many professional organizations of psychologists, physicians, other health care providers, teachers, and those in related professional specialties. In these organizations' communication forums such as listservs, chat rooms, and blogs, we also see tirades aimed at the pharmaceutical industry for perpetuating "the myth of ADHD." Comments are made chastising psychologists and physicians for continuing to diagnose this disorder and propagating this myth among the lay population. These declamations seem to correspond with or immediately follow newspaper articles regarding the conduct of drug companies, publicity surrounding some tragedy of a young person being treated with medication for mood or behavior, a story about incompetent diagnosis, or even coverage of research on the diagnosis and intervention of ADHD.

A few school districts have been "caught" providing biased and non-scientifically based information as well. Just several years ago, one public school district sent home a letter to all parents in the district criticizing the use of psychopharmacological treatments with children (specifically for ADHD and autism) and recommending that parents not follow the recommendations of their pediatricians, psychiatrists, or psychologists. This letter accused these professionals of "falsely labeling youth with the psychiatric diagnosis of ADHD" and placing children (anyone under 18 years of age) on medication as a means of intervention; however, the letter includes no real discussion or qualification of the issues. We would direct readers to the wealth of objective scientific literature regarding the etiology and treatment of ADHD in children, and we ask that those who hold the belief a priori that ADHD is a disorder created by drug companies and mental health professionals for profit try to approach this research literature with an open mind. We find no conclusion other than that ADHD is a real disorder that, when unrecognized, untreated, or mistreated, has severe consequences for many individuals; and, though not in every case, for many (about 30–40%), it is a lifelong experience.

The U.S. Surgeon General, the American Medical Association, the American Psychiatric Association, the American Academy of Child and Adolescent Psychiatry, the American Psychological Association, and the American Academy of Pediatrics, among others, all recognize ADHD as a real disorder and one that necessitates accurate diagnosis and treatment by appropriately licensed, certified, and trained professionals. In 2002 more than 85 leading scientists from around the world who study childhood psychopathology issued a consensus statement on ADHD as well, concluding that it was indeed a real disorder. Their statement first emphasizes that ADHD does exist worldwide, and not just in western societies (as some critics claim in support of it being a made-up disorder). Just as we have concluded that ADHD is real from our own review and our own peer-reviewed scientific work in the behavioral and brain sciences, these scientists from around the world concluded: "We cannot overemphasize the point that, as a matter of science, the notion that ADHD does not exist is simply wrong. All of the major medical associations and government health agencies recognize ADHD as a genuine disorder because the scientific evidence indicating it is so overwhelming."[1] You can read this brief but sensible, direct consensus statement at: http://www.russellbarkley.org/adhd-consensus.htm. You will also see on Dr. Barkley's website, where this page appears, a list of links to good sources about ADHD. We respect and recommend these sources.

LEGITIMATE CONCERNS EXIST

Nevertheless, legitimate concerns about ADHD diagnosis do exist, just as they do with any mental health disorder, and should not be dismissed by professionals in practice or by those who research this disorder. In the case of any disorder requiring medication, the potential for abuse is present. For example, college students may seek stimulant medication to help them study or student scholarship athletes may find temporary benefits to their endurance and focus in medications prescribed to individuals with ADHD. In addition, some individuals who may not have appropriate symptoms seek a diagnosis for other gain, such as to receive ADA accommodations at work or disability qualifications for supplemental income or educational support, to improve their ability to work night shifts, or simply to concentrate better or work longer hours on the job. Such behavior is abhorrent at all levels and does much damage.

In addition, ADHD may be overdiagnosed or incorrectly diagnosed, creating controversy in the minds of the public and in a very small group of medical and mental health professionals. We propose that the public controversies over ADHD largely stem from inadequate diagnosis and misdiagnosis of ADHD, especially in children who actually have other disorders that should be treated differently, but which on the surface look a lot like ADHD.

In this book, you will find factual information about ADHD: what it is and what it is not; how it is best treated and managed; why it is so often incorrectly diagnosed; how diagnosis should be made; the controversies of diagnosis and treatment; solving the learning and social problems of individuals with ADHD; and how ADHD is seen under the Americans with Disabilities Act (ADA) and section 504 of the Vocational Rehabilitation Amendments of 1973, which grant individuals with ADHD certain rights.

WHAT YOU WILL FIND IN THIS BOOK

In the chapters to follow, we will address truths and issues in understandable terms from the standpoint of a neuropsychologist, a teacher, and a counselor. We will talk about the symptoms, identification, and suspected causes of ADHD. We will describe strategies and treatments that can help you cope with the challenges associated with ADHD, tap into the creativity and energy that often comes with ADHD, and achieve success. Educational issues and problems encountered in the classroom and how these can be addressed are dealt with in detail, in addition to issues related to work, vocational training, and employment. These aspects of the lives of persons with ADHD are especially important due to their impact on successful pursuit of life, liberty, and happiness, including relationships with others and creating a loving family, but also because the symptoms of ADHD are the most notable in more structured settings like schools, classrooms, and workplaces. We want to help you sort through the myriad of opinions and controversies about ADHD and the unscientific information. We use real-life illustrations and stories throughout the book. Unlike some of the information you may have learned from a textbook or gathered from the Internet, this book will provide factual and trustworthy information with concrete examples to make the information clear and enjoyable to read.

ADHD AND YOU

We appreciate the importance you place on the topic of ADHD. Your interest may be personal or professional. Perhaps you or someone you care about has a diagnosis of ADHD. Perhaps you suspect that a friend, family member, or even you yourself may have ADHD. You might be a professional who works with individuals with ADHD such as a counselor, teacher, or doctor and you would like to know more about the disorder and strategies to help such people have successful lives.

If your interest is personal, you may be one of the 3–6% of individuals in the United States diagnosed with ADHD or suspected of having ADHD, or you may have a child, spouse, friend, or colleague with the disorder or with symptoms of the disorder. Rest assured that ADHD is a common but livable disorder. An ADHD diagnosis does not equate with a diagnosis of failure; indeed, individuals who show symptoms of ADHD can ultimately achieve greatness as many have. Famous people like Terry Bradshaw (quarterback), Paul Orfalea (founder of Kinko's), Ty Pennington (host of *Extreme Makeover: Home Edition* as well as a noted philanthropist), Woody Harrelson (actor), and countless others have publicly acknowledged their ADHD diagnoses. This book is designed to take you from wherever you are now—whether you suspect ADHD in yourself or others or simply desire to understand ADHD—to learning about ADHD and beyond.

You will master skills to make you more effective in your life or in fostering the lives of those you love who may have ADHD.

WHAT IS ADHD?

We have established that ADHD is real, but what is it? ADHD is defined as a neurobiological, or brain-based disorder related to the self-regulation of behavior. ADHD is characterized by hyperactivity, inattention, distractibility, and impulsivity that affects the cognitive, academic, behavioral, social, and developmental functioning of children, adolescents, and adults.[2] In the following sections we characterize ADHD as: (1) associated with deficits in self-regulation, hyper-

From the Teacher

Why is it important to understand that ADHD is real? When my students have a "name" for ADHD they seem to no longer wonder why they struggle in ways their peers do not. Although you might think that a diagnosis would make a child feel bad—I haven't seen it work that way. Instead, a light and a spark returns to a child who previously appeared to be losing self-confidence. The child will say things like "that is my ADHD" or "I am like this because I have ADHD." The "name" gives a reason to a child who has been trying so hard to do what a teacher asks and has been unsuccessful. Now they know "why" and that "why" seems to bring relief.

activity, inattention, and impulsivity; (2) consisting of four subtypes; (3) a diagnosable condition consisting of six decisions; (4) biological; and (5) a common behavioral disorder for children, adolescents, and adults.

ADHD is associated with deficits in self-regulation, hyperactivity, inattention, distractibility, and impulsivity (see Table 1.2).

Table 1.2: Some Definitions You Will Want to Keep in Mind.

Term	Definition
Self-regulation	The exercise of control over our voluntary actions and behavior including impulse control, directing attention, delaying gratification, raising and lowering our level of voluntary arousal, and controlling our mood. In practicing self-regulation, the executive system of the brain mediates our thoughts and actions and decides which should be expressed to the outside world.
Hyperactivity	Behaving at an excessive rate relative to what is required in the current circumstances. Excessive restlessness and movement in general are quite common expressions of hyperactivity. Usually hyperactivity refers to behavior observable by others but at times can refer to hyperactive thought patterns, (having too many ideas too quickly).
Inattention	Difficulty or an absence of the ability to direct attention or regard to a desired object or event in your immediate environment; also, difficulty determining that attention is required or best directed to a particular object or event.
Distractibility	An inability to resist moving attention from one object or event to another too rapidly and inappropriately, to the extent that it disrupts concentration; being constantly drawn to attend to many different competing objects or events in the immediate vicinity and being unable to discern which are the most important.
Impulsivity	Classically, impulsivity reflects acting overtly without giving due consideration or thought to the consequences of the act. Simply put, acting (including speaking) without thinking. You may have heard the comment in reference to an inappropriate quip, "He put his mouth in gear before his brain." This would represent impulsivity.

Self-regulation is a major task of what is called the executive system of the brain, and its failure to function properly is the key to understanding ADHD. The brain is quite an energetic organ, constantly generating thoughts and potential actions; the executive system is largely responsible for evaluating the appropriateness of these potential behaviors for the immediate circumstances and mediating expression of these thoughts and actions.

The brain regulates behavior in many ways. Most prominent in the executive system is the process of monitoring and controlling our immediate actions, sometimes based on what we have learned in the past about good decision making, and sometimes from the immediate feedback we receive from the world around us—much like the filter that keeps adults from saying things out loud in situations where children might blurt out what they are thinking. Children with poor self-regulation disrupt an entire classroom. They are often impulsive, hypersensitive to transitions, and tend to overreact to minor challenges or stressors. Self-regulation is the brain activity that keeps mature adults from grabbing at a plate of cookies that passes by, an option that young children seldom exercise in such an instance. You have seen many young children who simply cannot wait for something they want—it is always now, now, now—and when denied by others they respond emo-

From the Counselor

Understanding the reality of ADHD helps *everyone* assist individuals with ADHD to lead successful lives. The controversy that surrounds the issue only prolongs the beginning of treatment. I have listened to parents, teachers, and other professionals debate the issue at length. Should the child be on medication? Should the child be given modifications for assignments? Should the child be "taught" to do things, such as organize his materials, when other children do not receive the same instruction? These debates only hurt the child or adolescent by lengthening the amount of time that the individual goes without treatment and needed supports.

tionally and do not modulate or self-regulate their emotional responses.

Sometimes **hyperactivity** is also present. If you are a parent of a young child with ADHD, you are probably very familiar with hyperactivity. Individuals with ADHD who are hyperactive constantly appear to be restless, demonstrating this through such activities as pencil tapping or jumpiness, or simply have an overabundance of energy. Clinicians often note that the parents of ADHD children make such comments as "It seems like he is driven by an engine that is always running."

People with ADHD may have extreme difficulty with **inattention** or focusing on one task or may even be so **distractible** and **inattentive** to the demands of their environment that they work on the wrong tasks.

Not everyone with ADHD acts just the same way. Most persons with ADHD have problems with self-regulation, hyperactivity, inattention, distractibility, and impulsivity. However, the prominence or degree of each of these issues varies greatly from person to person and also tends to shift with age. For example, although impulsivity is common to nearly everyone with ADHD, children are more likely than adults (and boys more so than girls) to be hyperactive, whereas adults are more likely to have issues controlling attention. Because not everyone has the same symptoms, ADHD is divided into four subtypes according to which symptoms are most prominent. We will examine these four subtypes in the following section.

ADHD Consists of Four Subtypes

Because every individual is unique, ADHD can look and behave a little or a lot differently for each person. Not every person with ADHD will have every symptom, nor will any symptom be present to an equal degree with others. In fact, ADHD is not just one disorder. There are actually four subtypes of ADHD. Each helps us recognize and understand the specific behaviors related to ADHD that are demonstrated by the individual, although nearly all persons with ADHD will have problems of varying degrees with inattention, hyperactivity, and impulse control (see Table 1.3). Getting the diagnosis right is crucial to getting the treatment right! How this is accomplished is the topic of Chapter Four.

Table 1.3: Types of ADHD.

ADHD-Combined type or ADHD-C	Individuals with ADHD-C demonstrate behaviors associated with both hyperactivity and inattention-impulsivity
ADHD-Predominantly Inattentive or ADHD-PI	Individuals with ADHD-PI have problems accentuated by inattention.
ADHD-Predominantly Hyperactive-Impulsive or ADHD PH-I	Individuals with ADHD-PHI have the most difficulties with hyperactive and impulsive behaviors.
ADHD-Not Otherwise Specified or ADHD-NOS	Physicians, psychologists, and psychiatrists assign a diagnosis of ADHD-NOS when individuals have "prominent symptoms of inattention or hyperactivity-impulsivity that do not meet criteria for ADHD."[3] Basically, this category is used when the diagnosing clinician is absolutely convinced that although an insufficient number of the diagnostic criteria are present, ADHD is present, and the severity of the existing symptoms are extraordinary and warrant a diagnosis.

ADHD Is a Diagnosable Condition Involving Six Decisions

People who diagnose ADHD are typically medical doctors or clinically trained psychologists. A parent, teacher, or school counselor cannot diagnose mental disorders, but they do provide important information. When a diagnosis of ADHD (or any other mental disorder) is being considered, the most common practice in the United States is to follow the diagnostic criteria prescribed by the American Psychiatric Association's *Diagnostic and Statistical Manual of Mental Disorders* (known most often by its acronym, DSM),[4] the "bible" reference work for mental health providers. The doctor diagnosing ADHD makes several decisions related to the diagnostic criteria prescribed by the most recent edition of the DSM, known as the DSM-IV-TR.[5] Figure 1.1 provides an overview of these six decisions, but we will not go into details of the diagnostic process here as Chapter Four covers each in depth.

ADHD Is Biological

ADHD is a result of the person's biological makeup, just like red hair or physical stature. Strategies cannot be used to "change" biology, but the symptoms can be improved by various strategies, skills, interventions, or by other means, such as medication. Adults, children, and adolescents with ADHD who lose keys or forget to turn in homework are not lazy, obstinate, or disobedient; they have ADHD, a medical disorder. For these individuals, it is not a matter of will—it is not true that "he could pay attention if he wanted to," or that "she can sit still and listen if she would just make up her mind to do so." It may appear that during certain tasks the attention span is fine. Actually the ADHD brain is structurally (biologically) different and will operate differently than a "typical" brain without additional assistance.

The idea of a biological basis for ADHD problem behaviors is sometimes challenging for people to accept in part because ADHD behavior can look a lot like ordinary problem behavior that people learn to overcome or that is regarded as a lack of will or discipline. For example, when a child receives a diagnosis of ADHD one parent may feel relief at finally "understanding" the

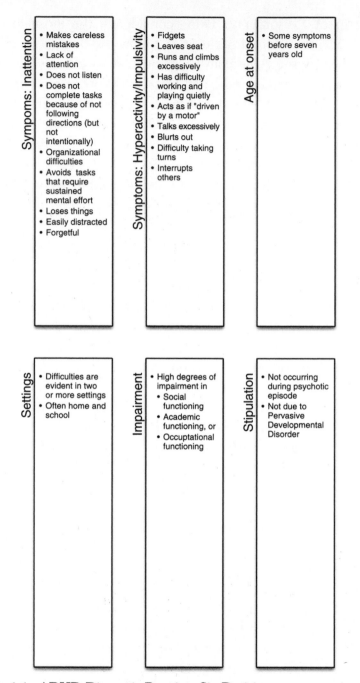

Symptoms: Inattention
- Makes careless mistakes
- Lack of attention
- Does not listen
- Does not complete tasks because of not following directions (but not intentionally)
- Organizational difficulties
- Avoids tasks that require sustained mental effort
- Loses things
- Easily distracted
- Forgetful

Symptoms: Hyperactivity/Impulsivity
- Fidgets
- Leaves seat
- Runs and climbs excessively
- Has difficulty working and playing quietly
- Acts as if "driven by a motor"
- Talks excessively
- Blurts out
- Difficulty taking turns
- Interrupts others

Age at onset
- Some symptoms before seven years old

Settings
- Difficulties are evident in two or more settings
- Often home and school

Impairment
- High degrees of impairment in
  - Social functioning
  - Academic functioning, or
  - Occuptational functioning

Stipulation
- Not occurring during psychotic episode
- Not due to Pervasive Developmental Disorder

Figure 1.1. ADHD Diagnosis Requires Six Decisions

problem, yet the other is irritated by what is perceived as a "crutch label" for not trying or not having enough discipline. The second parent may look around and see other children who "control" themselves and be frustrated that his or her child is not exhibiting self-control and now has an "excuse" not to learn to do so. This fundamental misunderstanding about what ADHD is and what it means for learning and development and intervention greatly affects how successfully the disorder is handled. It is not uncommon for individuals with little knowledge of ADHD to sometimes misinterpret or misrepresent the disorder. ADHD is not an excuse for problem behavior and the diagnosis is not a crutch. A diagnosis provides information about treatment options and how to improve behavior problems most effectively and efficiently. For example a child who "hits" out of impulsivity requires different treatment from a child who "hits" because he or she has been taught that hitting is OK. More on interventions will be addressed in Chapters Five through Nine.

With the idea that "knowledge is power," let's move on toward understanding more about ADHD. The greater the level of understanding, the more you will possess skills and strategies for successful living with ADHD. If you would like to read more about the biological basis for ADHD, we suggest you check out any of the following technical or medical articles or solid sources written in terminology intended for those without professional training in clinical diagnosis or the neurosciences.

ADHD Is a Common Behavioral Disorder for Children, Adolescents, and Adults

ADHD is one of the most common mental health disorders of childhood. The DSM-IV-TR reports that 3–5% of children in the United States have ADHD.[6] The Centers for Disease Control report that the prevalence of ADHD (the number of children and adults with the condition) ranges from 5% to 10% across

Table 1.4: Medical and Nonmedical Articles Explaining the Biological Nature of ADHD.

Medical Articles	Nonmedical articles
Hale, Loo, Zaidel, Hanada, Macion, & Smalley. (2009). Rethinking a right hemisphere deficit in ADHD. *Journal of Attention Disorders, 13*, pp. 3–17.	ADHD.org.nz. The Neurobiology of ADHD http://www.adhd.org.nz /neuro1.html
Arnsten, A.F. (2009). Toward a new understanding of Attention-Deficit Hyperactivity Disorder. *CNS Drugs, 23 Suppl 1*, pp. 33–41.	Ellison, K. (September 22, 2009). Brain scans link ADHD to biological flaw tied to motivation, *The Washington Post.* http://www .washingtonpost.com/wp-dyn /content/article/2009/09/21 /AR2009092103100.html
Curatolo, P., Paloscia, C., D'Agati, E., Moavero, R., & Pasini, A. (2009). The neurobiology of attention-deficit/hyperactivity disorder. *European Journal of Paediatric Neurology, 13*, pp. 299–304.	*ADHD and the Brain* YouTube video, AnswersMedia, LLC http://www.youtube.com /watch?v=u82nzTzL7To

the United States. In a class of 20, at least one student, such as Joey, would have ADHD (see Figure 1.2). In addition, ADHD continues into adulthood for about half of all people.[7] In a workplace meeting of forty adults (see Figure 1.3), at least one person would be expected to have enough symptoms to be diagnosed with ADHD.

HISTORY OF ADHD

ADHD is not a new or even a modern disorder—what is new is its formal recognition and the development of effective treatments. It has been described in individuals throughout history. We often find that studying some of this history is helpful in

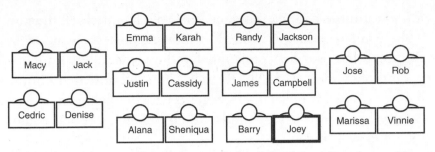

Figure 1.2. Three to Six Percent of the School-Age Population Have ADHD

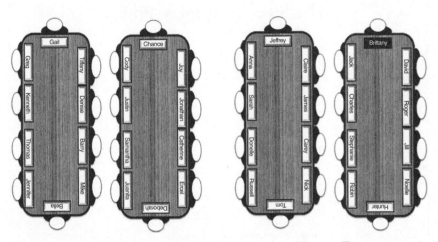

Figure 1.3. ADHD in Adults Is Common but Not as Frequent as in Childhood

learning about the disorder, but also we also understand if you choose to read ahead and skip over these details!

The Earliest Mention of Behaviors Similar to ADHD

So when did psychologists, psychiatrists, and researchers first begin talking about individuals with behaviors similar to the previous examples? Interestingly, descriptions of individuals who demonstrated behaviors closely associated with ADHD can be found centuries ago. For instance, in 1865, Heinrich Hoffmann, a physician in Germany, wrote the following nursery rhyme about Philip, which provides comic relief and understanding for many parents of children with ADHD today. You will note that Philip's behavior and Philip's father's reaction to his behavior over a hundred years ago is very similar to child behaviors and parent reactions seen today.

The Story of Fidgety Philip

"Let me see if Philip can
Be a little gentleman;
Let me see if he is able
To sit still for once at table."
Thus spoke, in earnest tone,
The father to his son;
And the mother looked very grave
To see Philip so misbehave.
But Philip he did not mind
His father who was so kind.
He wriggled
And giggled,
And then, I declare,
Swung backward and forward
And tilted his chair,
Just like any rocking horse;
"Philip! I am getting cross!"
See the naughty, restless child,
Growing still more rude and wild,
Till his chair falls over quite.
Philip screams with all his might,
Catches at the cloth, but then

That makes matters worse again.
Down upon the ground they fall,
Glasses, bread, knives, forks and all.
How Mamma did fret and frown,
When she saw them tumbling down!
And Papa made such a face!
Philip is in sad disgrace.
Where is Philip? Where is he?
Fairly cover'd up, you see!
Cloth and all are lying on him;
He has pull'd down all upon him!
What a terrible to-do!
Dishes, glasses, snapt in two!
Here a knife, and there a fork!
Philip, this is naughty work.
Table all so bare, and ah!
Poor Papa and poor Mamma
Look quite cross, and wonder how
They shall make their dinner now.

—Heinrich Hoffman

First Scientific Credit Given

Scientific credit for the first serious attention paid to ADHD is given to Drs. George Still and Alfred Tredgold. In 1902, Dr. Still described 43 children in his clinical practice who had serious problems with sustained attention. Dr. Still described problems with: passionateness, spitefulness-cruelty, jealousy, lawlessness, dishonesty, wanton mischievousness-destructiveness, shamelessness-immodesty, sexual immorality, and viciousness—descriptions very similar to those previously identified in this chapter using more current language. Dr. Still believed that these children displayed behaviour that represented a major "defect in moral control" and that was chronic in most cases. Much as researchers do today, Dr. Still noted a greater proportion of males than females (3:1) in his sample, and he observed that the disorder appeared in most cases before 8 years of age. However, in the early 1900s—and on through the 1950s—common consensus was that problem child behavior was a result of poor parenting, and no mental health condition similar to ADHD was included in the first edition of the DSM in 1952.

First Research Evidence

In 1958 the first research grant on the use of medication with childhood mental health disorders was awarded to Dr. Leon Eisenberg who recruited an instructor in pediatrics and medical psychology, Keith Conners, to collaborate. Dr. Conners's research confirmed the positive effects of methylphenidate (Ritalin) and in 1961, Ritalin was approved by the Food and Drug Administration (FDA) for use in children with behavior disorders.

In the 1960s and 1970s, amid a flurry of discussion focusing on poor parenting as the cause of hyperactivity in children, research in the field began to flourish. Dr. Virginia Douglas argued that the impact of deficits in sustained attention and impulse control were as important as symptoms of hyperactivity on the functioning of children. During this time period, Dr. Paul Wender, a research psychiatrist for the National Institute of Mental Health (NIMH), described Minimal Brain Dysfunction (MBD), the term for ADHD at the time, as characterized by six deficit areas: motor behavior; attentional and perceptual-cognitive functioning; learning; impulse control; interpersonal relations; and emotions. In 1971, Dr. Wender hypothesized that the likely cause of Minimal Brain Dysfunction (MBD), the name for behaviors associated with ADHD at the time, were neurotransmitter (for example, dopamine, norepinephrine) deficiencies in the brain. In 1973, building on Dr. Wender's hypothesis,

Dr. Mortimer Gross suggested that medications known to increase the levels of norepinephrine in the brain might also be of benefit to individuals with MBD. In 1978, ADHD was first included in the DSM-II and named Hyperkinetic Reaction of Childhood.

Advanced Research Technologies

The 1980s and 1990s brought increased research technology, new medication use, and two new editions of the DSM. Solid research began to establish the possible causes of ADHD as genetics and brain abnormalities. Advanced research technologies provided the means for investigating brain activity of individuals with ADHD. The role of dopamine and norepinephrine deficiencies in individuals with ADHD was confirmed and studies revealed "patterns of underactivity in the prefrontal area" of the brain.[8] At the same time, medication designed for use with depression and anxiety—which affect similar neurotransmitter systems—began to be used to decrease the symptoms of ADHD.

In the third edition of the DSM,[9] the name was changed to Attention-Deficit Disorder as three separate disorders: Attention-Deficit Disorder (ADD) with hyperactivity; ADD without hyperactivity; and ADD residual type. In the DSM-III-R,[10] the name was once again changed to Attention-Deficit Hyperactivity Disorder as one disorder with four subtypes: ADHD combined type; ADHD predominantly inattentive type; ADHD predominantly hyperactive-impulsive; and ADHD not otherwise specified. In addition, adult ADHD was first recognized in the DSM-III. Unfortunately, the term ADD has stuck in the minds of many and although its use is archaic and discontinued in the official nomenclature with the 1987 revision of the DSM, one sees and hears reference to it often in the lay press, among parents, and even in some professional resources.

ADD or ADHD?

In previous years, ADHD was divided into different subtypes, one of which was called simply ADD, or Attention-Deficit Disorder. However, research revealed that even those with ADD also had problems with other aspects of ADHD including hyperactivity and impulsivity, just to a lesser degree. The diagnostic term ADD was then dropped from all official nomenclature in the mid-1990s. ADD is now an archaic term in the profession though still popular in the lay press and on many lay websites.

TO SUM UP

Is it real? Experts in the field have established substantial quantities of evidence to support the reality of ADHD. Both behavior and brain structures are different in individuals with ADHD and in those without ADHD. ADHD is an identifiable medical condition and not simply "bad" behavior or a mythological creation by physicians or corporations to sell medication to children. ADHD can be reliably identified using proper diagnostic materials and criteria and ADHD can be managed and treated to ensure maximum success in school and life.

However, the media and others often may exploit the sensationalized topic of medicating children or the idea of mythological and nonexistent disorders and thus the "truth" about ADHD remains controversial. Some of this confusion comes from the reality that almost everyone experiences "ADHD symptoms" at some time or another. However, the chronic nature and degree to which the symptoms interfere with daily functioning is the defining difference. Temporary or passing inattention and/or hyperactivity is markedly different from the debilitating disorder that interferes with successful life functioning. Recognizing that ADHD is an actual condition helps us in determining effective and efficient treatment and helps individuals with ADHD in moving forward to overcome their challenges.

WHAT'S NEXT?

In the next chapter, we will further explore the nature of ADHD, specifically behaviors associated with ADHD, disorders often comorbid with ADHD, and functional impairment.

2

What ADHD Looks Like

Common Behaviors and Related Disorders

In Chapter One, you read about the characteristics of the primary symptoms of ADHD. In this chapter, you will learn about the common problem behaviors associated with the core symptoms, comorbid conditions, and functional impairment.

ADHD is a heterogeneous disorder, which means that the behavior of each child, adolescent, or adult with ADHD looks at least a little (and occasionally a lot) different from another's behavior. Individual people do not behave exactly the same way, although they may share some common behaviors. The shared behaviors that occur in nearly all cases are called a common conceptual core and are easily recognized in the formal diagnostic process. The behaviors of people with ADHD fall under the broad dimensions described in Table 2.1: (1) primary symptoms of ADHD, such as inattentiveness, hyperactivity, and impulsivity; (2) symptoms of comorbid conditions, such as depression or anxiety; and (3) "indicators of functional impairment," which means the ADHD interferes with the performance of common everyday behaviors necessary to adapt and thrive in life.[1]

Some experts and professionals will focus only on behaviors related to the primary symptoms. However, we believe that understanding and assessing *all* behaviors demonstrated by

Table 2.1: Behaviors of People with ADHD Fall Under Three Broad Categories.

Primary Symptoms	Inattention, hyperactivity, and impulsivity are primary symptoms.
Symptoms of Comorbid Conditions	ADHD with one or more additional condition, such as depression or anxiety.
Indicators of Functional Impairment	Behaviors associated with detrimental impact on social, academic, interpersonal, and/or occupational functioning.

individuals with ADHD—whether they are primary ADHD symptoms or not—is the key to more effective treatment and management of the disorder.

Every individual has strengths and weaknesses. Sometimes a particular characteristic or quality can be both a strength and a weakness. A person who is outgoing and self confident may have difficulty knowing when to stay in the background. A person who gets things done may be a person who overcommits. Most people associate the word "disorder" as a negative; although this book is primarily about overcoming and managing the problems associated with ADHD, we want to start off by mentioning the positives of ADHD. Sometimes, behavioral characteristics of ADHD are attributed to super-successful performance. People with ADHD will ultimately build resilience from the strength needed to overcome struggles. In addition, an individual with ADHD may learn more coping and compensatory skills, and develop them further, than someone without ADHD—in response to these challenges.

BEHAVIORAL STRENGTHS

Individuals with ADHD may have high degrees of *energy, focus, creativity, passion, exuberance, and multitasking ability*. This

energy is sometimes reported by successful people to be the source of their work ethic, and the superior performance they are driven to achieve. Ty Pennington, the host of *Extreme Home Makeover*, has noticed that his ADHD symptoms have helped contribute to his own—and others'—success. In an interview Pennington spoke of his experiences with ADHD, stating that he clearly believes some of his success comes from his ADHD "because I think, you know, we as human beings, especially when we have ADHD, we are creative, we have great ideas."[2] High energy is a strength when channeled in the right direction. With strategy training and self-recognition, individuals can identify and focus their energy to accomplish tasks, start new projects, create ideas for others, or lead groups through motivation.

Another behavioral strength for individuals with ADHD can be **focus**. High energy is often accompanied by **passion** and **exuberance** for specific interests. Individuals with ADHD are sometimes "hyper-focused" (that is, focused intensely for long periods of time) and passionate about or committed to specific causes or activities. One example might be a child engrossed in a novel or Legos™ or chess. The focus level is so intense that interrupting the child's concentration results in frustration, irritable responses, perhaps even aggression. If you are a spouse of an adult with ADHD, you might recognize a mate who spends lengthy periods of time working on a personally interesting task (for example, working on a car, or painting a picture) with intensive concentration and effort, but who is seemingly unable, or uninterested, in sitting down to watch a movie.

The ability to focus or lose oneself in a task is a behavioral strength for accomplishing work, solving problems, and creating. People with an overbearing passion for a particular pursuit are often criticized by others for ignoring other responsibilities while focusing only on the one pursuit. E. Paul Torrance, one of our favorite scholars (now deceased) in the area of gifted and talented children, noted that this can be discouraging especially to youth who are highly intelligent or highly creative, and he counseled them not to be afraid to fall in love with something and to pursue it with passion! We find this to be good advice and quite adaptive for anyone with ADHD as well. David Neeleman, CEO and founder of JetBlue Airways, relates this strength nicely about himself: "One of the weird things about the type of ADHD that I have is, if you have something you are really, really passionate about, then you are really, really good about focusing on that thing. It is kind of bizarre that you can't pay the bills or do mundane tasks, but you can do your hyper-focus area." He reports that he spends "all of his waking hours" obsessing about JetBlue.[3]

Multitasking is another strength. An awareness of simultaneous actions in others, or the ability to process and jump back and forth quickly between tasks, can put individuals with ADHD in leadership positions where rapid processing is a strength and quick associations lead to synthesis of knowledge in new and different ways. Although an often controversial figure, Glenn Beck has risen to prominence in his field. Beck works as a conservative radio personality and appears daily on CNN Headline News, and he is also the founder of Fusion Magazine. He often discusses his diagnosis of ADHD on his radio show. Pertinent here is a comment he made about multitasking: "I believe that my success in business is because I can process a million things at a time and move very rapidly."[4]

There are, at minimum, four areas of behavioral strengths for individuals with ADHD. One or all may be present. Energy, focus at the beginning of tasks or projects or intense focus on activities of interest, intuition or sensitivity, and multitasking are each tremendous gifts that can serve a person well in successful living or be used strategically to compensate for problem behaviors in the following areas.

PRIMARY SYMPTOMS

Primary symptoms are the "main" behaviors defined by the Diagnostic and Statistical Manual of Mental Disorders, 4th edition (DSM-IV)[5] that are causing concern or even problems. The broad primary symptom categories of ADHD are hyperactivity, inattention, and impulsivity.[6] Remember that for purposes of discussion, we use *categories* of symptoms because every person demonstrates hyperactivity, or distractibility, or impulsivity differently and these symptoms often change with age as our brains change. Within each of the broad primary symptom categories are unlimited numbers of observable behaviors. For example, within the hyperactivity category, you might see a million ways to express hyperactivity. The same is true for inattention and impulsivity. Primary symptoms are established by the DSM. As discussed in Chapter One, the DSM is "the" comprehensive source used by physicians, psychologists, clinical social workers, and other mental health professionals to determine if an individual meets the diagnostic criteria for a specific disorder. Within the broad primary symptom categories are specific behaviors that an individual must demonstrate to be diagnosed.

From the Counselor

I have always been concerned that while attempting to shape children and adolescents into functioning members of society, we ignore or even punish individual uniqueness and strengths. I believe that it is very important to reinforce and reward the positive characteristics of these youth when helping them learn to function within systems. This can be a daunting and frustrating task at times so we must be very aware of everything that we say to and about the individual. One method that I've tried that seems to help is to begin each conversation with the child or with others about the child with a discussion of strengths.

From the Teacher

It was so easy to get frustrated with Jason (a freshman student of mine): he couldn't pay attention to 5 minutes of a social studies lesson but was "locked on target" during chess. Before I knew much about ADHD I thought he was faking it. I learned that his hyper-focus abilities were related to his interest and I wish I had known to capture that interest and use it to his advantage in my class. He would have been unstoppable.

Behaviors Associated with Inattention

Inattention is the drifting of attention without focus. Individuals considered inattentive have difficulties attending, or paying attention, have a short attention span, and are easily distracted from some activities, such as monotonous or repetitive tasks, class work, or chores. Fully "paying attention" is composed of four processes. Figure 2.1 represents behaviors associated with inattention. Sustained attention (that is, the art of concentration) is particularly difficult.

Attention occurs without thinking when an individual focuses on an object, sound, activity, or thought for even a brief moment. For instance, when an infant hears a loud noise, he or she typically turns toward the sound, an indication of attention. This is called initiating attention or an orienting response. However, the infant might not "pay attention" or maintain attention to what created the loud noise for more than that second. The concept of attention has three components in addition to initiation: sustaining attention, inhibiting responses to distractions, and shifting attention (see Figure 2.2).[7] Individuals can experience difficulties with any of these four phases of attention. Attention is particularly important to learning and memory skills as well. Attention lays the foundation for memory—we cannot recall what we did not attend to!

You probably recognize inattention, but let's consider at least one example of inattention. Jeffrey is a fourth grader diagnosed

Figure 2.1. Symptoms of Inattention

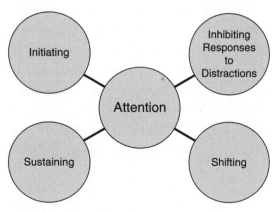

Figure 2.2. Components of Attention

with ADHD who has problems paying attention in class. Jeffrey has significant problems when his class assignment is to do long practice math worksheets. One day, given 20 long division problems, Jeffrey appears to be staring out the window. When the teacher picks up the papers, Jeffrey has completed all the problems; however, he did not follow directions. He only lists his answers and 50% are wrong. He was given instructions to show all of his work, but he did not. Jeffrey's teacher explains to Jeffrey that he didn't follow directions and made several careless errors. Jeffrey, looking confused, asks, "What did I do wrong? I did everything you said to do!"

Sustaining attention is the ability to concentrate on one thought, task, sound, activity, or object for an extended period of time. For example, watching a movie from beginning to end, practicing a speech, or solving a problem or a puzzle requires sustained attention. In terms of sustained attention, individuals with ADHD often exhibit attentional bias, which is when an individual prefers to pay attention to specific items, thoughts, sounds, or activities. This preference can interfere with attention when the person is focused on events, thoughts, or objects that are unrelated to the task requirements or that are a bigger priority for the individual. Have you ever seen a child intently watch a cartoon and "not hear" a mother's call or a student intent on an activity who misses the cue to move on to something else? The expression "lost in your thoughts" may refer to attentional bias. Individuals with ADHD have an attentional bias toward novelty. Often attention is diverted from monotonous but essential tasks, such as homework or brushing teeth, to more stimulating tasks or objects that are bigger, brighter, more intense, or louder—such as a bright picture in a textbook or a loud commercial on the television.

Inhibiting responses to distractions is another component of attention. The ability to inhibit responses requires the ability to use selective attention or purposefully paying attention to one object, thought, or activity. For instance, mystery novels or suspense movies contain information that is important and information that is incidental, or irrelevant to the plot. Attending to relevant cues and discarding irrelevant detail (actually called distracters) assists in problem solving, or in this case, unraveling the mystery. Some individuals with ADHD may have difficulty sorting (or discriminating) between the difference between relevant and irrelevant information. This difficulty would not be limited to recreational time but would cross into work also.

Shifting attention is the last type of problem associated with inattention. The ability to shift attention and the speed at which an individual shifts attention back and forth can determine the amount of work that is completed and affects the frustration level of the individual with ADHD, as well as those closely associated with the person.

Inattentive Behaviors Do Not Always Indicate ADHD   Inattention does not always indicate that the individual has ADHD; it is only one category of symptoms. In fact, most people experience difficulties attending, or paying attention, at some time. Fatigue, hunger, poor diet, medication, or tasks that are too difficult or too easy for the individual are all causes of difficulties attending. Several physical and mental health disorders, in addition to ADHD, are characterized by inattention, such as seizure disorders, hearing or vision disorders, schizophrenia, depression, anxiety, acute stress, brain injury or dysfunction, or sleep disorders. Even some common medications, such as diphenhydramine (better known as Benadryl, one of the most frequently administered medicines to children in the United States) can cause attention problems, irritability, and hyperactivity in some children.

Behaviors Associated with Hyperactivity

In medical terms, hyperactivity is defined as too much muscle or kinetic activity. Hyperactivity is demonstrated by an inability to sit still, difficulty engaging in quiet activities relative to age mates (most young children face such challenges), fidgeting, and excessively moving, talking, running, or climbing (see Figure 2.3). Common behaviors demonstrated by children and adolescents with hyperactivity include wiggling and moving around in the classroom, at the dinner table, or other times when sitting still is expected and age appropriate. When sitting becomes too much, children might get out of the seat and wander around the room or climb on the back of the chair or the table or other objects not designed for climbing. Children, adolescents, and adults with hyperactivity are notorious for excessive talking; at times, talking seems uncontrollable, even when silence is expected.

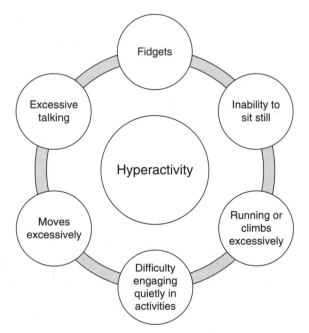

Figure 2.3. Behaviors Associated with Hyperactivity

Active Behavior Does Not Always Indicate ADHD Before determining that active behavior is hyperactivity and associated with ADHD, consider these factors. Developmentally speaking, active behavior is expected of young children. For an adult who has little experience with young children, they may appear overactive when they are not; conversely, overactive children may be considered "typical" when in fact they are not. Bright, curious, active children who are enthused about exploring and learning about their environment can be mistaken for being hyperactive as well, and the base rates (what is typical of children of the same age) of such behavior is crucial in determining whether the level of activity seen is in fact abnormal. The parents of clinically hyperactive children often spontaneously describe them as constantly on the go, almost "as though they are driven by a motor." Developmental norms do exist about the range of typical levels of activity. Using these norms provides the "big picture" of what is expected at specific ages or stages in development. Medication may be a consideration as well. Some medications cause hyperactive behavior. In addition, a medical diagnosis other than ADHD may better explain the hyperactivity in a particular person and should be considered.

Behaviors Associated with Impulsivity

Impulsivity, or behavioral disinhibition, is characterized by acting on impulse without advanced planning, thinking, or consideration of consequences. Behaviors associated with impulsivity (see Figure 2.4) include interrupting others while they are speaking, blurting out answers, and difficulty waiting for a turn. Impulsivity can interfere with problem solving or decision making at several stages. The person who quickly fires off an e-mail or feels compelled to resolve conflict immediately may be acting from impulsivity rather than thoughtful, more typical adult decision making. Immediate gratification may be a form of

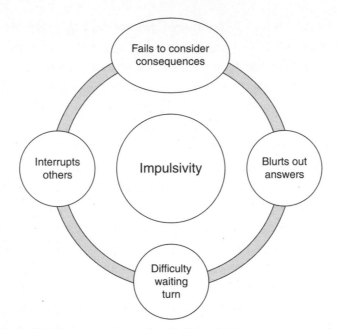

Figure 2.4. Behaviors Associated with Impulsivity

impulsivity or lack of impulse control—for example, the quick purchase of a nonpreferred shoe size or color rather than waiting for the correct size or preferred color to be shipped, or ordering a nonpreferred menu item. Impulsivity can manifest during problem solving, even significant decision making (sometimes called judgment). Problem solving, decision making, and judgment have an impact on nearly every area of daily living, with both short-term and long-term consequences. Failure to make thoughtful, reasoned decisions or choices can be damaging and can impair life functioning in many areas—for example, drinking and driving, marriage or partner choices, decision about having (or not having) children, attending or completing school, interactions and communication with colleagues, friends, and family members.

Impulsivity in decision making can be articulated as a series of steps or missteps. First, an individual may neglect to notice or consider all choices and select the first solution presented or considered. Guessing is another faulty decision-making technique. Typical adult behavior includes the expectation of "thinking through the problem" with a reasonable understanding of the consequences of various actions. A third misstep in ADHD decision making is to select a choice regardless of the consequences.

For example, Sonia is impulsive. In meetings at work, Sonia is often heard interrupting the person speaking. You may have heard someone described thusly: "If a thought pops into her head, it pops out of her mouth!" It may appear as if Sonia is rude or overly assertive. Sonia's coworkers comment that her remarks are impulsive, and she makes decisions quickly without thinking. These are common attributes of the adult with ADHD.

Impulsive Behaviors Do Not Always Indicate ADHD Impulsive behavior is not a diagnosis of ADHD. All individuals are impulsive at times, children even more so. Impulsivity does not always result in negative consequences. Just as anxiety (typically considered "bad") can propel us to action, create energy to move, or serve as an impetus to seek closure or end an uncomfortable circumstance, impulsivity can add spice and enjoyment to life such as the detour down a country road for scenery, the quick dance when favorite music comes on, or late-night ice cream. Also, impulsivity is associated with some other mental health disorders such as mania, personality disorders, and substance abuse disorders. Impulsivity can cause problems, such as when the impulse to detour is not down a country road but rather to turn the car around and go to the beach instead of to work or school.

COMORBID CONDITIONS

Interesting to note, a person with ADHD is highly likely to have *at least* one additional diagnosable condition. Individuals with

ADHD are frequently diagnosed with or exhibit behavioral symptoms of other mental health disorders, including mood disorders, disruptive behavior disorders, learning disorders or learning disabilities, or substance abuse. When two or more disorders exist in the same person, we refer to this as **comorbidity**. ADHD has high comorbidity with several other conditions including: depression, obsessive compulsive disorders, conduct disorder, pediatric bipolar disorder, Tourette's syndrome, oppositional defiant disorder, and others. You will probably recognize behaviors associated with comorbid conditions in many individuals that you know with ADHD.

Individuals with Pervasive Developmental Disorders (PDD), such as autism and Asperger's disorder, may also be diagnosed with ADHD at above-average rates. Problems with attention and impulsivity/hyperactivity are notable secondary issues to the more serious issues associated with the autism spectrum. Nevertheless, these ADHD-like problems require attention and resolution regardless of where they fall in a list of concerns.

ADHD and Mood Disorders

Individuals with ADHD might demonstrate behaviors associated with mood disorders, such as depression and anxiety. Depression is characterized by feelings of sadness, helplessness, and hopelessness. Individuals who are depressed often sleep too much or do not sleep at all, lose interest in activities that were previously enjoyed, lose or gain weight, experience a loss of energy, and have problems concentrating. Two to six times more children and adolescents with ADHD have diagnoses of depression compared to those without ADHD.[8]

Approximately one-fifth of youth with ADHD experience severe enough symptoms of depression to be diagnosed with a depressive disorder (see Figure 2.5). Understandably, researchers hypothesize that living with symptoms of ADHD might be the

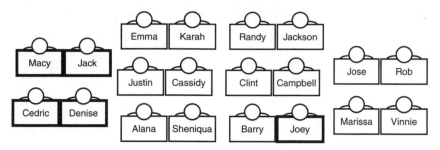

Figure 2.5. One-fifth of Children with ADHD Are Depressed

cause of depression; however, this has not been confirmed. We believe it is more likely to be related to the commonality in the brain chemistry issues associated with ADHD and depression and anxiety as well as obsessive-compulsive behaviors. We will explore this in more detail for you later.

Consider Cedric, who was diagnosed with ADHD when he was six years old. Cedric is now thirteen and his mother is very concerned about his behavior. He does not want to go out with his friends, he stays in his room, and he sleeps most of the day. Cedric says that he is a "loser" and he "fails at everything." He told his mother that when he looks at a test at school he begins to have problems breathing and feels like he is going to faint. It is becoming more and more difficult for Cedric's mother to get him up and off to school. Cedric's psychologist diagnosed him with ADHD, anxiety, and depression.

Anxiety is characterized by feelings of fear, worry, and uneasiness. Individuals with anxiety problems often talk about being afraid and worried to the degree that it affects their ability to function. This anxiety can be associated with stomachaches, headaches, difficulty sleeping, dizziness, difficulty concentrating, and difficulty breathing. Approximately one-fourth of youth with ADHD have diagnosable anxiety problems (see Figure 2.6).

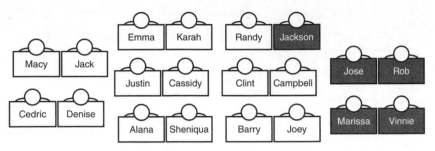

Figure 2.6. One-fourth of Children with ADHD Have Anxiety

ADHD and Disruptive Behavior Disorders

Disruptive behaviors are exactly as you might expect—behaviors that interfere with the activities of other people. Disruptive behaviors are common in ADHD but when persistent may also lead to later diagnoses of oppositional defiant disorder (ODD) or conduct disorder (CD). ODD is a consistent pattern of noncompliant, aggressive, and rebellious behavior towards authority figures which goes beyond normal child behavior. About 40% of children and adolescents with ADHD have oppositional defiant disorder. Teachers and parents often say these youth lose their temper easily, act aggressively, or defy teachers or caregivers. Many parents of children with ADHD report extreme frustration with defiant behavior. When this behavior occurs repeatedly in different situations for extended periods of time, practitioners can diagnose the individual with ODD in addition to ADHD. The individual will become resistant and disrespectful with authority figures such as school principals or police officers. Conduct disorder is represented by getting in trouble with law enforcement and illegal activity (for example, drug use or theft), cheating, and deceit or lying with no concern for anyone harmed by the behavior.

Kelby is a child with ADHD and disruptive behavior disorders. When Kelby's mother asks him to clean up his room, he says, "Hold on." When asked the second time, he screams, "No, not now, I'm playing a game." Eventually the conversation becomes very loud; Kelby throws the game controller, and refuses to clean the room. Kelby's behavior occurs repeatedly in different situations for extended periods of time, and he is eventually diagnosed with oppositional defiant disorder in addition to ADHD. As Kelby becomes older, he gets into trouble with the police. He begins stealing, lying, and becomes aggressive with his peers and other adults. Kelby is ultimately diagnosed with conduct disorder.

ADHD and Learning Disabilities

Children and adolescents with ADHD often have learning disorders. Learning disabilities are defined by a federal law, the Individuals with Disabilities Education Improvement Act (IDEIA) as a "disorder in one or more of the basic psychological processes involved in understanding or in using language, spoken or written, which disorder may manifest itself in the imperfect ability to listen, think, speak, read, write, spell, or do mathematical calculations."[9] Individuals with learning disabilities often have problems with reading, writing, or mathematical computations or application. About 25% of children in a class for learning disorders are likely to have ADHD. Individuals with learning disabilities most often have intellectual skills that fall in the average range or higher (about 10% of individuals with ADHD have IQs in the high average and superior ranges), and thus have the ability to learn typically, but their disability interferes with the rate and accuracy of learning.

For example, Sara's teachers often report to her mother that she can do her work, but she doesn't want to work hard. A teacher might look to performance in another subject area in support of the "lazy" theory: "Sarah is making straight As in math and if she would just apply herself the same way in reading she would do just fine." On the other hand, Sara says, "I've tried to do it, I just don't understand" or "I don't remember what the teacher said to do for homework."

In a recent study, we found that learning problems were the best discriminator between adolescents with ADHD and those without when their behavior was rated by teachers.[10] In this study, the biggest difference between adolescents without ADHD and those with ADHD according to teachers was not hyperactivity, impulsivity, or inattention, but that the adolescents with ADHD had learning problems and exhibited a variety of observable behaviors associated with difficulty in learning, such as problems with reading and spelling, and problems organizing, completing, and submitting assignments.

ADHD, Substance Dependence, and Addiction

Individuals with ADHD are at increased risk for addictive illnesses, BUT not (as many mistakenly believe) because they have experienced appropriate medical attention or prescription medicines for ADHD. Substance dependence or addiction is defined as "when an individual persists in use of alcohol or other drugs despite problems related to use of the substance."[11] Between 30% and 44% of individuals with ADHD abuse alcohol or illegal substances.[12] In addition, individuals who have ADHD as well as mental health disorders such as depression or anxiety have a higher incidence of substance abuse. Compared to peers without ADHD, individuals with ADHD experiment with addictive substances earlier and more freely.[13] This is believed to be related to impulsivity, higher tolerance or interest in risk taking, and potentially a self-medicating behavior. Children and adolescents treated with stimulant medications such as methylphenidate (popularly known as Ritalin) are actually at lower risk for later developing substance addiction.[14] In fact, some studies have found that treatment with stimulant medications decreases substance abuse and cravings.[15]

While serving as chief of psychology at a psychiatric hospital with both adult and adolescent substance abuse units, one of the authors (CRR) noted a high incidence of undiagnosed ADHD among many patients admitted for the use of cocaine and stimulants. Often these persons would remark during clinical interviews that they did not understand the "high" so many people described from using these drugs; instead, they would remark that when using amphetamines, for example, it was the first time they could sit, concentrate, and work on something productively in their entire lives. Often a part of breaking the cycle of addiction for these individuals was the use of medication. Treating physicians carefully selected medications for each individual to control their symptoms of ADHD, removing the need for their experimental, and detrimental, desire to self-medicate. Also, unlike street drugs, medical monitoring of the effects of these medicines was also provided so that changes could be made if undesirable side effects occurred or the medicines' effectiveness changed over time.

IMPAIRMENT IN DAY-TO-DAY ACTIVITIES

Functional impairment is the daily impact of ADHD symptoms on **social, academic, and/or occupational functioning**, and is a requirement for a diagnosis of ADHD. Understanding that behaviors associated with functional impairment are actually related to ADHD is an important step in understanding the individual as a "whole." For example, Melanie's ADHD contributes to car keys being left in a different spot on most days. Every day Melanie faces the stress of looking for keys, the frustration of not remembering where they were (no attention when they were put down), racing thoughts of anxiety about being late to work, noticing that her spouse and child are watching the frantic search, losing focus on the task of searching for keys and instead getting coffee, and finally finding the keys only to leave the coffee on the counter—the compounded stress felt by Melanie, her child, and her spouse exemplifies ADHD's impairment of daily functioning. ADHD affects functioning through difficulties with daily living skills, academic achievement, and interpersonal relationships with parents, peers, and significant others.[16]

Parents, spouses, children, and colleagues of individuals with ADHD in particular will relate to the deficit in daily activities experienced by this population. Individuals with ADHD have **difficulty following routines**. If following a routine is needed for daily functioning and NOT following a routine impairs or negatively affects life functioning, assistance may be needed in remembering typical activities such as brushing teeth, using deodorant, and taking a bath. The routines may be less obvious but equally important such as depositing a paycheck or paying bills on time, getting prescriptions refilled before they run out, or doing a mental check of "what do I need for the day" before walking out of the house to get on a school bus or go to work.

Difficulty with **short-term memory and inconsistent use of organizational skills** interferes with successful academic (elementary, middle school, high school, and university) and occupational functioning, and will also impair an individual's study skills and ability to begin, remain engaged, and complete tasks.[17] Problems with short-term memory affect the ability to remember daily activities, routines, or tasks. For instance, John is notorious for forgetting his reading book and spends a great deal of reading time not engaged with others in his class. Jack forgets to turn in his permission slip every day for a week even though it is in his backpack.

Difficulties with organizational skills are worsened by **ineffective time management skills and difficulties with neatness.** Time management difficulties can be seen in ineffective activity planning, tardiness, visible struggles estimating time, and an overestimate of the length of time intervals available. Sonja is tardy every day for her biology class, because she keeps thinking she'll have enough time to walk her boyfriend to the band hall and get to biology on time, despite evidence to the contrary. She truly does not "understand" why she is late and friends may joke with her that the space-time continuum does not apply to Sonja. Difficulties with neatness are demonstrated through problems with tidiness of households, automobiles, school materials, and assignments, and with frequently misplacing tasks and objects. When Nick opens his binder, it appears to "explode." Papers are not attached by the rings, much less located in the correct section divider. Along with his incomplete, complete, and graded assignments a missing sock might be likely to hit the floor. When his teachers ask for completed assignments, Nick is unable to find the assignments that he remembers completing and then he will spend significant amounts of time unproductively looking, going through all of the loose papers in his binder, saying over and over, "I know I did it. I did it at home last night." The teacher might sarcastically remark—funny that you "remember" doing it but can't remember where you put it. Ironically the same Nick who can't focus in class is very sincerely focused on looking for it. On multiple occasions Nick's mom has driven to school to turn in homework that was left on the kitchen table and never made it to the binder. These characteristics sometimes, but don't always, get better with age.

From the Counselor

Functional impairment is the key to everything about ADHD. The area of impairment is the focus of most counseling sessions.

ADHD impacts interpersonal relationships with significant others such as parents, peers, and spouses. We have dedicated an entire chapter to the impact of ADHD on friends and family (see Chapter Eight). Frustration and sometimes rejection occurs by the friends and family of an individual with ADHD. Individuals with ADHD may be rejected by peers because of behaviors that appear odd, different, aggressive, disruptive, intrusive, and noisy.[18] For instance, Sara in Ms. Swearingen's class has weekly fights with her friends because they tell her that she is weird. Brittany interrupts her colleagues, doesn't listen to the suggestions of others, and appears rude overall. Therefore, she does not have many friends in her workplace. Brittany often fights with her husband at home. He will say that Brittany doesn't care about his ideas or opinions and only does what she wants. He complains that Brittany never listens to him and always interjects stories of her own when he is trying to tell her about his day at work. In addition, a lack of emotional self-control, primarily in exciting or frustrating situations has a negative impact on family and friends and creates barriers to social relationships.[19]

From the Teacher

Teaching my students to "count to 5 before they speak" is a great way to keep them from blurting and interrupting others. It is this verbal river that seems to be the most problematic in developing and keeping friends. My students with ADHD just don't look like they are listening.

TO SUM UP

In this chapter, we have discussed the perspective of strengths in looking at ADHD, and discussed some of the behaviors demonstrated by individuals with ADHD using categories of primary symptoms, symptoms of comorbid conditions, and functional impairment. Within this framework comes the power to diagnose, build on strengths, and address problems. Despite the fact that people with ADHD have problems with activity levels, impulse control, and attention, they all act a little differently, because the degree of each problem varies greatly from person to person. ADHD is a heterogeneous disorder, meaning that the behavior of each child, adolescent, or adult with ADHD looks at least a little (and occasionally a lot) different from another's. Individual people do not demonstrate exactly the same behaviors in exactly the same way, although they may share some common behaviors, which are called a common conceptual core and are easily recognized in the formal diagnostic process. A key to diagnosis of ADHD, as not everyone with attention, impulse control, or activity problems has ADHD, is the notion of functional impairment—the symptoms (behaviors) seen must have a significant adverse impact on some important aspect of activities of daily living in the social, educational, vocational, or interpersonal domain.

WHAT'S NEXT?

In the next chapter, we will discuss how ADHD can affect a person's relationships with family and friends and how to be sure those relationships are optimized. The frustrations of parenting a child with ADHD are also noted and explored.

3

How ADHD Affects Family and Friends

ADHD has an impact on every aspect of an individual's life and also the lives of friends and families. ADHD is a life-long disorder with challenges and unique characteristic strengths. Some of the many reported challenges for parents include stress, frustration, self-esteem problems, depression, and even marital discord. Parents often argue about disciplinary approaches, because children with ADHD appear to be nonresponsive to parental correction (when really there is a biological difference between the ADHD and non-ADHD child). Parents may experience frustration or disagree in attributing "cause" to the behavior problems. In fact, according to the *Parenting Relationship Questionnaire*[1] (developed by Dr. Reynolds, one of the authors of this book), parents report more frustration in relating to and disciplining their children with ADHD than did parents for any other "type" of disability. Remember that as we discuss discipline in this book, we mean correction and teaching (*discipline*, from the Greek, means teaching). We don't mean corporal punishment when we say discipline and we don't advocate the use of punishment unless all other forms of reinforcement and intervention have been tried. Punishment will only assist a child in "doing" what he or she can already "do" and biologically/

From the Neuroscientist

I have seen many parents, but mostly dads, frustrated with failed discipline, who tell me, "He could behave if he wanted to, why doesn't "he" listen!" As we have noted, the energetic ADHD brain doesn't work that way—it is not that your child will not listen or does not want to behave. Your child's brain is sending very different messages and routing him or her off in many different directions all at once. Understanding that ADHD is in fact a brain disorder eases parenting stress and enhances understanding of these children and their brains. Each of us, after all, is governed by our brain and it dictates all behavior.

physiologically a child with ADHD may not be able to "do" some of the things you ask. Although true for parenting any child, it is especially important that parents present a unified front and consistent disciplinary strategies when managing children with ADHD.

Parents may also experience frustration when their children with ADHD have problems with friends. Because friendships may be difficult, the child of a parent with ADHD is also adversely affected. There may be increased demands that ADHD places on personal relationships and on parenting responsibilities for caretaking or accommodating challenging communication and behavior. Finally, this stressful relationship is two-way, so that more frustration, anger, and conflict can beget more problematic behaviors in the individual with ADHD, perpetuating a cycle of increasingly dysfunctional interactions.

Being a family member or friend of an individual with ADHD is a daily challenge unlike any other. As a parent you may experience the frustration that comes with constant reminders to follow directions or finish a task and the feeling that you are sucked into conflict or negative interactions over and over again, seemly without end and without control. As a sibling, you may be challenged by a brother or sister who seems to be out of control, blurts out, hurts feelings, has lots of accidents with your toys or property, or injures him- or herself frequently. If you are a child of a parent with ADHD you may feel frustrated by promises that are not kept or the promises to change and disappointment when that change never takes place. In each of these cases you may feel like your person with ADHD is his or her "own worst enemy."

Remember that ADHD is not a "yes" or "no" condition; there are certainly degrees to which ADHD may affect personal relationships. The impact may be small or great, so these chapters represent discussions of possibilities, not predetermined or

From the Teacher

I see so many parents at their wits' end come in to school. They are looking for answers about what is wrong, or they are looking for solutions. I want to tell them, it is going to be fine. ADHD is a chronic condition that requires management just like diabetes or vision problems. Your child is not bad, or mean, or determined to thwart your efforts at parenting. Your child needs medical attention and behavior modification to be successful. Let's work together and teach this child strategies that will serve him or her lifelong.

predicted problems. Friends or romantic interests may be puzzled by the interrupting, atypical social skills, or lack of follow-through by the individual with ADHD. Risk-taking behaviors or "getting into trouble" may put a strain on relationships. Parents of non-ADHD children may need information to facilitate better understanding, or they may just perceive the child with ADHD as ill-behaved and not want to be responsible for him or her. Parents and friends of individuals with ADHD may feel conflicted about their own emotions and reactions to a loved one with ADHD. We've heard parents sometimes say, "I love my child, but I'm not sure I like him." This is an understandable feeling during times of intense parenting. Children with ADHD are a challenge as much as they are a gift, and there is no reason to feel concerned by your own mixed feelings. It is not uncommon for peers of people with ADHD to describe them as overbearing.[2]

If you are a friend and not a parent, you want to help your friend but may find his or her behavior so frustrating that you give up trying to help. To paraphrase a saying, those who need help most may ask for it in a way that is unlikely to produce help.[3] Problems with friendships are very common. In fact, 52% of individuals with ADHD earn a rating as "rejected" by peers.[4] This peer rejection is significant when compared to typical peers. This does not mean that the person is a problem, but that the behavior is the problem. The cycle of peer rejection (see Figure 3.1) may also lead to more behavior problems as a child or adolescent understandably feels sadness, frustration, or anger at the

Problematic or
atypical ADHD
behaviors not under
control of the child

Rejection from peers,
frustration, and
distancing of parents
or caregivers

Feelings of frustration
and sadness

Acting out behaviors
in response to peer
rejection or lack of
approval from parents
and caregivers

Time passes and new
task demand is
presented, i.e., friend
tries again

Friends and parents
feel "confirmed" in
their emotional or
physical distancing

Figure 3.1. Peer Relationship Cycle

peer rejection and may act out intentionally. This is an ironic and unfortunate consequence of the behavior which is not under their control.

Children with ADHD "look and act" different from non-ADHD peers in obvious ways by age 7.[5] These differences are probably most related to an inability to self-regulate or to shift roles, both of which involve recognizing social cues such as facial expressions and body posture. Specific behaviors that cause these problems include inattention, immaturity, hyperactivity, impulsivity, poor emotional regulation, and aggression.[6] Most of these problem behaviors can be targeted for change through strategy training. However, the most effective treatments for peer problems include stimulant medications to address the physiological origins of the problems and include social skills training to learn new behaviors, combined with contingency management to reinforce their use.

From the Counselor

So many moms and dads, spouses, or friends are struggling to maintain a positive relationship with the person suffering from ADHD. Understanding isn't enough when you feel disappointed or let down or wonder "why can't he just be like everyone else." It is easy to get depressed or develop low self-esteem thinking that somehow if you were a better parent, spouse, or friend, the ADHD would go away. It won't. The person with ADHD needs strategies to manage the disorder and the family and friends need their own strategies and support.

INTERVENTION AND COPING STRATEGIES

Using a multimodal approach is the best option for improving the effects of ADHD behaviors on peers and families. Medication improves the biological aspects of ADHD, social skills training develops new behaviors to replace the problems that interfere with friends and family relationships, and contingency management creates an environment to reinforce use of the new behaviors and eliminate problematic negative interactions. These interventions should be implemented in every setting where a child is affected.[7] See Chapter Five for a comprehensive discussion of nonbiological interventions, Chapters Six and Seven for interventions effective in schools, and Chapter Eight for effective parenting strategies.

There are some aspects of ADHD that have great implications for families and friends. First, individuals with ADHD are more likely than not to have a parent with ADHD.[8] This means that as a parent of a child with ADHD, you or your spouse may have ADHD and this has implications for treatment. The same behaviors of inattention and trouble with follow-through that your child experiences may prevent you from fully implementing treatment plans. You may also be at risk for increased alcohol consumption[9] especially after interactions with your child. This may create a negative cycle—alcohol consumption can and will interfere with effective parenting and will create more deviant behaviors in children.[10] Alcohol consumption in response to stressful interactions with a child will also model a form of coping that you may not want for your child. If a young child sees alcohol consumption as a "relaxer" then you might expect to see a teenager with ADHD "self-medicate" with alcohol. Other issues include marital stress, more so than marriages with non-ADHD children.[11] Untreated maternal depression is also a factor in a child with ADHD not doing well. Because parents and caregivers are so important in the outcomes of their children, untreated maternal depression is a tremendous factor in childhood problems. If you believe you are suffering from depression, we encourage you to visit your physician and seek help. Depression will manifest itself in ways that essentially make the parent absent from the child's life and you are too valuable to be absent. Absent or nonparticipating fathers will contribute to increased problems as well.[12] To the degree that you are able, children with ADHD (like all children) need stability and structure in parenting relationships. Not overly harsh, punitive, authoritarian, or unyielding but stable, structured, and authoritative parenting. Permissive is not a good idea either, by the way. Think "middle ground"—responsive and structured with reason.

One of the challenges in parenting a child with ADHD is to recognize that your family has a child with a "Ferrari-engine brain" and that makes your family "atypical" from a numbers standpoint. You are in the minority. Atypical is not bad. Atypical means you have specific needs and challenges and also gifts. Although, unfortunately, in some segments of our society, a family who seeks "counseling" or "parent training" is seen (by some) to reflect personal failure or deficiency of some kind. *This is not so* and particularly not so in a family of a child with ADHD. Consider this scenario. If your child was reading at age 3, advanced rapidly through grade levels at school, and far exceeded peers by many years, perhaps ready to enroll in college by age 12 or 14, ideally you would seek outside advice from experts about the best way to manage the challenges associated with a very young child developing so rapidly. If you were the parents of a child with a medical condition requiring specific and particular care, you would seek advice from doctors or nurses and perhaps be asked to attend training on how to manage this condition. ADHD is a neurologically based condition requiring the same level of attention to maximize the potential of your child. This is not a difference you caused; it is a physiological condition. As such, there is a level of expertise needed that typical families don't need. There are specific demands and challenges associated with ADHD and those challenges probably require knowledge and additional support to be met.

Because there is such misinformation and stereotyping, let me give you one more "plug" for family counseling, parent training, individual counseling, or all of the above, and one more example story. Here is the analogy: to do anything well takes instruction and practice. In parenting we may have neither: we may (or may not) have read a book about "what to expect" with babies or "developmental stages in children" to prepare us, we may subscribe to any number of parenting magazines or have parents or friends with whom we share and receive "advice." Each of these sources may be terrific but are not typically devoted exclusively to the issues of you, your family, or your child. A counselor who specializes in ADHD has read many books and seen hundreds (maybe thousands) of clients just like you. This experience allows a good counselor or therapist to provide customized planning and strategizing for your family. If you want to get really good at something, you generally use a professional coach or trainer. This is true for "getting in shape" or making sure your child is the "star" of the soccer team. Personal trainers and coaches are in the same league as a counselor or trainer; the only difference is the topic. For whatever reason, our culture sometimes views counselors and therapists only as folks who "fix" problems rather than viewing them as people to help provide skills to make something the best it can be and maximize personal potential.

Example: A doctor friend of mine was going through a difficult time with her child. She is brilliant by all accounts with a successful career, a strong marriage, and a lovely son. When I asked "who she was seeing" for treatment of this problem she said, "No one." When I asked why, she responded that she didn't know where to start. This puzzled me until I thought about it more deeply. If I need a dentist, I ask a friend or call my insurance. I may not be able to ask a friend for a referral to a counselor and I may not have insurance. So here are some suggestions. Check first with your insurance for providers and do not be deterred if the person answering the phone is unclear. Ask for service providers in your area who specialize in ADHD or are listed as family counselors. Ask your family physician—they may have a list of providers or would be "in the know" about who is in your area. In fact, they may have someone in the building.

Use the Internet for a list of counselors (just like a dentist). Call first and ask a few key questions: (1) Do you work with families of children with ADHD and how often? (2) Do you have any specialized training or knowledge of ADHD (if so what is it)? (3) What is your philosophical approach? (Look for someone who says something about cognitive-behavioral, or ask if they are behavioral or cognitive-behavioral in their approach.) Avoid anyone trying to sell you vitamins, crystals, or other products.

One common and very effective support program is called "parent training" (for lack of a better term), and although no one treatment works for all things or in all circumstances, parent training is certainly effective for improving behavior in children with ADHD.[13] Parent training is also associated with improving family functioning overall, decreasing stress, and increasing self-esteem.[14] The greater the parental agreement about childrearing, the fewer problem behaviors, the greater the marital adjustment, and the fewer marital conflicts there are.[15] Getting on the "same page" about expectations can happen with education and skill development. This relationship between parental dissension and behavior problems goes both ways. Parent conflict increases problem behaviors and problem behaviors increase parent conflict (see Figure 3.2).

There are many levels and degrees of conflict, however, and this is not to say that parental disagreement is responsible for the behavior of the child. The point is that research shows us that, combined with our inability to resolve conflict, the more

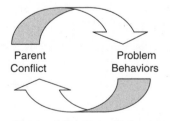

Parent
Conflict

Problem
Behaviors

Figure 3.2. Parent Conflict and Problem Behaviors

Figure 3.3. Comparison of Parental Conflict Over Child to Degree and Frequency

frequent, the more severe, and the more related to the child the conflict is, the greater the relationship between our behavior as parents and our child's acting-out behavior.[16] Not sure where your parenting interactions fall? Some problem interactions to look for include aggression, negative feedback to each other, argumentativeness, noncompliance toward each other, and ignoring one another.[17] Consider marking an "X" on the three scales in Figure 3.3 for where you think your spouse or partner interactions fall.

It is typical for a parent to think or wonder, "How am I doing, am I doing the right thing?" or "Is this normal?" and "Will my child be OK?" After all, most of us only have our personal experience or the children of friends for comparison. So if you are in a place where you want to consider or examine your own level of functioning, consider asking a professional for access to any of the following measures. The assessment called Parenting Stress can serve as an index of parent-child stress.[18] Parenting self-esteem can be measured in the Parenting Sense of Competence.[19] Other areas, which may benefit from assessment, include measures of marital satisfaction (Locke-Wallace Marital Adjustment Scale[20]) or overall knowledge of ADHD (Test of ADHD Knowledge[21]). Other assessments that can lead to the development of personal improvement plans might include the

Parenting Sense of Competency Scale.[22] Parenting Relationship Questionnaire (PRQ)[23] can provide a thorough look at how you relate to your child and how you see your child relating to you and give you information on how this compares to similar factors among other parents of similarly aged children. Specifically, the PRQ looks at parent-child attachment, communications, involvement, parenting confidence, disciplinary practices, relational frustration, and satisfaction with school.

There are two basic types of parent training, individual or one-on-one sessions and group sessions. The basic premise in parent training is to explicitly provide families with strategies and techniques to prevent and remediate problem behaviors at home and at school. These techniques can empower families to feel more in control, more positive, and more optimistic. These characteristic changes in turn predict better outcomes for children with ADHD. Basic social learning principles are involved, and although this chapter is not meant to serve as a replacement for seeking training, we will provide an overview here.

First, parents learn to identify and manipulate the antecedents and consequences of problem behavior. Antecedents are those things that occur before problem behavior. Consequences are those things that occur afterward. This is easily remembered as A-B-C, Antecedent—Behavior—Consequence. For example, see Figure 3.4: Mike's mom asks him to unload groceries, Mike says yes, but asks to get a drink first and then gets distracted and forgets to come back to help. Mom unloads all the groceries by herself.

This A-B-C chain demonstrates a task request—an escape behavior—and a negative reinforcer (the removal of something aversive, such as unloading groceries). In order to change this behavior, both the antecedent and the consequence can be changed. Antecedent: "Mike can you help me unload groceries immediately, without doing anything else? Come straight here." Behavior: Mike complies, or if he doesn't and instead asks to do

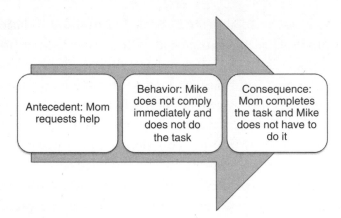

Figure 3.4. Parental Behavior and Child Behavior

something else, Mom says, "No. Immediately, without doing anything else, come straight here." Or if Mike is allowed to get a drink and wanders off, Mom needs to leave the groceries and go find Mike to redirect him to finish the task. Ideally, a structured system would be set up where following directions immediately is reinforced with access to privileges and not following directions has negative, natural consequences.

Family scenarios are likely more complex than a simple A-B-C and may involve **temporally distant setting events** (things that took place earlier in time and set the stage for problems to occur). Because they occur earlier in time, this makes them less easily identifiable. Here is the same scenario made more complex. Mike jumps off the school bus after a demanding day at school. He is hungry and hyped up about a new computer game he wants to download. Mike's mom has barely beaten the bus home from work and needs to unload groceries from the car and start dinner. Mike says "Hi, Mom" and asks to download his game. She would like help unloading groceries but would rather not have conflict and doesn't have time or energy to chase Mike down, so instead says "Yes—sure, but please pick up your coat and backpack and hang them up" as a way to feel some parenting satisfaction for teaching responsibility to Mike. Dad enters with two small children just picked up from day care. He is equally drained from work and a long car ride home with small, tired, hungry people in the back seat. When Dad sees Mike downloading videos and Mom unloading groceries, he gets frustrated and blurts out, "Son, what have I told you about helping your mom!" As he walks to talk to Mike, Dad trips over the backpack left on the floor. Mike recognizes he has (1) forgotten to do what his mom asked, and (2) not met his father's expectations. Emotionally he does not regulate well and instead gets angry and feels hurt and start to argue and tear up. This provokes Dad to say, "I'll give you something to cry about—your mom is too soft on you." Mom is now involved and the family conflict escalates. Mike eventually slams a door to escape the fight and gets punished by serving time without friends after school until he can make better choices. Mom retreats feeling isolated and sad that home cannot be a happy, peaceful place. Dad is unhappy with the family interactions as well and thinks he should "just stay out of it" rather than try to parent with his wife's interference. Frustration, conflict, and withdrawal then proceed between the parents, adding to the difficulties of an already difficult task (that is, parenting Mike well).

There is a chain of events here that are occasioned by mood, fatigue, hunger, dispositions, and expectations. The antecedents to the problem behavior "Mike pick up your backpack and coat and hang them up" are lost in the melee of interaction. The antecedent here is a request by Mom, in this case, to "hang up a backpack and coat." The consequences of punishment are removed from the problem behavior (not following directions immediately) and perhaps not fulfilling the behavioral expectations of the family for "helping." To improve this situation two things should occur. Like the simple scenario described first, the behavior of not following directions should be addressed with clear expectations, consistent follow-through, and reinforcement for performing. Consequences should be related to the problem and quickly administered. So, for example, the consequence for downloading video games rather than follow directions means no video games the rest of that afternoon, or perhaps for 24 hours (not a week, a month, and so on. Be sure consequences are reasonable in magnitude!). Unloading groceries should also be a clear expectation, perhaps written down as one of 3–5 family expectations for "helping" or "responsibility," which would also include hanging up a backpack and coat. Mike should have to go back and pick up the backpack and the coat and help with the groceries as well. Changing antecedents to the escape behavior may involve parents making an agreement to not jump to conclusions. Or to only review behavior each evening with a behavior point sheet. Parents might also agree to discuss any problems later, when alone, and not in earshot of Mike.

From the Neuroscientist

Often parents expect children to notice chores or other things around the house that need to be done or help that can be offered, and just do it. In reality, the children do not notice—they are not shirking responsibility, they just really do not see it. Remember, the first two words in ADHD are "attention deficit!"

Organizations such as Children and Adults with Attention-Deficit/Hyperactivity Disorder (CHADD) and Attention-Deficit Disorder Association (ADDA) provide opportunities learn more, access support, and develop coping skills and strategies.

PEER FUNCTIONING

Friends are important for all of us and especially for children. Friends help children learn social skills like cooperation and conflict resolution and how to be successful in the school environment. Problems with friends predict a host of future problems ranging from dropping out of school to problems adjusting to life after school, especially positive adjustment to work environments.

Because the problems of ADHD interfere so drastically with friendships, and because social reputations at school can be established quickly and remain in place for extended periods of time, social functioning, development of friends, and maintaining friendships is critical. Every aspect of ADHD has implications for friends.

Inhibition

Inhibition is sometimes simply the ability to hear that voice in your head that says "don't do that" or "don't say that." For example, Ralph is a fabulous friend in a one-on-one situation, but will frequently say inappropriate things in public or social groups. His friends have a hard time "excusing" his semi-offensive behavior and are put in an awkward position of saying things like "that is just Ralph" or in the equally awkward position of reprimanding a friend such as "I can't believe you said that." Ralph feels that because his statements are "true" or "right" as a reflection of his opinion, he isn't sure why he can't speak as he wishes. Ralph will then get defensive or difficult socially. Eventually most of the guys in the social circle leave Ralph out of group activities where they would have to be "responsible" for Ralph's verbal behavior.

Working Memory

Working memory is the ability to keep information at hand for problem solving or reasoning. Karen is a successful and generally well-liked teenager. She has many casual friends who say nice things about her. But Karen does not function well in group work at school and her casual friends do not include her in after-school activities. Her ability to contribute to a team or comprehend multicomponent assignments makes her the last pick for class teams. Karen notices the reluctance in her peers and responds in kind by not extending herself to develop deeper relationships.

Emotional Self-Control

Emotions reflect feelings. When emotions control the person, rather than the person controlling the emotions, problems occur. Disposition, mood, or sentiment appears to make up what others would consider "personality." Adrian is a likeable young boy. He is bright and a good athlete. But when confronted with coaching or criticism he flies off the handle at teachers, coaches, and other students. Faced with waiting in line to practice layups, rather than wait his turn Adrian pushes a good friend in the back and knocks him over. Upset at his own impulsivity he gets angry and cries, storming away from the game. His inability to wait, his frustration with himself for not waiting, and his lack of self-control create reoccurring problems which interfere with sports, recess, birthday parties, and siblings, among other issues.

Motor Control

Motor control is the internal process that executes complex motor sequences and responses or behavior, which, chained together, make up goal directions, motivation, and persistence. Levi seems directed to other students in high school and is rejected by most peers and adults on campus. Although he scored above average in a measure of intelligence, Levi is that kid who "can't get it together." He blows through idea after idea, never following through on any of them. His plans range from the fantastic, such as becoming an astronaut, to the pragmatic but unlikely, such as opening his own video store. Neither of these career paths is out of the question, but Levi is uninterested in taking or completing the coursework necessary to attend college and become a pilot. His interest in video games is fleeting and there will be bursts of activity in collecting games but no systematic approach to what would be required to open a business. As such Levi appears flaky and even "weird" to other high schoolers. His girlfriends don't last long because, for all his talking about romantic dates, he rarely delivers on his ideas.

FAMILY FUNCTIONING

Families are affected by children with attention or hyperactivity problems as early as preschool age.[24] Children appear more non-compliant and the parent-child interactions are more negative and conflict-ridden.[25] These types of interactions lead to more stress for parents, which creates an environment for further negative conflict.

The best way to interrupt this cycle and to prevent long-term problems is to work diligently (perhaps through training) to: (1) increase the number of positive interactions with children, (2) reduce conflict in parenting practices, and (3) improve consistency in parenting practices. These three things can dramatically change a child's social and academic performance.[26] Determining and teaching clear expectations for behavior at home and in all routines and establishing predictable and consistent family environments makes home life more positive. This creates a more positive circle of interaction (see Figure 3.5).

It seems that every area of family life is affected by ADHD in one of the family members. Family activities are less frequent or less functional. A child with ADHD can be the source of frustration in simple activities like eating out or going to a movie, or in more complicated functions like vacations and team commitments. Consider Beth and Darek, parents of a darling 3-year-old boy Keeland. Going out is a challenge as Keeland will not stay seated in a high chair, or remain interested in eating for

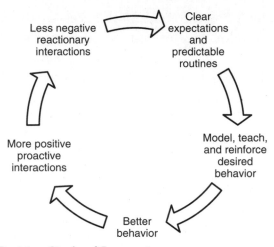

Figure 3.5. Positive Circle of Interaction

more than a few minutes. So Beth and Darek begin taking turns, one at the table eating and the other walking or chasing Keeland as he enjoys the wonders of the sidewalk outside. By age 6, when other boys are managing a meal at the table, Keeland still can't sit still long enough for the family to get through a meal. Over time Beth and Darek begin to argue about whether or not more punishment is needed. Beth begins to bargain more with Keeland and Darek begins to get harsher. Dinners out are a thing of the past because there is too much conflict to make it worthwhile. As more social events get removed from the routine, family stress increases.

Keeland and his mom had several play date opportunities when Keeland was younger because Mom was playing alongside Keeland, moderating his play behavior. A typical scene would be in a park, where children play while parents observe and correct continually, such as "Keeland, share your toy" or "Keeland, play nice" or "Keeland, wait your turn." But now that Keeland is older and play with friends is less parent supervised, there is no more Mom to govern Keeland's play behavior. No one to regulate sharing, playing nice, waiting a turn. Without this "voice over,"

Keeland fights with his friends and has trouble sharing, playing nice, and taking turns. Parents of Keeland's friends report that he makes messes, uses inappropriate language, seems "out of control," is too loud, breaks toys, cries, and is difficult to settle down. Keeland does not appear to attend to adult redirection and is perceived as not listening or being noncompliant. The other parents express concern that their children will pick up bad habits or learn inappropriate behaviors. Eventually Keeland isn't invited back. As the circle of friends grows smaller, Keeland is missing the developmental stages of learning conflict negotiation, how to pick up social cues from peers, and how to self-regulate. Mom feels the frustration for herself and her child. This scenario is why disclosure with other parents may help negotiate or prevent some of these problems. You may have a skill set other parents don't. You may need to say, "If my child starts to get loud, you need to touch him on the shoulder to get his attention" or "Don't be afraid to remind my child to take a turn" or "Be sure to tell my child about any house rules because he struggles with knowing how to act in new environments." This precorrection gives other parents permission to dialogue with your child and you about behaviors, and may avoid rejection and facilitate understanding and a cooperative approach. After all, most parents are hesitant to parent someone else's child.

Darek was a high school athletic star and had hopes for his son to perform well also. Although 20 years ago Darek struggled with attention, reading, and academics in school, got in trouble a couple of times, and was suspended once for a fight, this behavior is nothing Darek would consider abnormal for a boy. Darek's sports participation kept him interested enough in school that he didn't give up or drop out and was able to progress through the grades. Now that Keeland is old enough to play local sports, Darek is eager to coach him in the driveway or the back yard but Keeland doesn't listen to his dad. Instead of taking directions he argues that he is doing it the right way. Darek grows increasingly frustrated. Keeland will play for only a little while before wanting to create new games with the ball, imagine new rules, and create elaborate stories about how to play ball. Darek ends up frustrated because he perceives his son isn't "trying." Eventually Darek and Keeland end up in a fight and quit playing ball. Over time Darek gives up and Keeland misses out on the parenting of his father and the sports skills which may keep him interested in school. Although Darek recognizes some similarities between himself and his son, he is overwhelmed by Keeland's needs. A fixed limit on the coaching may help Keeland focus and Darek not be frustrated, such as 7 minutes of catch without changing rules or inventing a game, followed by 3 minutes of "We will do it your way son."

RECOMMENDATIONS FOR FRIENDS AND FAMILY

The adverse effects of ADHD are not restricted to just the individual; family members and friends are affected as well. The increased rates of negative in-school and post-school outcomes have implications for the individual and the social support people around them. Dropping out, school suspension, and expulsion occur at a frequency that is more than double for individuals with ADHD.[27] Rates of substance abuse, incarceration, attempted suicide, grade retention, and job dismissal are close to 50% in individuals with ADHD.[28] The parenting responsibilities and friendship implications for these statistics may seem overwhelming. However, individuals with ADHD are also some of the most talented and interesting contributors in our communities. These individuals sometimes have amazing abilities and the behaviors associated with ADHD may make them particularly well suited for certain tasks and careers.

There are strategies to mitigate the risk associated with ADHD. The earlier the strategies are employed the more likely they are to be effective at preventing other problems that may go along with ADHD, such as a failure to learn or thrive socially. Although any one strategy demonstrates improvement, a multifaceted approach certainly provides greater effects. Stimulant medication, family training, and behavior modification techniques generate a strong response to the condition. Early and sustained intervention of predictable routines, clear expectations, instruction, modeling of social skills, and contingency management can prevent a certain degree of peer rejection and negative interactions with family members. Successful negotiation of friends and family relationships provides a solid foundation for individuals with ADHD to have more and better life experiences.

Keeland is seen by a physician and, with multiple sources of information from family members and teachers, is diagnosed with ADHD. Medication treats the impulsivity, excessive motor activity, and distractibility. Keeland's mom, Beth, precorrects Keeland before going to restaurants about the expected behavior of sitting through a meal and gives Keeland a digital timer to keep track. Sitting through the meal without disruption means a choice of dessert for the family to share. If Keeland is disruptive, the meal is continued without punishment except for the loss of the reinforcer (Keeland choosing dessert). Dad Darek plays ball with Keeland without excessive talking and coaching. Dad reminds himself to keep the corrections to a ratio of one negative to four positives. The family will start play date arrangements again, for short periods of time with structured activities, while Keeland develops more social competency. The family has a predictable routine and the negative interactions have significantly decreased. Although Keeland's earlier established reputation will take some time to overcome, his ADHD was addressed early enough to prevent academic failure. This interception in his school life with a multifaceted approach will serve as a protective factor against risk.

TO SUM UP

Although this chapter discussed how ADHD may have a negative impact on family and friends, we want to stress that being a parent, spouse, sibling, or friend of an individual with ADHD can have many positive aspects as well. As we discussed in Chapter Two, individuals with ADHD can be filled with excitement, energy, creativity, passion, and exuberance. Focusing on the joy brought into your life by these characteristics can make the "bumps in the road" less difficult. Parents of children with ADHD often experience stress, depression, frustration, anger, and marital discord. Research on the relationship between parents and children with various disabilities shows that parents of children with ADHD report high levels of frustration with their parenting skills and in their relationship with their child. However, we discussed ways to parent more effectively and how you can focus on the positives in your child's life, as well as in your relationship, and thus avoid concentrating on your frustrations with him or her. We ask parents to avoid letting their negative emotions overshadow the good moments that occur.

In addition, by working together parents can overcome issues relating to the likelihood that one parent will also have ADHD. Often parents in this situation find that laughter is the best medicine. Though not diminishing the negative impact of multiple individuals with ADHD living in the same household, it is important for all to be able to laugh when things become chaotic, and to then regroup, and try again. We recognize that individuals with ADHD are often rejected by peers or have difficulties with friendships; however, you can encourage friends to focus on the fun and continue to help the individual with ADHD learn new coping skills. The situation does not have to be bleak and overwhelming, although at times it will feel so no matter what! With a multimodal treatment approach, medication can be beneficial, parents can learn to create a structured environment with consistent expectations providing positive and negative responses to behavior, and the individual with ADHD can learn to function successfully within his peer group via training, consistent guidance, and reinforcement. We encourage you, as a parent or friend of an individual with ADHD, to focus on the strengths, increase positive interactions, reduce conflict, and increase consistency in all of your interactions but especially in your disciplinary practices.

WHAT'S NEXT?

Part One has given you an understanding of what ADHD is, common behaviors and related disorders, and how ADHD can affect relationships with those closest to us. In Part Two, we will discuss diagnosis and treatment, which, it is important to remember, should be based on the best research available.

Getting Help

4

Is It Really ADHD?

Getting the Right Diagnosis

The truth is, ADHD can be difficult to diagnose accurately. Your clinician has no shortcuts, no quick blood tests, no brain scans, no five-minute questionnaires, and no brief interviews to use with your child, you as a parent, or you as an adult that have acceptable levels of accuracy in the diagnosis of ADHD. Nevertheless, accurate diagnosis is certainly achievable, and when you select a professional clinician who knows not only ADHD but other disorders that commonly mimic ADHD, accurate diagnosis becomes the norm. In this chapter we will teach you why getting the diagnosis right is so important as well as what to look for in getting a proper evaluation, which will always (a word we do not like to use!) be a comprehensive evaluation to determine the right diagnosis when symptoms that could be ADHD are at issue. We have reviewed the diagnostic criteria for ADHD and the various subtypes in a previous chapter, and we will try not to repeat that information here. Rather, we focus on the diagnostic process and how and with what tools diagnostic information is gathered when the job is done well.

WHY ACCURATE DIAGNOSIS IS SO CRITICAL

Effective treatment of any disorder depends upon accurate diagnosis. This statement is absolutely the truth—the relative importance of the level of detail and specificity of an accurate diagnosis, however, is not the same for every disorder. Take, for example, the diagnosis of most common infectious disorders by primary care physicians. You probably recall getting ill, perhaps with a sore throat, and going to your doctor. Following a brief physical examination, she tells you this has been going around and prescribes a particular antibiotic, but you were also probably told that if you were not better in 48 to 72 hours, to call the doctor's office. In about 7 to 14 days, you are well. In this case, diagnosis of a general class of disorder, a "throat infection," is typically sufficient and specific enough for successful treatment. There are reasonably broad spectrum antibiotics that kill most bacteria residing in airways that cause such infections, and it is not necessary to know exactly which bug is causing yours. However, if you do not improve quickly, your doctor will need to move to a more accurate diagnosis. She will likely need to culture or grow the bacteria so it can be identified specifically so that an antibacterial agent that will kill this particular bacterium can be identified and prescribed. There are presentations where immediate culturing and identification are urgent, such as in the case of bacterial pneumonia, which could proliferate into a life-threatening illness if the wrong antibiotic is used initially for treatment.

In the case of ADHD, just as with the bacteria above that were not identified correctly, very specific, accurate diagnosis is required so that we can abide by the first guiding principle of all health care providers: First, do no harm! If we diagnose ADHD when it is not present, especially when we mistake another disorder for ADHD, we run the risk of doing great harm. There are many emotional and behavioral disorders, some of which are also disorders of brain function, that look like or mimic ADHD on the surface. That is to say, many of the behaviors we see in these disorders look similar to those we see in ADHD. In some cases, as we will explain later, the medicines for ADHD can make people with certain other disorders not only worse, but potentially more difficult to treat once the correct diagnosis has been ascertained. Just as a fever does not always mean a bacterial infection, problems with attention do not always mean ADHD! If these behaviors and their history and the environments in which they occur are not assessed carefully and in detail, we may just get it wrong and call it ADHD when it is not. We will come back to this crucial issue later in this chapter. First we want to look at the issue of normal levels of inattention, impulsivity, and behavioral activity for anyone at any age. As you probably have noticed, everyone commits impulsive acts, everyone has moments of inattention, and everyone can be hyperactive at different times. How do you know when it has reached beyond the level of normal and has become an indication of a disorder? How do you know that your physician is not just creating psychopathology from what are typical variations in behavior?

What's Typical Behavior?

When diagnosticians of various types (psychologists, psychiatrists, neuropsychologists, physicians) attempt to answer this question in the realm of disorders that affect behavior and emotions (such as ADHD), they typically look at the three aspects of the behavior listed in Figure 4.1.

Once we answer these questions, we can make a sensible and often empirical scientific judgment about whether the behavior (or more likely, the cluster of presenting behaviors) represents a variation of normal behavior or whether it has risen to a level of severity and impact on your life that qualifies it for the diagnosis of a disorder. The first two questions are answered by

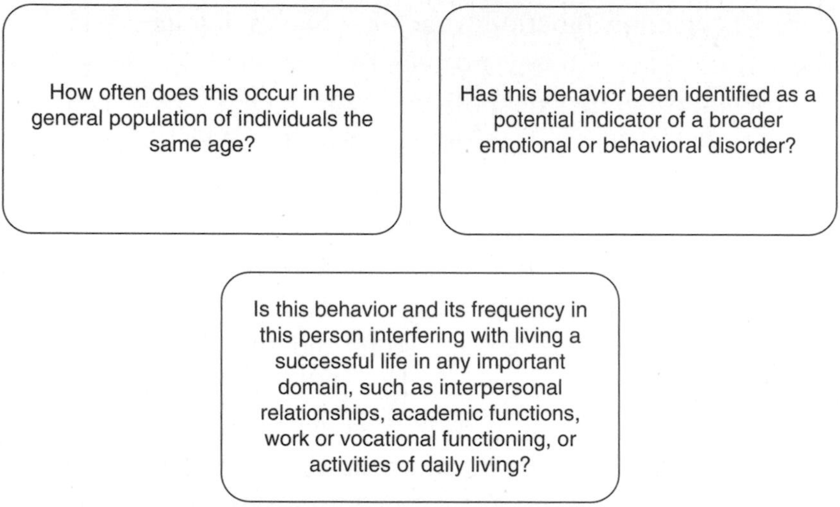

> How often does this occur in the general population of individuals the same age?

> Has this behavior been identified as a potential indicator of a broader emotional or behavioral disorder?

> Is this behavior and its frequency in this person interfering with living a successful life in any important domain, such as interpersonal relationships, academic functions, work or vocational functioning, or activities of daily living?

Figure 4.1. Three Aspects of Behavior Evaluated

research on the frequency rates of many different human behaviors to which the clinician can compare the observed behaviors of the individual in question.

How Often Does This Occur in the General Population of Individuals the Same Age? Have you ever tried to compare your behavior or the behavior of your child to that of others of the same age? It is an impossible task to do through simple observation. Determining what is typical requires observations of thousands of children, as all children demonstrate different behaviors at different times. Therefore, answering the first question requires access to a database that provides reference points for what is typical for hundreds of different behaviors and their rates of occurrence. These databases also identify the typical rates of occurrence of clusters of these behaviors—not just one behavior at a time, but how often they occur together. Such databases allow the clinician to determine whether the behaviors are common in frequency or more or less frequent than occurs in the general population of persons the same age, and this is always

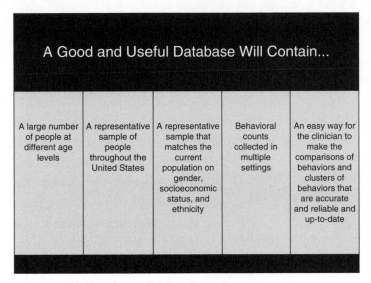

A Good and Useful Database Will Contain...				
A large number of people at different age levels	A representative sample of people throughout the United States	A representative sample that matches the current population on gender, socioeconomic status, and ethnicity	Behavioral counts collected in multiple settings	An easy way for the clinician to make the comparisons of behaviors and clusters of behaviors that are accurate and reliable and up-to-date

Figure 4.2. A Good and Useful Database Contains

important in any behavioral or emotional diagnosis. Databases like these exist, but there are very few that are of high quality and that represent the behavior of people in the United States at large. To be accurate and allow for solid diagnostic determinations, any such database includes behavioral counts that meet at least the criteria in Figure 4.2. This database provides the clinician an easy way to make the comparisons of your behaviors and clusters of behaviors to that of people who are similar to you and that are accurate and reliable and up-to-date.

From the Counselor

I have often had teachers tell me that a child is demonstrating behaviors associated with ADHD. However, without the teacher completing a rating scale and comparing the results to the "norms" provided in test databases and the clinical judgment of a trained professional, I cannot know for sure that the teacher is correct.

A good and useful database will contain behavioral counts based on a large number of individuals, including a large number of persons at different age levels to enable age-appropriate comparisons—the frequency of "inattention," for example, is normally not the same in a 3-year-old as it is in a 13-year-old or a 33-year-old. The people in the database (we will refer to this as our *sample* or *sample of individuals*) whose behaviors are counted should be representative of people at different ages throughout the United States as a whole and not just one state, or even one region. Otherwise, the database would only be useful in that one state. For example, if we were concerned about the frequency with which a 5-year-old in California acts quickly without thinking, comparing that child to a database that only included 5-year-olds from Tennessee and none from California would not give us an accurate answer to our question. The people in the database should also represent the current population on other characteristics such as gender, ethnic background, and socioeconomic status.

We also want such databases to include behavioral counts obtained in multiple settings, because the frequency of a behavior can vary substantially from one setting to another. For example, the frequency of talking out while another person is talking may be much more common at home than at school, or at work if an adult.

To be maximally useful, the database should also provide the clinician with an easy way to make the comparisons of behaviors

From the Teacher

Many parents have asked me if their child has ADHD. As a teacher, I can attest that it is impossible to observe children and determine who is more hyperactive, impulsive, or inattentive than other children of the same age. I can tell you when certain children behave in a hyperactive or inattentive manner, but determining what is different from the norm is difficult. In addition, I cannot tell you for sure that the child has ADHD. There are too many other things that could be causing the problem and that is not my training. It takes a trained clinician to make this determination.

and clusters of behaviors that are accurate and reliable and up-to-date.

Databases like these are expensive and time consuming to build and they can also become dated. While there is no clear rule, to be useful in diagnosis any such database should be updated every 10–15 years as the frequency of some potentially important behaviors may change as society and the daily activities of all of us change over time.

Databases such as those described here are typically developed and maintained by commercial test publishers. One role that commercial test publishers play in the diagnostic process is to develop, maintain, and revise these databases to keep up-to-date on psychological measures of behavior and emotion. These are used often in the diagnosis of disorders of behavior and emotion and are referred to most commonly as *behavior rating scales* and *self-reports of behavior*. When your clinician is completing an evaluation for ADHD, you will probably be asked to complete one or more behavior rating scales. If you are the parent of a child being evaluated for ADHD, you and your child's teachers will be asked to complete rating scales (this will be done separately, because children often will actually behave differently at home and at school—and also with one parent versus another). If you are an adult being evaluated for ADHD, you will complete a rating scale, and your parent, spouse, significant other, or another adult who knows you will complete rating scales. The other adult that is rating your behavior should know you well enough to rate accurately the frequency of many of your different behaviors. The rating scale that you complete for yourself is called a self-report. Self-report rating scales are just as they sound—they are completed by the person, responding to questions by rating the frequency with which they do certain things and feel certain feelings or have particular thoughts (thoughts and feelings are actually behaviors too, we just cannot see them). Often, these rating scales will go by another, perhaps even more familiar name. They may be referred to as *personality tests!*

For example, the Behavior Assessment System for Children, Second Edition[1] (usually abbreviated BASC-2) contains a database of more than 800 items or behaviors on which data from more than 13,000 individuals between the ages of 2 years and 21 years were gathered. In other words, to determine the typical level of behaviors represented by the 800 items (some represent the same behavior) for the different ages between 2 and 21, parents, teachers, and individuals completed the BASC-2 for 13,000 individuals. To ensure that a good comparison could be made to individuals across the United States, these individuals were chosen to match carefully the demographic characteristics of the population of the United States at large. When you complete a BASC-2 rating scale (or form) for yourself, your child, or a significant other, your physician or other clinician compares the frequency and distribution of the behaviors of the individual being evaluated to the frequency and distribution of the same behaviors in this database.

Has This Behavior Been Identified as a Potential Indicator of a Broader Emotional or Behavioral Disorder?   To answer this second question, clinical research is conducted that allows the diagnostician to look at a list of behaviors that are associated with a specific disorder such as ADHD. We gave you a list of some of these for ADHD in Chapter Two. Some of these might be interrupting others while speaking, acting without thinking, not waiting to take turns, being easily distracted, and not being able to stay seated, among many others. These behaviors were established as indicators of ADHD as the frequency or intensity of each of the behaviors in persons with ADHD is greater than the frequency of the behaviors in persons without ADHD. Fortunately, there is much clinical research on which behaviors distinguish one diagnostic group from another, such as telling the difference between depression and ADHD!

Is This Behavior and Its Frequency in This Person Interfering with Living a Successful Life in Any Important Domain, Such as Interpersonal Relationships, Academic Functions, Work or Vocational Functioning, or Activities of Daily Living? The third question we posed in Figure 4.1 is difficult to answer as clearly and as objectively as the others and is often left to the judgment of the individual, the parents, and the clinician. There are tests that assess quality of life as we experience it. These can be helpful, especially when we examine the frequency of things like behavior problems at home, school, and work, along with problems in daily living. Problems in daily living are often evident in such behaviors as remembering to brush your teeth, to bathe, to look both ways before you cross the street, and choosing clothes that match and are appropriate to the weather. These scales allow the clinician to compare these frequencies to those in the database, but ultimately some judgment must be invoked as to whether functioning in one or more of these areas has been adversely affected by ADHD. Also, some behaviors impair some people more than others. The truth is that you or your child may have learned to cope better with a particular problem behavior or have parents, spouses or other loved ones, teachers, or supervisors who are more tolerant of a behavior that others would criticize and find more difficult.

THE PERILS OF MISDIAGNOSIS, OR WHY WE NEED COMPREHENSIVE ASSESSMENT TO DIAGNOSE ADHD!

As we have indicated, there are many disorders that can look like ADHD on the surface but which, upon detailed

Bipolar Disorder (especially Early Onset Bipolar Disorder)

Tourette's Syndrome

Oppositional Defiant Disorder

Childhood Depression

Conduct Disorder

Central Auditory Processing Disorders

Anxiety Disorders (especially overanxious disorder of childhood)

Obsessive Compulsive Disorders

Acute stress reactions including grief reactions

Post Traumatic Stress Disorder, especially related to physical and/or sexual abuse

Fetal Alcohol Spectrum Disorders

Exposure to drugs in utero (including certain prescription drugs as well as illegal drugs)

Certain types of thyroid problems

Mild mental retardation

Drug abuse by the individual

Reactions to prescription medications

Head injuries including closed head concussion

Heavy metal poisoning (e.g., lead, mercury) and related toxic exposure

Sleep disorders

Certain diseases of the brain and spinal cord, e.g., meningitis

Figure 4.3. Disorders That Might Look Like ADHD on the Surface

examination, turn out to be something else. We will not attempt to list all of the possible disorders or reactions that can mimic ADHD, but those in Figure 4.3 are some of the more common, especially among children and youth.

We have seen much longer lists, and often these lists will include things like diet, eating too much sugar, and the like, but as we have said, there is little scientific evidence that such factors are involved in the development of ADHD symptoms. Another popularized mimic is called sensory integration disorder (sometimes abbreviated as SID). Our review of the scientific evidence leads us to the conclusion that SID, to the extent that it exists at all, is unrelated to the development of symptoms of ADHD.

Many of these disorders are easily ruled out or diagnosed quickly, especially diseases like meningitis which have other obvious symptoms. However, some are far more difficult to discern without careful systematic consideration, and misdiagnosis and treatment of ADHD in place of some of these disorders is especially problematic. Let's look at several of these.

ADHD, post-traumatic stress disorder (PTSD), and generalized anxiety disorders (GAD) in children can have more than ten behavioral symptoms in common. Children, especially boys, who have each of these disorders will often (not always) exhibit attention problems, act impulsively, be restless and fidgety, be irritable emotionally, and have learning problems and difficulty with memory. It is easy for a clinician, based upon parent complaints of these behaviors, to reach the more common of all of these diagnoses, ADHD, prematurely, in the absence of a careful, comprehensive evaluation. Misdiagnosis among these disorders can have serious consequences. PTSD and, to a lesser extent, other anxiety disorders stem from being overly vigilant and on high alert physiologically. In the case of PTSD, the limbic system of the brain, that part of the brain responsible for threat appraisal and our "fight or flight" response, is hyperstimulated by some external traumatizing event and remains that way for longer than normal. It is important for you to be able to tell the difference, as the effective treatments for PTSD as well as GAD are vastly different from the effective treatments for ADHD (you can read about nonmedication treatments with scientific documentation of their effectiveness for anxiety, attention problems, aggression, and a number of other behavioral symptoms in a treatment guide by Vannest, Reynolds, and Kamphaus[2]). If the correct diagnosis is PTSD or GAD and the wrong diagnosis of ADHD is given, the individual will not improve; however, in the case of PTSD the outcome is far worse than simply delaying effective treatment. Because certain brain systems that are affected by dopamine and norepinephrine (see Chapter Three) are heavily involved in PTSD and are already overly aroused, the use of stimulant medications such as Ritalin with these individuals can create serious problems. Not only may some individuals actually get worse, it may become more difficult to treat their PTSD in the future due to the even greater, more exacerbated state of arousal created by the incorrect use of stimulant medication. Treatments for PTSD are targeted at easing the arousal levels of the limbic system, which is in a constant state of alert in PTSD, and especially at changing the negative valence of stimuli in our environment that seem to trigger anxiety and panic in a person with PTSD over to a positive valence, a change that has to occur in the limbic system. The further enhanced arousal of an already overly stimulated system by misdiagnosis and inappropriate treatment with stimulant medicines violates the first principle of all health care providers: first, do no harm.

If principles of comprehensive differential diagnosis are followed, the probability of getting the diagnosis right goes up substantially. No one and no process of diagnosis is right 100% of the time, and our goal is to keep our errors to a minimum so that we get the right diagnosis and the treatment required in place as soon as possible.

THE DIAGNOSTIC PROCESS: WHAT IS NECESSARY AND WHAT TO EXPECT

The truth is, you cannot diagnose ADHD accurately in most cases with a brief or even an hour-long clinical interview. More information is needed than can be reasonably gathered in this time, and several forms of psychological or neuropsychological testing, or both, are needed to do the job well. The days should be behind us when the pediatrician diagnoses ADHD and prescribes medication for its treatment on the basis of parents or teachers complaining that "Johnny just can't seem to sit still," or that Susanna "cannot pay attention for more than a moment or two"—based on observation in a brief office visit during which the child is also seen to squirm in the chair.

The American Academy of Pediatrics (AAP) recognized the issues and complexity of the diagnosis in 2000, when the AAP released their official clinical practice guidelines on diagnosis of ADHD.[3] Noting that ADHD is a common problem and increasingly becoming a controversial one, the AAP recommended broad diagnostic work that is largely behaviorally based. According to the official practice guidelines of the AAP, the assessment of ADHD should include information obtained directly from parents or caregivers, as well as a classroom teacher or other school professional, regarding the core symptoms of ADHD in various settings, the age of onset, duration of symptoms, and

From the Parent

Although the days of pediatricians diagnosing ADHD based on parent report should be behind us, it has been my experience that many continue to do so. Though this is the pediatrician's ultimate decision, I believe that as parents, we have to be careful not to look for a quick fix. I have seen parents get to the point of great frustration with a child prior to having the child evaluated for ADHD. At this point, many parents go to their pediatrician, with whom they have a long-standing and trusting relationship, and when the pediatrician recommends a referral to a clinician with expertise in ADHD, the parent suggests that the child just needs to "try" medication to see if it makes a difference. The lessons here are that as parents, we must act more quickly prior to becoming overly frustrated and that we should trust our pediatrician's professional judgment to refer to a clinician with expertise in ADHD. Of course, the pediatrician should also know to refer the child for a comprehensive evaluation.

degree of functional impairment. In recognition of the common finding that ADHD may be comorbid with other problems, AAP stated that evaluation of a child with ADHD should also include assessment for coexisting conditions such as learning and language problems, aggression, disruptive behavior, depression, and anxiety. AAP noted then that as many as one-third of children diagnosed with ADHD also have a coexisting condition.

In making these recommendations, the AAP appears to recognize the need, as we do and as others have noted,[4] for a broad-based assessment of the behavior and affect of children suspected of having ADHD. These recommendations are highly similar to the recommendations psychologists and others have made since the early 1990s,[5] and they are highly consistent with diagnostic models proposed as the best practices for most areas of childhood psychopathology or behavioral and emotional disorders.[6] Diagnosis of ADHD then is a multistep process (see Figure 4.4). The following components of this process are recommended for inclusion by most who specialize in the area of emotional and behavioral disorders.

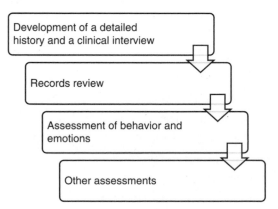

Figure 4.4. Diagnosis Is a Multi-Step Process

1. Development of a Detailed History and a Clinical Interview

ADHD does not just all of a sudden appear overnight. Some forms of emotional and behavioral disorders, such as PTSD, can do so, but not ADHD; however, ADHD might not have been noticed until your child was placed in a structured environment such as a preschool, kindergarten, or in the elementary grades. In addition, as an adult you might not have been diagnosed as a child, but you recognized symptoms of ADHD in yourself when your child was diagnosed. As Goldstein describes the process, this is not a quick or cursory "How long has he been acting this way?" but is a detailed discovery process designed to learn about the developmental history of the individual, others in the family, relationships with others, the context of the behaviors (for example, do they only occur at school or only around Mom but not Dad, only during religious attendance, only when the family goes out to eat, and so on), and how the behaviors of concern (*the presenting problem*, in clinical language) are affecting the person's ability to function appropriately in everyday life.[7] It is necessary to understand the presenting problems and to be able to trace your developmental course overall, because some other problems that may not have been of initial concern in the referral for ADHD assessment (for example, a period of normal language development that then stalls or even regresses) may appropriately take the clinician down a different diagnostic path. The diagnosis of emotional and behavioral disorders is very different from asking, "How long have you had a fever?" To obtain the necessary thorough narrative of the history and to understand and explore more vague symptoms that are indicative of different, perhaps even unusual disorders, takes time. Such an in-depth interview should be expected to take at least an hour of a clinician's time, and it would not be unusual for it to require up to two hours.

It is also not uncommon, especially for young children, for you to be asked to bring along a "baby book" or other record of development that you may have kept. Such contemporary recordings of development and behavior are especially helpful if you have more than one child. Research has shown, and we have noticed as parents, that it is easy for parents of more than one child to sometimes confuse key developmental markers or misattribute behavior to a particular child in a free-form interview about a child's development; thus, if you have any written records, take them with you. Completion of a structured written history is also useful, and some clinicians will ask you to fill out a developmental and history questionnaire in advance of the interview.

2. Reviews of Records

In the case of children and youth, it is common and almost always quite useful for your clinician to request a copy of prior medical and education records. Your child's medical records provide a history of illnesses and treatments that have occurred over a lifetime and are critical to determining the proper history and context of the behavior. A history of medication may be particularly important in establishing any relationships between your child's medical issues and current behavioral issues. Your child's school records are useful in multiple ways. School records can contain a wealth of information regarding the behavior of your child in a carefully structured setting. Often, structured settings are where the symptoms of ADHD are not only the most pronounced but result in the greatest degree of functional impairment. However, your child's school records also provide clear indications as to whether the evaluation should include a diagnostic workup related to learning problems. When children are performing well academically, as some children with ADHD in fact do, it may not be necessary to engage in the time-consuming

From the Clinician

Several years ago I received a call from some very anxious parents who wanted me to evaluate their child to see if he had ADHD. In setting up the appointment, they remarked that their son had done quite well in kindergarten the previous year, and they had no reports of behavior problems. However, the first-grade teacher was now reporting that he had great difficulty remaining in his seat, was restless and fidgety a good bit of the time, and seemed to be constantly distracted although she did not know by what. The teacher seemed convinced that this young man had ADHD and "needed medication." As part of the detailed history taking, it was determined that the behavioral changes seen were fairly recent and the parents had seen the distractibility as well. They also noted that he seemed to spend more time in his room by himself than they recalled previously. When the topic of changes in the family routines and related topics were discussed, it was revealed that his teenage stepbrother from another state had spent the summer living with the family. He had returned home just before school started. The parents indicated that the stepbrother had spent a great deal of time with their son during the summer and that they seemed to develop a close relationship. As it turns out, a clinical interview with the son revealed that the relationship had indeed been quite close and quite inappropriate. The teenage stepbrother had molested this young man on multiple occasions throughout the summer and threatened him with physical harm if he revealed what had been happening. The symptoms of ADHD that had become so apparent to the first-grade teacher were not symptoms of ADHD at all in this case. Rather, this young man received a diagnosis of post-traumatic stress disorder for which he was subsequently treated with significant success. A legal referral also ensued as is required by law in most states, and the episodes of molestation were confirmed by the appropriate authorities. Without a detailed history that included a discussion of the context of his life in the family and the routines and living circumstances of the family throughout this young man's life, the circumstances surrounding the changes in his behavior would not have been discovered and there is a strong chance that he would have been misdiagnosed with ADHD and received the wrong treatments.

task of assessing intelligence and academic achievement areas. However, if your child presents with ADHD-like symptoms and the school records indicate academic difficulties, your child should also be assessed for comorbid learning problems. Although it is not necessary to assess intelligence and achievement levels and related areas of cognitive skill in order to rule in or rule out a diagnosis of ADHD, you will recall that learning problems are common occurrences in individuals with ADHD. In order to ameliorate your child's functional problems in an academic setting and to facilitate later educational and vocational success, a comprehensive assessment of cognitive skills including educational skills and accomplishments must be conducted so that proper educational plans can be devised. Under current federal laws, you have access to your child's school records and can obtain copies directly or have them sent to the clinician who will be conducting an assessment of your child. Typically such requests must be provided to the school in writing and should be done several weeks prior to the child's appointment.

3. Assessment of Behavior and Emotions

It is also necessary to obtain assessments of behavior from those who know you or your child well (depending on who is being evaluated). What we mean by "well" is those who have a history of observing or interacting with you or your child over a period of weeks and possibly even months; that is, we don't mean "know you well" as in a deep understanding of feelings. This is about observable outward behavior and emotions that are made visible. For your child, this will typically be you, another parent or step-parent, and one or more teachers. This information is most likely to be gathered through the use of behavior checklists or rating scales that are linked to a database such as we discussed earlier in this chapter. For example, you might be asked to indicate whether your child "Interrupts others when they are talking," by checking one of four options: never, sometimes, often, or almost always. Typically, you would be asked to rate more than a hundred such behaviors (and on most scales, closer to two hundred). Why so many? Because accurate diagnosis is important. Five questions will not give you accurate answers. You need multiple questions that ask the same things in different ways and are designed to pick up nuances or details in the differences between ADHD-type behaviors and behaviors that mimic ADHD. Two hundred questions may sound like a lot but it is not as intimidating as it sounds, and usually takes no more than 15–20 minutes. The answer choices at first glance may seem rather subjective—what is "sometimes" versus what is "often"? Interestingly enough, thousands of research studies have demonstrated that these ratings have great reliability (accuracy) and validity (measure what they mean to measure). That is to say, people make the right decisions and know how to determine the difference between "sometimes" and "often." People like you, teachers, and even your child can and do respond accurately for the most part and the results of the ratings (which compose a pattern) clearly and accurately differentiate among individuals who have different emotional or behavioral disorders. Those with ADHD look different from those with conduct problems or depression—given that you use a good instrument as part of a comprehensive diagnosis and that it is interpreted by someone qualified to do so. For example, parent and teacher ratings can help the clinician determine reliably if the child has oppositional defiant disorder, ADHD, or both. Clinicians rarely interpret or give too much weight to any one behavior on such scales, which is good. Rather, they look at clusters of behaviors or groups of items that are known to go together to form known patterns. These clusters or groups of items are created by the developers of these scales based on large databases and comparisons of how individuals with different disorders are rated by those who know them well. Most often, the responses are entered into computer scoring programs that make quick, reliable comparisons to the database underlying each scale.

Most useful in the context of an initial diagnosis are what are referred to as *broad-band rating scales*, which include lists of behaviors that are not just associated with ADHD but that are also associated with many other emotional and behavioral disorders, especially those that might mimic ADHD. Additionally, broad-band rating scales include lists of behaviors for emotional and behavioral disorders that are commonly comorbid with ADHD. For example, a broad-band diagnostic rating scale might include lists of behaviors that correspond to hyperactivity, attention problems, aggressive behavior, rule breaking, but also include lists of behaviors associated with anxiety, depressive symptoms, emotional withdrawal, learning problems, self-esteem, social skills, highly unusual behaviors (such as hearing things that are not there or seeing things that are not really there), resiliency, and interpersonal skills. Different broad-band rating scales may cover somewhat different areas but this list of domains is typical or representative of what you might find generally.

Sometimes, you may be asked to complete what are referred to as *narrow-band rating scales*. A narrow-band behavior rating scale is one that is tied to a specific disorder, such as ADHD. A narrow-band behavior rating scale **does not** cover the broad spectrum of emotional and behavioral disorders. There are many narrow-band behavior rating scales with ADHD in their names. Typically, such scales will measure attention problems, hyper-activity, impulsivity, and possibly constructs such as conduct problems and rule breaking, but they do not assess the possibility of other disorders. ***The use of such a narrow-band scale in the initial diagnosis of a disorder like ADHD is dangerous.*** As we have discussed in several places in this book, including this chapter, there are many other disorders that share symptoms with

ADHD. The truth is—in order to get the diagnosis right, we have to look for all possibilities, consider different disorders, have access to a detailed history and knowledge of the context of your or your child's life, and then integrate this information to determine whether the ADHD-like symptoms we have documented are in fact being caused by ADHD and not some other disorder.

This is not to say that narrow-band ADHD rating scales do not have a role to play in the realm of ADHD. However, their role is best played in evaluating treatment outcomes. Once a diagnosis is made and you or your child begins treatment, narrow-band rating scales are well suited to help the clinician determine whether the treatment is working. Progress-monitoring techniques are also useful in this area and can be tailored to the problems demonstrated. A person knowledgeable about the individual's behavior may be asked to complete a narrow-band scale that focuses only on the ADHD behaviors we are attempting to change with treatment. Such scales are much shorter and more efficient than the broad-band behavior rating scales that are necessary for initial diagnosis.

Commonly Used Broad-Band Behavior Rating Scales   The most frequently administered broad-band behavior rating scales in the English-speaking world are the BASC-2[8] (mentioned earlier) and the Child Behavior Checklist (CBCL).[9] There are also many translations of these two scales in use throughout the world. Both of these behavior rating scales have strong databases to back up the interpretation of the scores derived from the clusters of behaviors that are measured, and both have been the subject of many research reports in scientific journals published in this country and throughout the world. The BASC-2 and the CBCL address in detail not only the behaviors associated with ADHD but also simultaneously evaluate behaviors that are associated with many different ADHD mimics. By using scales such a these, your clinician is less likely to be misled or to misdiagnose or misinterpret behaviors. A detailed analysis of the patterns of the clusters of behaviors assessed by each of these instruments enables the clinician to determine whether or not ADHD is the cause of the presenting problems or whether other disorders are more likely to be at the root of the problem.

Commonly Used Self-Ratings and Personality Scales   The BASC-2 and the CBCL each have a self-report form. A self-report is where the person demonstrating the challenges can indicate (1) the frequency with which he or she believes he or she engages in certain behaviors, and (2) feelings and emotions that he or she does and does not experience and how often this happens. How children and adults think and feel about their own behavior is also important in arriving at a proper diagnosis and enhances our overall understanding of the impact of any problem behaviors, thoughts, and emotions on daily life. Self-rating responses are used just like the other rating form responses and are compared to a database to detect differences. If you are an adult being evaluated for ADHD, the CBCL system has specialized forms for both behavior rating and self-report. There are far fewer good diagnostic rating scales for ADHD and related disorders available for use with adults. It is more common for clinicians to rely upon self-report when evaluating an adult for the possibility of not only ADHD but nearly any emotional or behavioral disorder. There is some movement under way, but occurring quite slowly, to enhance the use of rating scales completed by those who know the person well even for adults. This movement has occurred mostly among the senior population, because elderly individuals may be less able to evaluate their own behavior. However, over the last several decades, adult ADHD behavior rating scales have begun to appear. The use of such rating scales with adults is complicated somewhat by the necessity of obtaining permission from the person being rated to have another adult provide information on their behavior. How would you feel about the clinician asking your spouse, parents, or employer to rate your behavior? Sometimes this is a hard decision, but is probably the best way to evaluate your behavior. This has implications for the relationship between the two individuals (the one being rated and the one doing the rating), because under HIPAA and other health privacy laws, the person being rated has access to this person's ratings! If you are in this position and truly looking for accurate diagnosis, step back from "hurt feelings" and ask the rater to give an accurate rating of your behavior, regardless of the relationship. If you choose to access the ratings, remember that this was in the pursuit of your health and well-being. The rating was at your request and done to assist you in accessing treatment.

4. Other Assessments

In the majority of cases of referrals where ADHD is suspected as the diagnosis, the information noted up to this point will be sufficient for a clinician to arrive at an accurate diagnosis. There are occasions, however, when additional assessments might be necessary, although many of these are used only when ADHD has been ruled out and the clinician is searching for the correct, alternative diagnosis.

Remember that attentional problems and the ability or inability to inhibit impulsive responding are the key to a diagnosis of ADHD but are also found in many other emotional, behavioral, and neurodevelopmental disorders and, at low levels of expression, are also somewhat typical in the average person. One of the most common classes of tests used to assess attention and the ability to inhibit impulsive responding is the *continuous performance test* or CPT. A CPT is almost always administered via computer. If you are an adult taking a CPT, you will be presented with a constant stream of pictures or, in some cases, sounds. You will be given instructions as to when to respond to a picture or sound and when not to. Continuous performance test stimuli (pictures or sounds) will be streamed continually by the computer and there will be very little time in between stimuli for you to decide whether or not to respond to a particular picture or sound. To perform well on a CPT, you must pay particularly close attention and concentrate very hard and also resist the temptation to respond to all of the pictures or sounds. CPTs are very good measures of distractibility, the inability to maintain concentration over time, and the ability to inhibit impulsive responding. However, as we have noted, these problems may occur with many different disorders, and abnormal performance on a CPT does not always mean that ADHD is the correct diagnosis.

CPTs have another significant issue. CPTs are laboratory tests that occur in an isolated setting in a quiet room. They do not occur in the real world with all of the distractions that are constantly around us. Consequently, you could potentially perform well on a CPT in such an isolated and quiet environment even if you are impaired. The typical school classroom or job environment is quite different from sitting in a quiet, isolated office taking an important and potentially life-altering test.

There were times in the history of ADHD research that the CPT was held out as the gold standard for the diagnosis of ADHD. Some insurance companies and other third-party payers like HMOs and PPOs went through periods where they would only pay for an ADHD diagnostic examination that included a brief clinical interview and a CPT. Such thinking is now quite archaic, and such simplistic examinations are known to produce too many false positive and false negative diagnoses (that is, diagnoses that are just wrong). Although CPTs are highly sensitive to potential problems, especially distractibility and impulsivity, they do not measure them in a real-world environment, nor do they measure them in a way that is specific to their underlying cause.

When ADHD is present and there are other complicating factors, additional assessments may be needed to discover comorbid disorders, as discussed earlier, or to aid in treatment planning. A comprehensive neuropsychological assessment can be quite useful as an aid to treatment planning in cases of complicated presentations of ADHD. By complicated, we are referring to ADHD that occurs at the same time as problems with learning and memory in particular. Neuropsychological assessments are designed to evaluate the integrity of the processing systems and communications systems throughout the brain based on their actual function as opposed to looking at their structure. Evaluating function is much more valuable in understanding comorbid disorders and the determination of appropriate treatment plans for the learning and memory problems that are so common among individuals with ADHD than are static views of brain structures.

Various types of brain scans including such methods as magnetic resonance imaging or MRI and its various forms (sometimes abbreviated as qMRI, fMRI, or some similar designation), simple computed tomography scan (a CT or CAT scan, for computerized axial tomography), single photon emission computed tomography (SPECT), positron emission tomography (PET), electroencephalograms (EEGs), and brain electrical activity maps (BEAM) are typically costly and are not necessary for the diagnosis of ADHD. In the case of certain comorbid disorders, for example when a seizure disorder is suspected or there is a history of traumatic brain injury, which could include a closed head injury that produced a concussion or worse, one or more of these exams might be determined to be necessary by the examining clinician. However, such exams should be used sparingly and are not necessary for the diagnosis of ADHD.

IT TAKES A SKILLED CLINICIAN

As you can see, evaluation for ADHD requires many different resources. Once all the necessary information has been collected, it still takes a skilled clinician to combine the different sources and types of information to arrive at an accurate diagnosis and to know what, if any, follow-up examinations or tests are necessary. Typically, you should expect to receive a written report that details everything that has been done along with a listing of the results of any tests and an interpretation of these results. Before you begin the assessment process you may want to ask some questions about the assessments to be used and the training of the person interpreting them. Good clinicians appreciate questions about any aspect of the examination, results, or their interpretation and recommendations for treatment that you do not understand. Always remember that it is your child, your loved one, or yourself that is going to be involved in receiving treatment or other interventions, whatever the diagnosis. It is your responsibility to ask questions about any aspect of the process or its results that you do not understand. Clinicians who are resentful or hostile to your questions about their examination are demonstrating a quality you want to be aware of early. Consider rephrasing questions, but if you are not being argumentative and they are being defensive or hostile, consider going elsewhere. Thank them for their time and excuse yourself. If a clinician is difficult to reach during the diagnostic process, is not responsive to requests, or is not timely in working with you to explain conclusions and their bases or their recommendations for treatment, they may also be too busy to have developed the individual understanding of your particular case that is necessary to designing the most effective treatment plan for your situation. You may be well advised to seek help elsewhere. On the other side of the issue, if you struggle with attention, impulsivity, organization, and the like—even if it is your child under examination—consider seeking help from someone to make and keep appointments. Consider using a digital recorder or taking notes in all meetings (but do not lose the notes). Ask the clinician to provide written directions and to follow-up with you.

Comprehensive examinations that follow the professional guidelines of the American Academy of Pediatrics as well as other recommendations we have noted in the professional literature, such as those by Reynolds and Kamphaus, Goldstein, and others, do not always occur in practice. You can see how it would be difficult for most medical practitioners to spend the kind of time required to conduct these evaluations. Therefore, you should not be surprised if your pediatrician or family practitioner makes a referral to a psychologist, clinical neuropsychologist, psychiatrist, or other professional whose practice is devoted to conducting such comprehensive diagnostic evaluations. This practitioner would then typically send a written report not only to you but to the referring physician with a description of their diagnostic process, conclusions, and recommendations for any follow-up examinations and treatment. However, our field experience in hundreds, perhaps thousands of schools, tells us that too many clinicians continue to diagnose ADHD without conducting a comprehensive examination and do not follow the professional guidelines we have discussed. There are many reasons for this, but central to the issues are the pressures placed on medical personnel—in the current environment where health care is dominated by HMOs, PPOs, and similar third-party payer systems—to see a large number of individuals for a short period of time. At times there is also pressure from well-meaning individuals who self-diagnose and seek quick relief with medication. Although brief and efficient patient reports of illness are reasonably sufficient for many routine diagnoses encountered in health care settings when accompanied by a brief physical exam and review of systems, quick self-reporting and a cursory examination are not a reasonable expectation for accurate diagnosis of ADHD and many other emotional and behavioral disorders. The truth is, the diagnosis of ADHD and its common comorbid disorders can be difficult and takes a significant amount of time, training, and skill. Do not allow yourself or your family member to be shortchanged by a quick interview and rapid diagnosis of ADHD followed by getting out the prescription pad.

TO SUM UP

In this chapter we have acknowledged the myriad difficulties in making the correct diagnosis of ADHD and we have explained that there are no shortcuts, or 5 minutes to diagnosis, at least, none that yield accurate results. We also explained the need for accurate diagnosis, which is the key to getting the right treatment. The need to develop good databases to allow us to differentiate accurately between what are normal variations in behavior and behaviors that distinguish those with ADHD was also explained, in addition to the process used to collect and apply such information to diagnosis. We also told you, however, that a good clinical interview, developmental history, and a review of past records of development are important and cannot be replaced with other tests in the diagnosis of ADHD, just as behavioral test data cannot be replaced by an interview and the like. Getting the diagnosis right is a comprehensive process, and we have prepared you to avoid quickie diagnosis of such a complex behavioral disorder as ADHD.

WHAT'S NEXT?

In the next chapter, we take on the issue of medicine for ADHD. We first relate the known (so far) causes of ADHD, and explain that it is a neurobiological disorder—that is, a brain disorder—and what happens differently in the brains of individuals with ADHD. We then review how medication affects the brain, and why medication is useful in many cases. The side effects of the most common and most effective medicines for treating ADHD are also presented.

5

How Medication Affects the ADHD Brain

Is medication the answer, the cure, the sine qua non for ADHD treatment? The truth is, no. There is no one medicine or combination of medicines that cures ADHD. No medication alone should ever be considered "the" answer for treatment or control of ADHD symptoms. ADHD is a complex syndrome (that is, a specified combination of problems that co-occur in predictable ways). It is not a simple problem, and it does not have a simple answer. We wish we could tell you that we have the "magic" cure or that your search for answers will stop here. Complex problems— just like complex children, adolescents, and adults—require multiple approaches for maximum benefit.

If a physician has suggested that you or your child (or someone else that you know with ADHD) take medication, you may be struggling with the decision. The thoughts, "Medicate my child? or "Take medication to change my behavior?" are perhaps scary ones. You and your spouse, family members, or trusted friends may have differing opinions, which only adds to your apprehension. All of these reactions are normal. Whether you have a trusting relationship with your physician or you question your physician, the decision to use medicine as part of a treatment regimen for ADHD is one to be taken seriously and is a very personal decision. It is not like taking an antibiotic for a couple of weeks. Medicine as part of the treatment for ADHD becomes a long-term part of the lifestyle of the person with the diagnosis as well as that of other family members. We would like to help you focus on whether or not medication has a clear role to play in treatment or management of ADHD symptoms. To this question, generally our answer is: yes, most of the time, but not always. Parents and adults with ADHD will almost always face the question of whether to use medicine as part of the treatment regimen. Medication for ADHD has always been controversial, with massive amounts of misinformation and claims of "better" ways to treat ADHD (most of which will cost you significantly more money). Some raise moral objections, arguing that we should not medicate "behavior," or that we are placing children in particular into chemical straitjackets. The decision about medication for treatment of symptoms associated with ADHD is important. There are consequences either way, whether you choose "no medicine" or "medicine." This chapter is intended to provide clear guidance and objective information in making an informed decision. We have no horse in this race: we do not do pharmaceutical research; we do not sell alternative treatments; we do not have a vitamin or alternative therapy business. The decision belongs solely to you and your family. We intend to help you become well educated before you make that choice.

To understand the medication issue, we believe strongly that it is first necessary to have some understanding of the brain mechanisms that are affected by or are responsible for ADHD. Since ADHD is a disorder of brain function, we will take you back to "Brain 101," the class you may never have had. We will explain what we know about the cause of ADHD, how the brains of persons with ADHD are different from those without ADHD, and why medicine helps for most people with ADHD. We believe that understanding ADHD at the brain level will help you to make intelligent decisions about treatment and to evaluate more clearly the issues and objections to medicine for behavior.

We want to acknowledge up front that this will be the most intellectually demanding of all the chapters in this book. However, knowledge truly is power, and we want you to be as empowered as possible in making medical decisions related to ADHD, so bear with us as we delve into the brain, its structure and function, and what goes awry in the phenomenon of ADHD. Pay close attention to linking the text to the various drawings provided and do not be surprised if you occasionally have to read over something more than once.

WHAT CAUSES ADHD?

Why do children, adolescents, and adults have ADHD? The short answer is that, at this time, we really do not know exactly what causes ADHD. However, psychologists of various types, neuroscientists, developmental and behavioral pediatricians, and psychiatrists, among others have spent decades researching the topic. What we do know is that it is not your "fault." You did not "cause" ADHD by eating too much sugar or by your choice in parenting practices.

Evidence strongly suggests that ADHD is a genetic disorder. This means that it is in your genes, just like your hair color and eye color. Genes are transferred from one generation to the next. Genes are a segment of our deoxyribonucleic acid (DNA). Scientists are almost certain that ADHD is polygenic (meaning that many genes are involved—not only one). In just the last year, a gene associated with being able to inhibit an impulse to act has been located. Other genes that interact to produce ADHD-like symptoms are currently under scrutiny. The most common gene transfer in ADHD is from the father, but mothers are not in the clear. They too can transmit the ADHD gene group or constellation (and there is likely more than one constellation of genes that can cause ADHD).

Our genetic code, passed to us from our mothers and fathers, in combination with our environment and individual circumstances, dictates the development of our brain and its ability to function optimally (or not). Brain imaging allows us to see that the brains of individuals with ADHD actually are different in both structure and function from the brains of those individuals without ADHD or a similar disorder. You can picture "structure" as the light fixtures, wires, and switches in a house and "function" as the lighting and electricity. Both structure and function are different (remember the complexity of the problem) in the ADHD brain. All the pronounced symptoms you see, such as the problematic behaviors (like excessive movement and impulsive actions), are caused by real differences in the brains of individuals with ADHD compared to those without the disorder. Just as children look different on the outside because of their genes, their brains look different because of genes (we just cannot see those differences without very specialized imaging technology).

At a basic level, understanding that ADHD is brain-based with some details about ADHD and the brain will arm you to make informed decisions about medicine as a part of a treatment regimen. We will not attempt a course in genetics or in cellular neurobiology here, but we do consider it crucial to provide a basic understanding of the brain-based nature of ADHD. Understanding the information that follows will help you comprehend the apparent contradiction of why stimulants (that typically "stimulate" a person) work to enhance inhibition and self-control in the case of ADHD and reduce the rates of behavior in persons with ADHD. This understanding will help you talk more intelligently with your physician and with teachers and counselors and perhaps to ask them better questions. This understanding will also help you evaluate treatment options. Lots of people like to throw out terms like "research-based" or "brain-based." We would like you to be educated enough to protect and help yourself and your child or friends and family members. To understand the differences in the brains of individuals with ADHD from those without, we begin with a brief discussion of how the brain works.

HOW THE BRAIN WORKS

At its most fundamental level the brain "works" as a series of electrical charges. These electrical pulses are created and maintained by changes in the chemistry of each neuron. Neurons are a type of cell in the brain which can hold and transmit electrical signals. These electrical charges cause neurons to send impulses to the next neurons in the sequence to continue a chain of what are essentially commands to act—or not to act. You might picture a relay game where one child runs to the next and passes on a message. The chain continues until the message is received at its destination. If we look at Figure 5.1, we see a schematic drawing of a typical brain cell or neuron. It has a large circular-shaped area called the cell body. The cell body houses the nucleus of the cell. In the nucleus, the cell consumes oxygen and glucose and manufactures other chemical needs (this is also called the metabolism of the cell). A long extension (the axon) leaves the cell body, and appears like the tentacle of an octopus. The axon has insulation (the myelin sheath) just like the wires in a house have insulation around them, enabling it to carry electrical charges more efficiently. This tentacle (the axon) reaches out to other neurons until nearly touching them with its axon terminals. If you saw the animated film *Finding Nemo* you may remember the scene of a school of jellyfish floating in the sea. The long tentacles carried electrical currents like a lightning storm, creating a problem for any fish who tried to swim through them. The brain is a series of neurons with axons (tentacles) extending out and with axons coming back from other neurons. Communication is electrical at first but then is mediated by the chemistry of the neuron. This electrical communication stops at the gap between the nontouching axons and becomes chemical. This is an important point. The electrical impulse becomes chemical to complete the communication circuit.

When the neuron is activated, it releases specific chemicals (called neurotransmitters) at the axon terminal that cross over a microscopic chasm known as the *synaptic cleft*, forming a neural

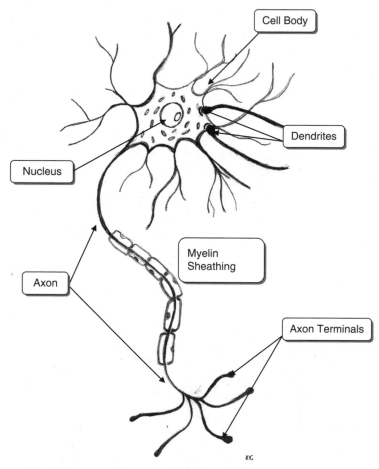

Figure 5.1. Schematic Drawing of a Typical Neuron

synapse—you can remember synapse by picturing that space between the bulbous end of the axon or tentacle and the dimple on the next neuron in the chain. The neural synapse is a place where the neurons connect and communicate with each other. Once across this gap, these chemicals, called *neurotransmitters* (chemicals that transmit a message to the next neuron, telling it to act or not act), cause the next neuron in the sequence to continue the message; or, sometimes, the neurotransmitter may block the neuron from contacting the next neuron. In their normal state, neurons transmit information in only one direction, from the nucleus of the cell (see Figure 5.1) outward via the axon. Figure 5.2 illustrates how communication occurs as neurotransmitters are released, cross over the synaptic cleft, and are received by the next neuron in the sequence. Once they have done their job, the neurotransmitters are released and may be taken back into the issuing neuron by the reuptake pump as shown in Figure 5.2.

Neurons are not randomly connected or just scattered around in the brain. They exist in systems within the brain that are very well organized. The brain organizes neurons in two very

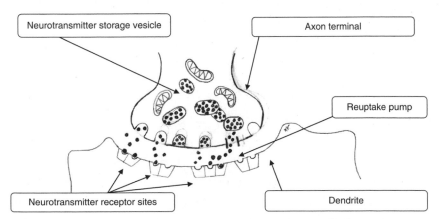

Neurotransmitter storage vesicle

Axon terminal

Reuptake pump

Neurotransmitter receptor sites

Dendrite

Figure 5.2. Depiction of Chemical Neurotransmission—the Space Between the Axon Terminal and the Dendrite Is Called the Synaptic Cleft

fundamental ways, creating essentially two address systems for sending messages that can interact to alter behavior. These two address systems are referred to generally as the brain's physical address system and its chemical address system.

The Physical Address System of the Brain

The physical addressing system of the brain is the actual physical layout or architecture of the neurons themselves and the connections they make with other neurons. Neurons form these connections in groups or clusters that allow communication among distinct anatomical regions of the brain. These regions perform different activities in order to work smoothly and in a coordinated fashion. These patterns of connections are called many names but they all refer to the same thing. Some of the names you may read or hear are things like "pathways in the brain," "association fibers," or "projection fibers." Typically the names will reflect the location and the direction in which they carry communications—mostly up and down, side to side, or back to front, and vice versa. To make this simple we will refer to them all as *neural pathways* (but remember this is not a technically or specifically accurate term), because, like a path, they all lead from one place to another. We behave or perform differently based on which physical address system is active or inactive.

The Chemical Address System of the Brain

The brain operates also via the chemical secretions of neurons. Not all neurons secrete or release the same neurotransmitters and not all neurons are willing to accept the same neurotransmitters. Remember that a neurotransmitter is literally just as it sounds from its name. It is a molecule that travels across the synaptic cleft into a receiving site (or port or dock, if you will) of an adjacent neuron, causing it to transmit the electrical charge of the neuron on to the next neuron in the pathway or to cease transmitting signals; that is, some neurotransmitters energize the next neuron in the chain and some enervate the next neuron. There are classically 16 different neurotransmitters in the brain, but with many slight variations of each of them. Depending upon which neurotransmitters are released and which are accepted by the receiving neuron, our behavior will be different. The neurotransmitters most implicated in ADHD are dopamine, nor-adrenaline (also called norepinephrine), and less often, serotonin. Different neurotransmitters are present in different concentrations in different parts of the brain and in different neural pathways. This becomes very important when choosing medicines to affect brain function.

On the one hand, dopamine and noradrenaline release tends to facilitate neural action; that is, it causes the neuron to pass along a continuing signal. On the other hand, a neurotransmitter like GABA (short for gabaminobutyric acid) has a soothing effect on neurons and modulates neural transmissions. You may have heard of the drug propofol. This is a commonly used and largely safe anesthetic popular among surgeons for brief surgical procedures in particular, but is also notorious for being the drug that was implicated in the death of the pop star Michael Jackson.

Propofol acts very much like GABA in the brain and is a bit of a GABA mimic, soothing neurons to the point of stopping them from transmitting signals to one another. In unduly large doses, it stops the nerves that energize the diaphragm to breathe from receiving and acting on the needed neural impulses properly. This is why it is ill advised and never recommended to administer propofol to anyone outside of a clinically controlled setting where supplemental oxygen is readily available along with medicines to counteract the effects of the propofol, the situation that is alleged to have happened with Michael Jackson.

Let's recap a bit. Brain communication for "how to behave" is electrical and chemical in nature and occurs in structures called neurons. Neurons are laid out in particular patterns in the brain that create neural pathways. The actions of neurons in these pathways are controlled by the secretion or release of neurotransmitters. Neurotransmitters are released and accepted in different concentrations in different pathways. This is very important when it comes to medicines that affect the brain. Different neural pathways are affected in different ways by the choice of a medicine. Some medicines will help facilitate one particular neurotransmitter over another such as dopamine versus serotonin versus norepinephrine, for example. So, depending upon the physical address and the chemical address associated with a particular neurotransmitter, different brain systems, and hence different behaviors, will be affected more or less strongly by the chosen medicine.

As we noted earlier, Figure 5.2 shows a schematic of how neurotransmitters function. This bears reviewing again now that you know about the brain's address systems. The axon terminal releases a neurotransmitter in response to an impulse received via its own dendrite—the receiving site of the neurotransmitter coming from the communicating neuron. The neurotransmitter seeks out and is attracted to a receptor site designed to receive this neurotransmitter (not just any neurotransmitter will fit into just any receptor site). If the receptor site is successful in capturing the neurotransmitter, then the target neuron will pass along the intended message. Then the neurotransmitter is released from the receiving neuron and may be reabsorbed by the neuron it came from. This occurs via the reuptake pump, which is depicted as a gate in the schematic drawing. Sometimes, neurotransmitters are taken back into the issuing neuron by this pump or gate too early, before they have had a chance to pass along the message and do their job! Some medicines are designed to prevent this from happening. You may have heard of medicines called reuptake inhibitors, the most common and perhaps famous of these being Prozac. Prozac is an

SSRI, a selective serotonin reuptake inhibitor, and it blocks the neurotransmitter serotonin from being pumped back into its originating neuron, leaving more serotonin in the synaptic cleft, making it more likely to be captured and able to transmit its message to the connecting neuron.

For the sake of argument, and putting stereotypes aside, picture a large "high school" party of people milling about communicating information. There are rooms of people with different interests who do different things (for example, perhaps one has athletes, another the chess club, and another the more political or activists types). As people come in the doors and enter the commons area (synaptic cleft) they look for the "right" room. Only certain people will feel comfortable in certain rooms. Rooms have a capacity; as people enter and rooms fill up, some people return out the door, and people may or may not have time to communicate before they are out of the room. Some rooms are full. Other rooms may be empty. The balance of people in the common area helps accommodate the flow of the people in and out of the rooms. This flow of communication is what makes the social network of the school work. Too little or too much is a problem. This school example is admittedly a simplistic illustration of the chemical systems of the brain, but we think it helps to illustrate some of what goes on.

The truth is, ADHD occurs when these physical and chemical systems are disturbed in particular ways. The brains of persons with ADHD are different structurally and chemically when compared to the brains of persons of the same age who do not have ADHD or a similar brain disorder. We will explain more in the following sections.

BRAIN DIFFERENCES IN ADHD

In the previous section, we explained how the brain functions, and you are probably asking, "OK, so how are the brains of individuals with ADHD different?" The answer is that individuals with ADHD have differences in structure and function in their brains as compared to those without ADHD. These differences were uncovered with the advent of modern brain-imaging methods in the late 1970s. Since then, imaging methods have advanced, and so has our understanding of these differences. Two kinds of neuroimaging methods have been the most useful. The first is structural imaging, which allows us to look at the actual physical structure of an individual brain and calculate with reasonable precision the size and exact location of each brain structure. The second is functional neuroimaging, which allows us to see the brain in action, as it metabolizes or consumes food and oxygen, and carries out other metabolic activities such as manufacturing neurotransmitters.

Figure 5.3 is a schematic drawing of the surface of the left hemisphere of the brain that we will use to illustrate some basic

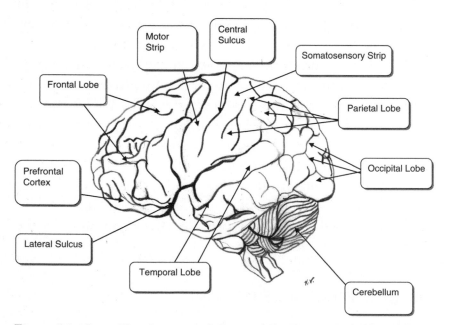

Figure 5.3. Some Key Anatomical Areas of the Brain—Left Hemisphere, Exterior View

structures. The brain can be divided in different ways, but most commonly is seen as consisting of four lobes, the frontal lobe, the parietal lobe, the occipital lobe, and the temporal lobe. Each lobe has specific responsibilities but to work well, each part of the brain must communicate well with other parts of the brain, and thus neural pathways are crucial to a coordinated brain.

From the Neuroscientist

Structural Differences

Individuals with ADHD have slightly less brain volume (meaning fewer neurons and fewer connections) in the frontal regions of the brain as compared to persons without ADHD, especially on the right side. The frontal lobe is a center of action in the brain. It initiates and organizes behavior, but it also is responsible for inhibiting behavior that is not appropriate or useful at a particular time. As such, the frontal lobes are the point of coordination of the executive system of the brain—the brain's coordination and decision-making system. Although other parts of the brain can also act (for example, the limbic system of the brain controls our "fight or flight" response when we perceive danger), the frontal lobes can override most any voluntary

This difference in the density of the frontal regions of the brain in individuals with ADHD is an average difference, and it will not be true of every person with ADHD. When it occurs, it indicates that there are fewer connections among neurons in these regions and quite possibly fewer neurons altogether. This is important in ADHD because the right prefrontal areas in particular have major roles to play in the organization of behavior and in the inhibition of unwanted behavior. If there are fewer neurons to help make these decisions and fewer connections to other parts of the brain, our behavior will be more disorganized than otherwise, and we will be more apt to "act without thinking." The neurons that are in these areas then must work harder to help us organize and control our behavior. Unfortunately in ADHD, these brain regions tend to work less hard instead!

system of action in the brain. The prefrontal regions in particular have strong roles to play in the inhibition of activity (that is, stopping us from doing something) and the direction and control of attention via its many neural pathways to other parts of the brain. The frontal regions of the brain are the most widely and influentially connected parts of the brain.

The parietal, occipital, and temporal lobes receive information from the outside world, process it, and develop an understanding of this information, and provide integration of this information into schemas (that is, an organized pattern of thought) that the frontal lobes can understand and use for decision making. The parietal lobes concentrate on tactile and sensory input along with helping out with spatial ability (how well we can judge and manipulate space, distance, and objects mentally) and are home to the somatosensory strip seen in the figure. The occipital lobes concentrate on visual input and helping us locate objects in space, and the temporal lobes concentrate on speech and language sounds usually in the left temporal lobe and nonlanguage sounds most often in the right temporal lobe. (These brain parts perform many other functions as well, but this much of an overview should be sufficient for our purposes here.)

Kesler and her colleagues[1] reviewed studies using methods designed to allow the calculation of the amount and density of brain tissue present in specific areas of the brain. Following this review they concluded, as have others, that individuals with ADHD have slightly less brain volume in the frontal regions of the brain as compared to persons without ADHD. The differences get smaller with age up to at least age 22, but some small differences in brain volume in the frontal and prefrontal cortex remain evident. In these regions, then, the physical address system of the brain is disturbed in persons with ADHD. This is particularly important because these are the very regions of the brain, especially the right frontal areas, that carry heavy responsibilities for organizing behavioral plans, executing them properly, directing attention, and stopping us from behaving (the act of inhibition) when that behavior is not adaptive or appropriate to our circumstance at the time.

Functional Differences

Differences in the metabolism (the conversion of food and oxygen to energy in the cell, manufacturing, and release of neurotransmitters) or functional activity of several brain regions also are different in the brains of persons with ADHD. There are now different methods of actually observing brain systems in action. These methods track blood flow and the consumption of oxygen and glucose for the most part. We assume that the parts of the brain that increase their need for blood and its nourishments are becoming more active at different times. The changes in metabolism can be seen with clarity on such images. When studies that compare the metabolism of key areas of the executive system and related brain systems are reviewed, the results are not always 100% consistent, but a general consensus has emerged from this literature. The regions of the prefrontal cortex, especially on the right side, that communicate between this region and the cingulate (see Figure 5.4) on through the remainder of the basal ganglia, including the very important portal of communication known as the thalamus, and on to the cerebellum show generally inefficient or decreased metabolic rates.[2] This should be clear when you view Figure 5.4.

The primary difference is an imbalance in the levels or perhaps the use of the neurotransmitters dopamine and noradrenalin or norepinephrine. These differences occur mostly in the prefrontal cortex and its connections through the basal ganglia, thalamus, and on to the cerebellum. In some individuals, it appears that serotonin may also be involved. These neural pathways are depicted in a schematic drawing in Figure 5.4, and

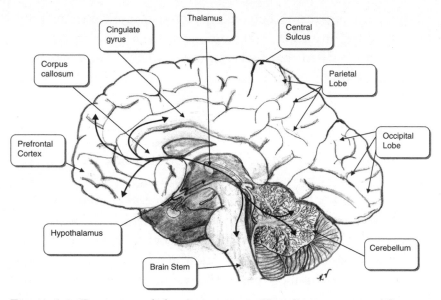

Figure 5.4. Depiction of the Approximate Key Communication Circuits in the Brain That Perform at Suboptimal Levels in Most Cases of ADHD (Shown as Darker Lines with Arrows)

have a great deal to do with the control of motor behavior, attention, and the inhibition of behavior—all key aspects of our ability to self-regulate our behavior. In Figure 5.5, we have provided a schematic drawing of the major dopamine pathway in the brain, and you can see that it overlaps substantially with the neural pathway that is impaired in ADHD. Now we also know that the chemical address system of the brain in persons with ADHD is different as well.

Here we see also the interaction of the brain's physical addressing system and its chemical addressing system. The actual volume of physical brain matter is slightly less for the average person with ADHD in the important prefrontal cortex, which is very rich in dopamine receptor sites. This section of the brain and its major connections to other important self-regulating structures do not appear to use certain key neurotransmitters as

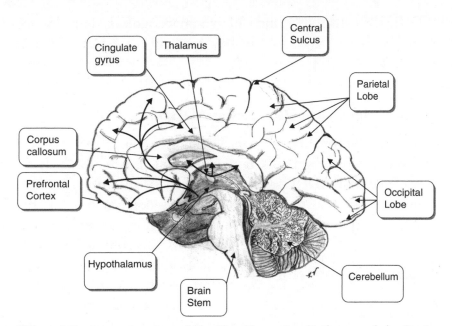

Figure 5.5. Approximation of the Key Dopamine Pathways of the Brain (Heavier Lines with Arrows Show the Dopamine Pathways)

effectively as is required to sustain normal levels of brain function. The truth is this interaction between the problems in the physical address system and the chemical address system is what causes ADHD—but what causes this to happen? The truth here again is that we are not yet certain, but it is almost certainly genetic in most cases.

There can be other causes as well. Difficulties during pregnancy can cause these brain regions not to develop properly. Prenatal exposure to cocaine, methamphetamines and related drugs, certain prescription drugs, alcohol, tobacco, premature delivery, significantly low birth weight, excessively high blood lead levels, other environmental toxins, and birth or early postnatal injury to the prefrontal regions of the brain have all been found to contribute to the risk of developing ADHD to varying degrees. Still, the consensus among the scientists who study

ADHD most rigorously, and with whom we agree, is that genetics play the largest role in the development of ADHD in the population.[3]

A Little More on the Genetics of ADHD

The brain abnormalities seen in ADHD are thought to be genetic in nature.[4] Since the 1970s, researchers and clinicians alike have speculated that ADHD is primarily a genetic disorder. Research from the 1990s to today provides strong confirmation of this hypothesis, but a specific genotype or faulty genetic profile has yet to be confirmed through replication, although suspicious patterns were identified in the 2000s. Sam Goldstein has provided a succinct and clear review of the various genes that are suspect in ADHD as well as describing inconsistencies in some of the findings.[5] If you are interested in more technical details, we encourage you to consider reading his review work.

First-degree relatives (parents, siblings, and children) of individuals with ADHD are eight times more likely to have ADHD than the average person in the population with no such relative with ADHD. In other words, if individuals with ADHD have children, these children will be eight times more likely than others to have ADHD. This

From the Counselor

I have known teachers and others at school who become frustrated with parents of children with ADHD for not making sure that the child goes to bed on time, has lunch money, or comes to school with all their supplies and homework. Considering the genetic nature of ADHD, this is a very common occurrence. I try to stress to teachers that the parent is not intentionally "neglecting" the child's needs. It is very important for parents of children with ADHD to stay in close communication with the teacher to assist the teacher in understanding the struggles that take place at home. Both the parent and the teacher are usually trying very hard to do the best thing for the child.

genetic component intensifies family problems created by the interpersonal relationship difficulties of individuals with ADHD. If both the parent and the child have ADHD, problems seem to multiply. For example, if Alyssa has ADHD and forgets to do her homework, depending on her mother with ADHD to remember and prompt her to complete her homework is sometimes a lost cause. Alyssa forgets. Mom forgets. The next morning, Alyssa is upset because she forgot her homework, blames it on Mom for not reminding her more than once, and Mom is even more upset for forgetting to remind her.

WHAT DOES NOT CAUSE ADHD?

Have you ever felt like ADHD is your fault? Maybe you wonder if you are to blame for your child's ADHD, or your own? Maybe you have been told that your child has ADHD because you are an incompetent parent? The fact is that diet and bad parenting DO NOT **cause** ADHD. Many have heard that children and adults with ADHD eat too much sugar or food with red dye and that this is the reason they have ADHD. Parents might hear, "If you would simply control your child's sugar intake, the symptoms would disappear." Even adults with ADHD are asked, "Did you eat too much sugar today?" Although the claims of diet-induced ADHD surface in the lay press and even in scientific journals from time to time, no reliable scientifically based connection has been established between food and ADHD. Certainly, if you are gluten sensitive and exposed to gluten, you may become irritable and consequently have attention problems—but, this is not ADHD. If your diet causes your blood sugar levels to fluctuate widely and rapidly, you may also experience attention problems and restlessness, and even impulse control problems—but these are temporary states and are not ADHD!

In addition, some contend that particular diets can cure ADHD. Diets used to try to eliminate certain naturally occurring elements such as salicylates are one example. The Feingold Diet (named after its founder) is a popular one. However, carefully controlled studies of these diets have demonstrated that very, very few children respond to such diets. Often, such dietary changes require substantial changes in the entire family routine and alter the focus of the family in many ways. We suspect the improvements seen with some people who have ADHD in these circumstances is due more to the lifestyle changes and a changed focus of the family than to the dietary changes. In scientific circles, some such effects are referred to as Hawthorne Effects, and are related to simply making large changes that are believed to help—when we do that, often things do change in the expected way, but not for long periods of time! We are unaware of any studies meeting current scientific standards that demonstrate that diet causes ADHD. There is a small percentage (about 2–3% of individuals who are diagnosed with ADHD) who do in fact have food allergies that may cause them to have attention and behavior problems. We always recommend that an allergist or related physician test for these allergies prior to attempting any special dietary control or related treatment of ADHD. You will hear and read anecdotal reports of miracle cures via special diets and supplements surrounding ADHD. The science to back up such claims leaves much to be desired,

From the Counselor

Some of the saddest appointments of my career have been spent with a mother who has been told that the reason that her child with ADHD is overactive, does not pay attention at school, or does not make excellent grades is because she is not doing her part. The mother has done everything that she can do without more information. Explaining the fact that ADHD is brain-based, that we have scientific evidence to prove it, and that there are ways to help always seems to be the most important starting place. Take the blame away and focus on what to do to help the child. We do not believe it is possible simultaneously to "fix blame" and fix problems!

and these approaches seem to survive only on personal testimony and anecdote. The truth is that in March 2011, the Food and Drug Administration (FDA) once again reviewed the scientific evidence regarding the effects of food dyes and colorings on children's behavior and concluded there was no significant, reliable scientific evidence to support the claims that such substances cause ADHD or other emotional and behavioral disorders. If you see a diet or similar program advertised for ADHD treatment, and it looks and feels like the infomercial for two-second ab workouts, listen to your gut. If you spend money on these easy cures, you can expect some temporary effects at best, mostly because you expect to get them, and chances are they will soon pass.

The National Resource Center on ADHD is a program sponsored by a sound nonprofit organization known as CHADD, Children and Adults with Attention-Deficit Hyperactivity Disorder. Membership includes people with a diagnosis of ADHD as well as parents, other family members, and a host of clinicians who treat ADHD along with leading scientists who research ADHD. CHADD tracks research on suspected causes as well as treatments and treatment attempts related to ADHD. Based on this work, CHADD maintains position papers on many proposed treatments and supposed cures once there is enough information to reject or support their use. If you want further information in this area, you can access their position statements on the Web at: http://www.help4adhd.org/en/treatment/complementary/WWK6.

Successful treatments and interventions for individuals with ADHD must be multimodal; that is, they must have different components that affect different aspects of the person's weaknesses. Typically this would include teaching parents how to cope with their child's ADHD behavior, the use of behavioral intervention strategies, education for the parents and the individual with ADHD about the disorder, the development of an appropriate educational plan, and medical interventions in many but not all cases.

In addition, "bad parenting" does not lead to ADHD—undisciplined children and those reared in chaotic environments where rules are inconsistently applied if at all, and where guidance is not given, may end up with such an incorrect diagnosis of ADHD. These children may have problems sitting still and paying attention, but it is not because they are children with ADHD. In these cases, the behaviors seen are most likely learned, serve some purpose, and are changed via behavior therapy approaches most effectively. Parents (and adult children) reading this book will be glad to hear that if you had or would respond to the numerous comments by your closest relatives and friends to "just take that child in the other room and make him stop that," it will not or would not change the behavior for more than a few seconds or minutes at best. Punishment, physical or otherwise, is especially ineffective in treating ADHD behaviors. However, this does not mean individuals with ADHD do not respond to punishment, only that the behaviors they exhibit that are caused by their ADHD will not change because of punishment.

HOW DOES MEDICATION WORK TO AFFECT ADHD?

Different parts of your brain control different bodily and mental functioning. Some parts of the brain control easily understood activities such as muscle movement or hearing. However, the prefrontal cortex and the pathways illustrated in Figure 5.4 (the areas affected by ADHD) control complex thoughts and behaviors (especially behavioral initiation), including attention, decision making, inhibition, and certain aspects of motor behavior. For instance, when Joey is asked to do something that he does not want to do, such as to take out the trash, he makes a quick decision based on the consequences of his actions. He considers the consequences before acting. Understanding that if he takes the trash out everyone will be happy and the house will not stink or that if he refuses to take the trash out his parents will become angry and the house will begin to reek is a complex thought. However, if Joey is a youth with ADHD, his decision-making process may suffer, and instead of getting to the part about consequences, he just reacts impulsively and storms off to do whatever it was he wanted to do right that second, thinking he will take out the trash later. Of course, later never comes without many parental reminders—because Joey gets distracted by all the other choices in his environment and forgets about the trash.

The systems of the brain formed by the connections among the frontal regions, (the cingulate and on through the thalamus to the cerebellum) are crucial to the self-regulation of behavior and to the proper function of the executive or decision-making systems of the brain. When these areas are not at the proper level of arousal and are under-aroused, slow, or sluggish in their functioning, behavior caroms out of control. Medications that increase the arousal level of this part of the brain, such as dopamine and noradrenalin facilitators (like Ritalin and Strattera, the two most frequently used medicines for ADHD), and even many of the antidepressants, work because they disproportionately increase the arousal level of that part of the brain that coordinates our ability to recognize and regulate our own behavior and to benefit from environmental feedback.

The two major groupings of medicines that are used for ADHD (of course there are others that are used in a small percentage of cases) fall into the categories of stimulants and reuptake inhibitors. Both types of medicines can be effective in most cases of ADHD but stimulants seem to be the most effective for the largest number of people. Ritalin is by far the most frequently used stimulant in the treatment of ADHD. Why, then, would Ritalin not be used all of the time in all cases? There are several reasons. First, not everyone responds the same way to the same medicines and this is why there are typically many variations of each patented medicine for many diseases and disorders. Second, the side effects of medicines are different for different people. Some people also tolerate some side effects better than others. With all of the individual differences in degree and nuance of response and reaction and tolerance of side effects, multiple choices are needed to find the best medicine with the best fit for each person.

Stimulants

Stimulants have been used for many decades in the treatment of ADHD and were among the first medicines tried. For the first thirty or more years, we did not know why they worked. Their effectiveness was characterized as a paradox because no one understood why a stimulant calmed individuals with ADHD. Now we know.

History of Research on Stimulants   Numerous researchers date the true beginnings of psychopharmacological treatment of what is now known as ADHD to the 1930s and the discovery of stimulant treatments. The effectiveness of stimulants was discovered by accident when several new amphetamine compounds were being tried out as headache treatments in children. The researchers began to notice that youth with behavior problems reacted favorably to these medicines. However, very little research was done on these or other psychiatric drugs until the 1950s. In 1956, the National Institutes of Mental Health created the Psychopharmacological Research Branch (PRB). Subsequently, the prominent pioneer researchers in this arena, Leon Eisenberg and Keith Conners, completed a series of state-of-the art scientific studies of the efficacy of the stimulant Ritalin for treatment of ADHD and found it to be effective. In 1961, the FDA approved Ritalin officially as the first medicine with a clinical indication for treatment of ADHD. Even so, much was written during these years arguing that ADHD was the result of poor parenting. In the early 1970s, Paul Wender, a child psychiatrist, began to write about the links between neurotransmitter deficiencies, especially dopamine and norepinephrine, and ADHD. Ritalin and related stimulants facilitate dopamine and norepinephrine in the brain (among several other neurotransmitters) and these neurotransmitters are concentrated in the areas of the brain believed to be under-aroused or inefficient in their use of dopamine and norepinephrine among individuals with ADHD.

How Does a Stimulant Medication Work? When we write that a medicine facilitates a neurotransmitter, we mean it does something to help its appropriate use in the brain. This can happen in many different ways. Indeed, stimulants seem to act on multiple neurotransmitter systems in multiple ways, which is likely why they are so effective for so many people. If we look back at Figure 5.2, we can see that there are many possibilities for facilitating neurotransmitters. Stimulants can, for example:

- Result in **increased** production of neurotransmitters so more is available for use
- Cause **more neurotransmitters to be released** by the storage vesicle into the synaptic cleft
- **Increase the receptiveness of the neurotransmitter** receptor site, making it more likely to capture and use the neurotransmitter
- Cause the neurotransmitter to **stay in the receptor site longer**

All of these actions will increase the arousal of those parts of the brain where the affected neurotransmitters are concentrated.

This increased arousal, in the case of ADHD, enhances our ability to regulate our own behavior, giving us better voluntary control over what we do and to what we pay attention to and for how long. We see this occur not just in the behavior we observe, but also in the brain itself. Sophisticated images of brain metabolism have shown that the areas we noted in the earlier figures and text in this chapter that are under-aroused in the ADHD brain do show increases in their metabolic rates when stimulant medications are given.[6] The effects on neuroimaging take about six weeks or so to be seen, but clearly substantiate our thinking as to how these medicines work.

The truth is, stimulants work because they increase the arousal levels of the key structures of the brain that are responsible for the self-regulation of behavior, enabling us to adjust our attention and behavior to our immediate circumstances, to inhibit responding or behaving when it is best to do so, and to benefit more from the feedback of our environment and the people in it.

Reuptake Inhibitors

Reuptake inhibitors were first used clinically as antidepressants. Different reuptake inhibitors target their effects to different neurotransmitters, but the most likely ones to be affected are dopamine, serotonin, and norepinephrine. Most reuptake inhibitors will affect all three of these to some extent and others as well. Strattera, the most widely used of the reuptake inhibitors for treatment of ADHD, has the most narrow, specific effects, and targets norepinephrine almost exclusively. Once again, if we look back at Figure 5.2, we see an opening on the axon terminal labelled reuptake pump. This pump, ideally, takes the used neurotransmitter and pumps it back into the neuron for recycling. Sometimes, it may capture neurotransmitter molecules that have yet to carry out their mission of activating or communicating with another neuron. A reuptake inhibitor blocks this action so that more neurotransmitter remains in the synaptic cleft. Reuptake inhibitors may also extend the time that a neurotransmitter is retained by the receptor site.

The end result in brain function is similar—reuptake inhibitors, in the case of ADHD, increase arousal levels of systems that are similar to those affected by amphetamines or stimulants such as Ritalin. The effects, however, are not as pronounced, nor are they apparent as quickly. Stimulants can begin to work within about thirty minutes of oral administration, whereas reuptake inhibitors can take anywhere from 10 to 21 days to show improvements that are significant.

> **From the Neuroscientist**
>
> When a child or adult takes medication for ADHD, the medication actually assists the brain in doing what it is supposed to do. Just as glasses assist eyes that have problems or braces change the placement of teeth and the alignment of the jaw, the right medication creates a state of "normal" for an individual with ADHD. The arousal level of the control mechanisms that are so important to our ability to regulate our own behavior is increased to what are normal levels for individuals without ADHD.

Stimulants Versus Reuptake Inhibitors

If you determine that medicine has a role to play in the treatment of ADHD for yourself or your child, careful consideration is due to which medicine should be given, and this decision should be between you and the primary treating physician. Your physician should be willing to discuss different issues with you, such as the benefits of particular medicines and their potential side effects.

Ritalin is typically a first choice of most physicians because it is the most likely to be effective and has the strongest effects. However, Ritalin has to be administered 2–3 times a day in most cases (unless a sustained release dose is used, and the sustained release forms may not be as effective—this issue continues to be debated, and our clinical experience suggests the sustained release forms are not quite as effective), so it will end up having to be administered at school for school-aged youth. Ritalin also suppresses appetite in most youth and meals have to be scheduled around medicine schedules, which is not hard, but at times can be inconvenient for busy families. Ritalin (and when we say Ritalin here we really refer to most stimulant-class medicines for ADHD) may also cause sleeplessness and in some individuals causes increased irritability. This often wears off over time, but can be a problem for some. For some years, it was believed that Ritalin produced growth suppression. If this does occur it is a temporary effect. Children who take Ritalin will reach their normal size; it just may take a little longer.

Some reuptake inhibitors have many side effects as well, but Strattera is preferred because it has the least severe side effects. It has a lower side effect profile because it affects fewer chemical systems in the body and is very narrowly targeted to norepinephrine. Table 5.1 summarizes the most common side effects of Ritalin and Strattera. Side effects attributed to Strattera differ somewhat for children and adults so we have broken these out in the table. Other rare or unusual side effects occur with both of these medicines; therefore, this is not intended to be a complete list. You should talk to your physician if anything unusual happens after you or your child begin any new medicine, and medicines for ADHD are no different in this regard. Also, some people can tolerate some side effects better than others or may find one side effect less problematic than another. This may create a personal preference for one medicine over another. That said, Ritalin remains the most effective medicine for control of the symptoms of ADHD and works for a larger percentage of individuals with ADHD than other medicines.

One other feature of these medicines deserves mention. Ritalin and other stimulants can be abused. They have the same

Table 5.1: Side Effects of Ritalin and Strattera.

Side Effects	Ritalin	Strattera (Children)	Strattera (Adults)
Dizziness	X	X	X
Nausea or vomiting	X	X	X
Decreased appetite or weight loss	X	X	X
Insomnia (trouble sleeping)	X		X
Headache	X		
Drowsiness	X		
Abdominal pain	X		
Nervousness	X		
Upset stomach		X	
Tiredness		X	
Mood swings		X	
Menstrual cramps			X
Problems passing urine			X
Constipation			X
Dry mouth			X
Sexual dysfunction			X

effects and are similar to what is sometimes referred to as "speed," and can be abused just as methamphetamine is abused. Ritalin also has "street value," meaning it can be sold—illegally, of course—on the street. It is a controlled substance and is sometimes sought after by those who want its arousal effects for long-distance driving, all-night studying, working late shifts, or in other circumstances where they want to stay up and not sleep. Studying under such circumstances is of dubious value. Fatigue later adversely affects test performance, and some of the learning may not be recalled unless Ritalin is taken at the time of the exam as well. Strattera does not have such abuse potential and is preferred especially in adults who have any history of addiction issues or who are at increased risk of addiction or abuse (addiction potential also runs in families for a variety of substances, especially alcohol, and so has a genetic component as well).

Neither medicine should ever be prescribed without a complete physical examination by a medical doctor or without your doctor knowing all other medications and any vitamins or supplements that you or your child may be taking. Certain other health conditions, especially those involving major organs like the heart, liver, and kidneys, preclude the use of one or both classes of these medicines. Both medicines can interact in serious ways with certain other drugs and supplements as well, as is true with most prescription medication. Before starting a new medicine, always tell the physician about anything you take, prescription or not, legal or not. No exceptions—leave nothing out!

Does Medical Treatment for ADHD Lead to Drug Abuse in the Future?

Many parents are alarmed that the use of medicines, especially stimulants like Ritalin, may lead to a future of drug dependence, abuse, or addiction in their children's lives as teens or adults. This issue has been the subject of intense scientific and public scrutiny. There is a great deal of literature addressing this issue. The scientific evidence seems clear enough at this point. Dr. Laura Dean of the National Center for Biotechnology Information conducted a thorough review of this scientific literature recently at the request of the National Medical Library, an agency of the National Institutes of Health.[7] Her conclusion was that "in teenagers and young adults, the use of stimulant ADHD drugs in childhood is not linked with alcohol abuse, smoking or substance abuse later on in life." We agree based upon not only our knowledge of this scientific literature, but also on our own clinical experiences with adolescents and young adults. Some percentage of children and youth who are diagnosed with ADHD and take stimulant medication will grow up to engage in substance use and abuse. This is unfortunately true for our entire population. However, the evidence says that when this occurs for persons with ADHD, it is for reasons other than their exposure to stimulant treatment for ADHD. The truth is, the

From the Neuroscientist and Clinician

Having been chief of psychology and director of neuropsychology at a psychiatric hospital that housed, among other units, treatment units for various addictions, I found that it was not uncommon to see teens and young adults who were using various illegal drugs to self-medicate. Many of these youth had undiagnosed disorders such as ADHD, depression, or even bipolar disorder, and were attempting to manage their behavior and feelings on their own with the use of street drugs as opposed to proper, professionally managed care. I can recall quite vividly more than one young adult who told me they just did not understand all the fuss about cocaine (and in some cases methamphetamine), since they did not experience the rush or the high that other people described to them. Instead, they remarked on how it calmed them. The failure to diagnose and to treat ADHD can have very bad consequences, one of which is to lead to substance abuse problems. I once evaluated a medical resident who had become addicted to amphetamines and who clearly had undiagnosed ADHD. He was clear that it was only when he discovered and used amphetamines that he was able to sit still and study for long periods of time, or indeed to sit and attend to anything for any real length of time. During his medical training, he realized he had ADHD but was not willing to seek professional diagnosis or treatment for fear of ruining his medical career, and so he continued to self-medicate until he was caught. This young man, with proper diagnosis and treatment, was able to return to his residency, and is now a high-functioning, well-respected psychiatrist.

treatment of correctly diagnosed ADHD via stimulant medications such as Ritalin does not cause future substance abuse issues.
Treated ADHD may put you at lower risk for self-medicating or
risky impulsive behaviors such as drug experimentation.

TO SUM UP

Some people and some organized groups object on philosophical
grounds to treating behavioral problems such as ADHD with
medicine: "We shouldn't medicate behavior!" Some even try to
take such arguments to the level of a moral objection, promoting
fear about "zombied-out children" or guilt that parents are
"dodging responsibility" or putting their children into a "chemical straitjacket." However, once we understand that ADHD is
truly a disorder of the brain, the organ that controls behavior,
we understand the ridiculous nature of such arguments and
objections. Using medicine as one component of a comprehensive treatment plan for ADHD is no different from using insulin
as one part of a comprehensive treatment plan for diabetes. A
person with diabetes cannot simply will the body to produce
more insulin. A person with ADHD likewise cannot simply will
the brain to produce more dopamine or norepinephrine or
increase the density of the right prefrontal cortex.

We agree with the general conclusions of organizations like
CHADD as well as several federal government agencies, such as
the FDA (Federal Drug Administration) and the NIDA (National
Institute on Drug Abuse), that medicine properly prescribed and
properly taken as directed by the prescribing physician has a role
to play in most cases of ADHD, provided the medicines are toler-
ated well. However, medicine should never be the only approach.
As we have said and will say again, the truth is multimodal treatment plans are crucial to success when ADHD is the diagnosis.
Medication can create a more normal operating state for the
brain but it will not teach reading or math, and medication will

not undo bad habits if such habits and ineffective or problematic coping strategies were learned, and medication will not create new social skills. What medication will do is allow the individual to benefit more fully from all learning opportunities: academic, functional, and social.

WHAT'S NEXT?

In the next chapter, we will address nonmedical or nonbiological interventions that work in the management of ADHD—not as a cure. Targeted behavioral interventions are noted to work best, but these come in many forms and each is reviewed to direct you to the right source for the right help—and by right, we mean effective!

6

Nonmedical Interventions That Work

As we mentioned in Chapter Five, medication can be very effective in helping people live productive lives with ADHD, but there are also very effective nonmedical interventions that you can use with or without medication. These interventions are based on scientific theories that explain why individuals behave the way that they do. The interventions in this chapter are known to decrease inattention, hyperactivity, impulsivity, and other ADHD-like behaviors . . . but not to cure ADHD. Because ADHD is a neurobiological disorder, the truth is that any child will be affected for a long time, and a third or more throughout his or her lifetime. Behavioral interventions are used often in schools and community settings, such as private or state-funded counseling practices, by parents of children with ADHD, and by individuals diagnosed with the disorder who want to implement self-help strategies.

Your previous attempts to change your own behavior or that of others with ADHD may have left you feeling frustrated and wondering why you were unsuccessful. You might blame yourself when interventions do not work—when the reality is that the intervention is actually ineffective for decreasing hyperactivity, inattention, and impulsivity or helping individuals with ADHD cope and learn new strategies. In this chapter, we begin by telling you about some of the ineffective, yet often advertised and promoted interventions for ADHD. You probably have heard about some of these interventions and wondered if using them might help, or you may have even tried some of them.

From the Teacher

Behavioral and cognitive-behavioral interventions are important because my students sometimes come to class without the strategies they need to be successful. When students develop self-management skills (as an example) I can help them practice that skill in school. I can't hand them medication and I don't want to. I want to be able to help them develop the skills to be successful in my class and beyond. Sometimes medicine makes my students feel as though "it is the medicine" that makes them successful rather than their own skills and efforts. In conjunction with stimulant medication, teaching skill sets and strategies is a win-win because both the student and I feel empowered by our own actions.

After reviewing interventions that do *not* work, we will discuss behavioral and cognitive-behavioral strategies that are effective. Behavioral therapy, as proven by research and endorsed by the American Academy of Pediatrics (AAP) guidelines, can be effective in treating the core symptoms of ADHD.[1] Although cognitive-behavioral interventions are not necessarily effective for decreasing inattention, hyperactivity, and impulsivity, evidence suggests that they are effective in reducing the negative impact of ADHD on daily living skills such as learning, performing simple daily tasks, behaving safely, being organized, and developing and using good social skills. If you are interested in interventions specific to schools and classrooms, we will refer you to Chapters Five and Six, and for specific interventions for parents to use at home and in the community to Chapter Eight. When you, or a professional you are working with, select behavioral or cognitive-behavioral strategies, the age as well as the developmental stage and any comorbid conditions (such as depression, anxiety, and oppositional defiance) should be considered.

WHAT WILL NOT WORK?

You (and millions of others) may have tried numerous highly publicized techniques to decrease or in some cases "cure" hyperactivity, impulsivity, or inattention that have simply not been proven effective. Approximately 19.6% of parents report trying alternative treatments (those different from the most common and standard treatments) with their children with ADHD.[2] Naturally, many parents hope to find remedies that do not involve giving children psychotropic medications. Even though medication use with ADHD has a history of more than fifty years of effectiveness and safety treating individuals with ADHD, some parents are reluctant to try medication or use it as prescribed. Many worry that medications are overprescribed and others are concerned about side effects, such as decreased appetite, insomnia, and stomachaches. However, the use of alternative treatments (such as diets and herbs) is not the answer to this dilemma and often leads to feelings of frustration and increased family discord when the treatments do not change any behavior, especially when some of these treatments require massive changes in established family rituals and interaction patterns.

You can read many reports of alternative therapies advertising that the approach will "cure" ADHD. However, as we have

From the Counselor

From a counseling perspective, behavioral and cognitive-behavioral interventions are important because as educators, we need to be able to teach children skills that will increase their opportunity to be successful both in and out of school. We do not have the option (or the desire) to prescribe medication or make that decision for parents. In addition, I've worked with many adolescents who REFUSE to take medication. So we value interventions that we can use to teach individuals with ADHD to function successfully on a daily basis.

stressed, ADHD is a neurobiologically based disorder and no simple cure has yet to be determined. Some find this disappointing, but it is vitally important to remember and encourage the development of the positive characteristics associated with ADHD, especially as we attempt to decrease the negative aspects.

What Research Tells Us About Diets and Supplements

Eating healthy is good for you. There is no doubt about that, but specifically avoiding sugar does not make a person with ADHD less hyperactive, impulsive, or inattentive.[3] For over two decades, researchers have evaluated the possibility of a connection between sugar and hyperactivity, but a large majority of research discounts any association between sugar and hyperactivity.[4] The most influential study on the topic was conducted and published by Mark Wolraich, M.D. Dr. Wolraich is a professor and chief of the Section of Developmental and Behavioral Pediatrics at the University of Oklahoma Health Sciences Center and is a major contributor to the American Academy of Pediatrics' primary care physician's guide for ADHD. In 1985 Dr. Wolraich's research team evaluated the effect of sugar on 16 boys with ADHD for three days and found that sugar did not increase hyperactivity.[5] In 1986, Drs. Milich, Wolraich, and Lindgren reviewed several studies of sugar and ADHD and found that results were as likely to indicate that sugar actually decreased hyperactivity as to have increased hyperactivity.[6] In another study in 1994 investigating mothers' perceptions of hyperactivity, researchers gave 31 children a drink containing a sugar substitute but told half of the mothers that the child had been given a sugary drink.[7] The mothers who were told their child had consumed sugary drinks all rated their child as being more hyperactive whether the child had a sugary drink or not! If you have a child with ADHD, you may believe that your child is more hyperactive after consuming sugar, but the reality is that the typical perception of parents is that children are more hyperactive after sugar intake, even though scientific evidence does not indicate that the child's activity level actually increases.

Only a few small research studies have investigated the use of vitamin supplements and herbal remedies for ADHD. Some recommend doses of vitamins that are far above the minimal daily requirements recommend by the federal government. However, such excessive doses of vitamins or minerals can be dangerous and the safety of many megavitamins has not been proven.[8] Therefore, we urge you to use caution and diligent care and to speak with your doctor before you give children anything "herbal" or otherwise. The herbal supplements we have seen advertised for curing ADHD have no properly controlled scientific research to support such claims of cure, and there is no reason based upon the known neurobiology of ADHD and the chemical nature of these herbs to even suspect they might actually cure ADHD.

Some contend that gluten-free diets decrease the symptoms of ADHD. Though this may be true for some, the key here is to pay close attention to the word "symptoms." There has not been any research conducted on this link and so there are no results to support or discount the effectiveness of gluten-free diets as a treatment for individuals diagnosed with ADHD. The link is highly doubtful. Doctors recommend that people with celiac disease, or gluten intolerance, avoid gluten. Gluten intolerance might mimic the symptoms of ADHD, as many people with celiac disease have anemia which creates a lack of concentration and can adversely affect decision making, sometimes making them appear impulsive, and individuals who are allergic to gluten may become irritable in response to gluten. In addition, B vitamin deficiencies and magnesium deficiencies can cause behavioral changes in children. However, if you find that inattention, hyperactivity, and impulsivity are cured by a gluten-free diet, then it is not likely that the person actually had an accurate diagnosis of ADHD. As we have noted in earlier chapters, misdiagnosis of ADHD occurs and we suspect strongly that reports of cures with diet and herbs are really affecting people who did not have ADHD to begin with.

Punishment Is Ineffective

A less publicized and advertised recommendation that is often heard from family and friends is punishment. If you have a child with ADHD or you were a child with ADHD, we are sure that at some time in your life, a relative or friend has suggested that punishment or "more discipline" is the answer. As a parent of a child with ADHD, you might have felt criticized or condemned for your child's behavior, especially when others suggest the cause is simply a lack of punishment.

You can be reassured that a lack of punishment did not cause you or your child to have ADHD, and punishment is not a cure. You have probably noticed that punishment does not create lasting change in the behavior of individuals with ADHD, especially during childhood, and this observation is supported by research.[9] Why? For several reasons. To begin with, although most people believe they have a thorough understanding of punishment, most do not understand how to determine if an action is truly punishing. **Punishment** is defined as the removal of a positive reinforcer or the presentation of an aversive stimulus (doing something to the person that they find aversive or do not like)[10] after a behavior occurs that **decreases the severity or frequency of the behavior**. To say that the punishment was effective, you would actually have to say that the punishment (and not something else) caused a decrease in the behavior. Consider the example of punishing your son with ADHD for not completing his homework by taking away his television time. If this happens to result in his homework getting turned in, you might assume that it was the loss of television time that sparked the behavior change. However, how much additional monitoring occurred that normally did not occur? This result could just as likely have been caused by adult monitoring that accompanied the punishment. In other words, you were simply helping him attend better to his homework. Also, if the problem were to return, the loss of television time would clearly not be an effective "punishment" in the classic sense, as it didn't act as a deterrent. You would then be challenged to up the ante. As punishment is typically ineffective for changing the behavior of children with ADHD, parents of children with ADHD will eventually run out of options for punishments that they are willing to deliver. Spanking or other corporal punishments for a child with ADHD in response to acting impulsively is simply doomed to failure; it will eventually frustrate you, make you feel awful, and teach your child some improper lessons about the use of force. Spanking will not alter a child's neurochemistry or result in increased arousal of the brain parts we discussed in great detail in Chapter Three for more than a few minutes—once the brain returns to its own normal state, the effects of any physical punishment are done.

The truth is that punishment is a poor method for teaching children the skills necessary to monitor and change their behavior. Research on the effects of punishment with children also tells us that punishment only works with most children when there is an immediate threat of punishment; if you are not present when the child has a decision to make, chances are that the probability of punishment will not enter into the child's decision-making process. You realize that you CANNOT "punish" diabetes or near-sightedness out of a person. Instead, we teach the individual to "cope." When we choose punishment in such situations, we lose the opportunity to teach. You may have noticed that when you punish a child immediately after the behavior in a calm, direct manner, the behavior briefly stops but eventually returns or worsens—if you do not also teach the child the appropriate behavior you would like to see. The truth is that the excitement and stimulation from punishment sometimes actually increase the negative behaviors of individuals with ADHD. When we model a punitive method of resolving problems by punishing a child for a behavior that may not be under his or her control, the result might be a trade of minor behavior problems for more difficult ones. For example, the individual might impulsively attempt to "escape" the punishment by being aggressive, running away, hiding information about problems, or lying.

When punishing your child with ADHD, you might have felt like you were in a vicious cycle. That is because punishment often leads to a **coercive behavior cycle** (see Figure 6.1). In this cycle of interactions, the parent, teacher, or employer gives a directive; the person receiving the directive does not comply (by choice or error); the other person becomes frustrated or angry, repeats directions or gives the directive louder, perhaps becomes

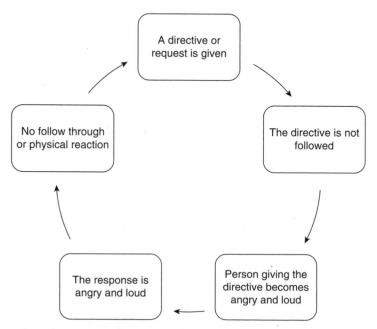

Figure 6.1. Coercive Behavior Cycle

aggressive and threatens; the person again fails to comply and may resist outright. Now what does the person giving the directive or request do? He or she has two choices: (1) physically make the person follow the direction, or (2) give in and withdraw the request or directive. You probably would not find either choice acceptable and neither choice is effective in changing behavior. The person giving the direction or request (parent, significant other, or boss) and the person not following the direction both become more and more angry and frustrated.

PSYCHOSOCIAL INTERVENTIONS AND ADHD

Professionals can help you in the journey to capitalize on strengths and decrease negative behaviors associated with ADHD and their impact on daily functioning. Effective psychotherapists can teach and support you and your family through the use of behavioral and cognitive-behavioral strategies. Therapists (counselors, psychotherapists, social workers) consider themselves "helping professionals" with

From the Teacher

When I punish a student in my class, even if I temporarily eliminate the problem, my relationship with the student is damaged and I seem to get less cooperation later. I don't want to "ride" my ADHD student into the ground with the constant verbal reprimands or threats to stop moving, stop talking, or remember the directions. It takes the fun out of teaching.

From the Counselor

In my work with individuals with ADHD, punishment only seems to worsen the problem. Natural consequences, such as removing access to risk-taking activities, helps prevent the individual from self-harm at the moment, but not long term. Individuals with ADHD often speak of unfair punishment for unintentional behavior. The anger and self-esteem issues that follow often become one more issue to be worked through in counseling.

the primary goal of nurturing the growth of or addressing problems of psychological and emotional well-being.

How to Select a Helper

If you decide to seek help from a psychotherapist, it is important that you carefully select a therapist. We recommend that you follow at least the following three guidelines.

First, ask for a referral. Ask your friends, your child's teacher, and others that you trust for recommendations. You may find that school employees are not encouraged to recommend one therapist, but many will be more than willing and happy to give you the names of three or more therapists that specialize in ADHD. Teachers and school counselors often have years of experience and knowledge of community agencies from working with other parents and children. In addition, your physician is an excellent source for recommendations. If you have health insurance, it is important to contact the company for a recommendation and to determine which providers are covered under your insurance.

Second, once you have recommendations from reliable sources and know which providers are covered by your insurance, speak to at least three therapists prior to making a commitment to enter a therapeutic relationship. In addition to asking logical questions about fees and availability consider asking the types of questions in Figure 6.2. Ask the therapist to discuss his or her years of experience and expertise with ADHD. Because individuals with ADHD are all different, it is important that you seek the assistance of a therapist that has expertise in the core symptoms of ADHD, impairment created by ADHD, and comorbid conditions. Therapy is not a cheap experience and should not be taken lightly. Remember that you are entering into a counseling **relationship**. Is this person someone that you feel you can trust? Are you comfortable talking to him or her about your

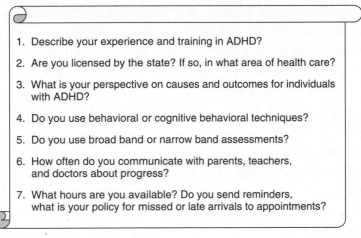

1. Describe your experience and training in ADHD?

2. Are you licensed by the state? If so, in what area of health care?

3. What is your perspective on causes and outcomes for individuals with ADHD?

4. Do you use behavioral or cognitive behavioral techniques?

5. Do you use broad band or narrow band assessments?

6. How often do you communicate with parents, teachers, and doctors about progress?

7. What hours are you available? Do you send reminders, what is your policy for missed or late arrivals to appointments?

Figure 6.2. Behavioral Strategies

behavior or your child's behavior without being embarrassed or feeling judged? Do you feel respected by the therapist?

Third, select a therapist with a behavioral or cognitive-behavioral orientation, which are the most effective in treating ADHD. Different therapists use specific techniques based on their theoretical orientations—which are reasonable and scientifically acceptable explanations of why people think, behave, and feel the way that they do. Psychoanalysis and other insight-based approaches are not effective for treating ADHD.

Behavioral and Cognitive-Behavioral Interventions

In the following sections, you will find information about behavioral and cognitive-behavioral interventions that are supported by research and are effective in changing the negative behaviors associated with ADHD and in increasing knowledge and skills to cope with ADHD. Therapists often implement behavioral and cognitive-behavioral interventions in sessions, school counselors often use these strategies, and some of the strategies can be used as self-help strategies.

Behavioral Strategies   Behavioral strategies are techniques that focus on changing what happens before the behavior (antecedents) and after the behavior (consequences). For example, think about on-task behavior. You might notice that when you are folding laundry (the task at hand) and your telephone rings or a text message alert beeps on your cell phone, you stop folding laundry (off task) and do not return to complete the laundry until you suddenly remember that it has to be completed (right before you plan to go to bed). The phone ringing or a distraction by another task demand would be the antecedent to the off-task behavior of not folding laundry; the consequence is not completing the laundry.

One example of how you and a professional can work together to change behavior using these strategies includes defining the problem or target behavior, identifying the antecedents and consequences, and setting up a new consequence that will support the desired behavior and decrease the problematic one. In the laundry example above, the target behavior is to complete the laundry, the antecedent is the telephone, and an effective consequence might be to use a list and reinforce yourself when the laundry is done. A similar variation is the use of behavioral contracts where you specify the target behavior that you would like to eliminate or modify, identify antecedents and consequences that maintain the behavior, then come up with a more adaptive replacement behavior, and then determine the reinforcement for using the replacement behavior (see Exhibit 6.1).

First, determine which behavior(s) you would like to change and prioritize one behavior as the **target behavior**. It is helpful to prioritize concerns and select one behavior that interferes the most with success and happiness. For example, Suzy is a high school student with ADHD who does not feel successful at school. Suzy has two concerns. She has difficulty with friends; the girls tell her she talks too much. She has difficult with schoolwork and is failing two classes, because she forgets to complete

---

Exhibit 6.1: Sample Behavioral Contract

Contract

I, _____(individual's name), on this date
_____, agree that I will do the following: _____
_____
_____
_____
_____.

By successfully completing this contract, I will receive or allow myself
to or give myself: _____
_____
_____
_____

_____   _____
Individual's Signature   Therapist's Signature

---

long-term assignments. The counselor and Suzy write goals to
address each of the challenges that Suzy mentioned, but determine to begin with the goal of turning in long-term assignments
on the due date, as this seems to be the most critical to her
success.

Next, identify and change the antecedents and consequences.
To determine the antecedent of the behavior, you have to determine what typically happens before the behavior. Environments
can perpetuate ADHD symptoms. Environments that are over-
stimulating, filled with distractions, or completely unstructured
challenge and tempt the ADHD mind. To begin changing behaviors, you can structure work and study environments in such a
way that distractions or temptations are minimized. You may
know individuals with ADHD who work well in private offices
or cubicles and others who do well with white noise in the

background, and still others who need completely quiet work environments free of distractions. Determining and creating the environment that best fits you or the individual with ADHD is the first step to structuring an efficient environment. Know that what works at one juncture may not always work either, so be prepared to reassess and revisit what you need.

Consider Suzy from the previous example. Suzy does not complete long-term assignments. Suzy has a calendar with short components of the long-term assignment that she is supposed to complete each day after school. Every day, Suzy goes to her room with the full intention of completing the task. Once in her room, she takes out the materials to complete the task and puts them on her desk beside her computer. Suzy then checks her social network page to make sure that she has not missed any important information. Three out of four times, Suzy never manages to return to the task (the problem behavior). Ultimately it is the day before the long-term assignment is due and she has not completed the assignment (consequence). To avoid the distractions created by the computer (the antecedent), Suzy could do her homework in another room that is quiet and free of distractions. If Suzy's homework requires the use of the computer, Suzy's parents can carefully monitor her work on the computer and encourage her to refrain from looking at distracting websites prior to completion of the daily task. However, Suzy actually believes (each and every time) that she will be able to quickly check the social page and get back to her work. In cases like Suzy's, it might be necessary for her parents to keep her computer in another room until the homework is complete. This makes computer time contingent on homework completion.

Consequences maintain behavior. Have you ever noticed that distracted behavior gets you away from a task that you find less engaging? Individuals with ADHD (and probably others) often "escape" boring responsibilities for something likely more entertaining. Determining the consequences that are maintaining the behavior is important. Think about Ali, who is asked to do some chores around the house, reasonable things for a 10-year-old. Her chore list on Saturday includes making the bed, bringing her dirty laundry to the hallway for washing, and violin practice. However, most Saturday mornings Ali is delightfully singing to her iPod®, happily dancing around in pajamas, flitting between her cats, fish, and hamster, and talking to her parents. Sometimes Ali starts a job like carrying her laundry to the hallway and then remembers something she wanted to show her parents. This type of scattered behavior continues through most of the morning until it is time to go to soccer practice. Then the family has lunch out, does some shopping, and goes home. By now it is early afternoon and Ali gets invited to a movie with a friend's family. When Mom and Dad get home, Mom gets the laundry because it needs to get done, makes the bed, and sighs when she looks at the violin. Dad says, "You've got to quit enabling her." Changing the consequences for Ali could involve redirection when Ali is distracted, using a list so that Ali can self-monitor, and not allowing play dates on Saturday unless jobs were finished. These consequence changes are set up not to avoid "punishment," but to create scenarios where Ali can be successful and learn strategies to do what she needs to do to be successful.

Sometimes the problem behavior, such as whining, hitting, or arguing with parents, needs replacing completely, so you would select a **replacement behavior**. Doing so involves identifying what function the behavior serves. If whining helps a child get his way, if hitting helps a child get access to a toy, or if arguing with parents means that the child is removed from the room or the discussion and thereby avoids something, the replacement behavior must be an appropriate method for achieving that same outcome. We must teach a behavior that can put a child into "power" or in a winning situation, allowing her access to a toy or even to escape an aversive situation. The replacement behavior must be easy to understand and have the same outcome for the individual as the problem behavior. Some problem behaviors continue because the consequences are reinforcing or rewarding. Other problem behaviors continue because the behavior allows the individual to avoid something that is challenging or unpleasant.

For example, as an adult with ADHD, you might find yourself blurting out the first thing that comes to your mind during meetings at work. Your coworkers indicated that this is very bothersome to them but your boss seems to smile and acknowledge the worth of your comments. You do not like to annoy your coworkers, but you like the positive attention from your boss. In order to find a replacement behavior that will work, you have to find a behavior that does the same thing for you (get positive boss attention). The replacement behavior might be to write down the thoughts and interject them at an appropriate time. Your boss would still value your comments and your coworkers might be more likely to provide reinforcement as you are not interfering with their ability to concentrate or participate.

As another example, Tamal, an eighth-grade student with ADHD, does not like his history class, because the teacher lectures for 30 minutes and then expects the students to answer questions in the back of the book. Tamal has trouble concentrating and becomes easily bored in the class. He has discovered that if he distracts other students in the class by thumping his pencil or talking to them, the teacher will send him to the principal's office. In the principal's office, Tamal sits by the secretary's desk and finds out everything that is going on in the school. Although one would expect the visit to the principal's office to stop Tamal's behavior, the opposite happens. Tamal gets out of class and this is worth anything negative that will happen in the office. As a bonus, Tamal actually enjoys the office. A replacement behavior would allow Tamal to escape history in an appropriate way, such as by using a hall pass to go to the bathroom, or asking for permission to listen to an iPod while answering questions in the back of the book. Or, with the help of parents and the office,

Tamal might be able to check in with another classroom and work interactively with a teaching assistant to learn the material and answer the questions.

Once you select the replacement behavior and practice it, you want to **reinforce** the use of the behavior. You can use reinforcers that are social, edible, or tangible. Natural reinforcers occur in the environment without any planning. Getting an "A" on a test because you studied naturally reinforces studying, at least for those who care about grades in school. Social reinforcers are expressions of praise from others (a pat on the back, a smile, clapping, nodding, and positive comments). Activity reinforcers allow individuals to participate in activities that are enjoyable to the individual (playing games, watching television, driving a car). Tangible reinforcers are items such as food, toys, stickers, balloons, awards.

For rewards or reinforcers to be truly reinforcing, they must be things to which the individual does not currently have access. For example, having the opportunity to eat edamame would be reinforcing to one of the authors of this book, but not to the others. Offering a child one piece of candy as a reinforcer may not be rewarding to a child who is allowed to eat all of the candy that his or her heart desires at home. To bolster the strength of a reinforcer a state of deprivation helps, and to increase new behaviors reinforcement must occur as close in time to the desired behavior as possible.

You will find, or may have already found, that using positive reinforcers is a bit tricky with individuals with ADHD, as they may respond differently than others to positive reinforcement. Individuals with ADHD respond best to *short-term* positive consequences and are not inclined to wait for *long-term* positive consequences. For example, Suzy (in the earlier example) is immediately reinforced by positive peer attention on her social network, but not so reinforced by the long-term positive consequence of good class averages. Suzy's parents can provide immediate reinforcement for homework completion by checking Suzy's homework daily and providing a reward, such as extra time on the computer at an appropriate time (or giving her the computer back once the homework is complete). Suzy's parents could also write a behavioral contract with her to outline possible rewards or reinforcers (as shown in Exhibit 6.1).

Cognitive-Behavioral Strategies   Unlike behavioral strategies that focus on changing only external antecedents and consequences, cognitive-behavioral strategies are founded on the concept that our behavior and feelings are controlled by **our thoughts** in addition to the environment. Cognitive-behavioral strategies are not useful in decreasing inattention, hyperactivity, and impulsivity, but are useful in helping you or your child cope with the impact of ADHD in specific areas such as organization, study, or relationship skills. Your therapist might use cognitive-behavioral interventions to identify and replace negative thinking, provide new thought patterns, and create coping skills. We will discuss three cognitive-behavioral techniques that are effective with ADHD: (1) cognitive restructuring, (2) self-management, and (3) problem solving (see Figure 6.3).

Cognitive restructuring is the process of changing negative thinking caused by numerous past experiences with failure and criticism. By definition ADHD begins in childhood; thus, many adults with ADHD have lived for years with criticism.[11] This criticism

From the Teacher

Behavior strategies help me teach a student the connection between behavior or choices and consequences. Some of my students come to school not making that connection naturally. They think things are just "unfair" or happen only to them randomly. Managing the environment and making explicit the relationship between actions and consequences helps set up my students for success. What starts as an external reinforcer, such as a token or a privilege, can soon become the naturally occurring things like good grades, more free time, and better relationships with friends and teachers.

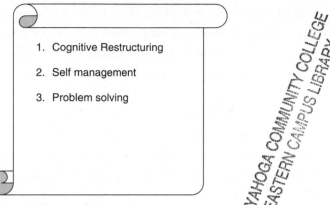

Figure 6.3. Cognitive-Behavioral Strategies

can become part of what you or the person with ADHD that you care about thinks and believes about yourself or him- or herself. Because we have only recently come to understand that ADHD continues into adulthood, minimal research is available to verify the effectiveness of any intervention with adults with ADHD; however, cognitive restructuring is emerging as one option.

> **From the Counselor**
>
> I like to use behavioral strategies with students. But I find it most helpful to combine behavioral and cognitive-behavioral strategies. I think it is most important to teach students new skills.

Cognitive restructuring begins with confronting and changing your negative self-talk. Do you ever listen to what you are saying to yourself or ask your child what he or she is thinking? Many people actually are more critical about themselves than others are of them. The first step in changing what you say to yourself is becoming aware of negative thoughts and treating them as a hypothesis to be proven or disproven and not facts. Once you become aware of a negative thought, then you automatically stop and think . . . is that true? If negative thoughts are proven correct, then you can learn new skills needed to change the negative behavior (that is, disorganization, lack of time management, distractibility, lack of effective problem-solving skills, ineffective communication skills).

For example, Gwendolyn, an adult with ADHD, tells herself that her friends do not really like her and ALWAYS make demeaning comments to her about behaviors that she feels are directly related to her ADHD. She tells herself that her friends always make fun of her for moving too quickly or interrupting conversations. Gwendolyn's therapist asks her to test the hypothesis that her friends always say negative things to her by documenting the negative things that her friends say. If Gwendolyn determines that her friends do not actually make a lot of negative comments, then she can replace the negative thought with a more productive one, such as "That was a joke and I am taking it too personally." If Gwendolyn finds out that her friends are making a lot of negative comments, then she can use problem solving to decrease the behavior that is being criticized. For example, Gwendolyn might determine that she does interrupt others and decide to work on interrupting less.

Another cognitive-behavioral strategy that you can use to decrease the impact of ADHD on everyday functioning is **self-management**. Self-management is a skill to assist you in managing your own behavior without relying on others for guidance or reinforcement. Self-management is especially important for adolescents and adults with ADHD who have difficulties managing distractibility, impulse control, organization, time management, and study skills. Each of these can be self-managed. Self-management involves counting the frequency or duration of a behavior that you want to increase. At times, remembering to document that you demonstrated the behavior might be difficult for individuals with ADHD. If this becomes a problem, then you can ask someone to help prompt you to record the behavior or you can use an electronic timer to cue you. If these strategies do not increase your compliance with the procedures, then you would want to select another strategy.

Using self-management, you follow a seven-step process (see Figure 6.4). First, select a self-monitoring form. Figure 6.5 is a sample self-monitoring form. Many forms are available in books or online and you can actually create one that better fits your needs. Self-monitoring forms are designed for the specific behavior to be monitored. You measure or count the occurrence

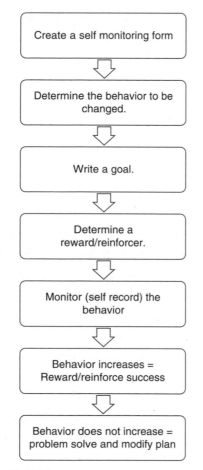

Figure 6.4. Steps to Self-Management

Problem Behavior:				
Goal:				
Week:				
Monday	**Tuesday**	**Wednesday**	**Thursday**	**Friday**

Figure 6.5. Self-Monitoring Form

of behaviors based on the frequency, duration, or whether or not a behavior occurs (yes or no). For example, arriving at class or school on time could be self-managed as frequency. How often did you arrive at school on time within a specified time period (a week, a month, and so on)? Self-managing an activity like studying, however, might be better accomplished by considering duration. How long did you study at one time period? Curbing the impulse to interrupt could be self-managed by asking yourself whether or not you interrupted someone—yes or no—perhaps within a specific time period.

In addition, you can self-manage with a calendar, appointment book, or task list. Many electronic versions of each are available for purchase, but some people prefer to use hard copies. It is important to use a self-monitoring system with which you are most comfortable so that you will follow through.

Second, define the behavior that is the most worrisome and which you feel motivated to change. The behavior is described in terms that are observable (or countable). Before writing the behavior to be changed on the self-monitoring form (see Figure 6.5), ask, "Can I count this behavior, thought, or feeling?" Once you decide that the behavior, thought, or feeling is most worrisome and countable, write the behavior at the top of the self-monitoring form, calendar, or task list. For example, Cannon, a sixteen-year-old with ADHD, is always late for football practice on Saturday mornings. Cannon decides to self-manage leaving the house on time. He puts a self-management form beside the back door of his house. He defines the behavior to be changed as leaving his house late for practice. When Cannon walks out the door on his way to practice, he simply puts a check beside the date if he is leaving on time or a negative sign if he is running late.

Third, you write a goal to increase or decrease the behavior. Just like the problem behavior, the goal must be observable. For example, Cannon writes the following goal: "I will leave my house by 7:30 on Saturday."

Fourth, decide how you will reward meeting the goal. The reward must be truly "rewarding" to you. For example, Cannon decides that if he meets his goal of leaving the house at 7:30 on Saturday morning, then he will go to the park and hang out with his friends after practice. If he does not meet the goal, he will go home and start his chores for the day.

Fifth, self-monitor the behavior. Use the self-monitoring form to document the behavior. Sixth, after a prespecified time included in the behavioral goal, check to determine whether you met the goal. If you achieved your goal, then self-reward. If you did not meet the goal, use the steps to problem solving in the next section of this chapter to determine what interfered with achieving the goal. Sixth, begin the process again. It is important for individuals with ADHD to repeat this process until the new behavior (the goal) becomes a habit. Individuals must consistently reinforce behaviors over extended periods of time for real change to occur.

Problem solving is a skill you need when considering all of the options for resolving problems and selecting the best option. Children, adolescents, and adults with ADHD often find solving problems challenging. You might have noticed that when the options become overwhelming, instead of facing the problem and attempting to find a solution, individuals with ADHD tend to avoid the issue. Following the steps for problem solving outlined on Figure 6.6, we are going to use the next example to illustrate the entire problem-solving process. Let's say that you

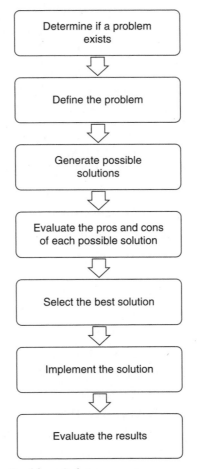

Figure 6.6. Steps to Problem Solving

are a college freshman with ADHD and realize that you are failing your English class. Your grade consists of one research paper and four exams. In November, you realize that you had not started your research paper and you made a 60 and a 70 on the first two exams. You feel overwhelmed and do not know where to begin. One way to address this would be to decide that because there is no way that you could possibly write the paper or pass the last two exams, you should go to the local pub for a few drinks. Of course, when you wake up the next morning the problem will still be there. Another approach would be to follow a seven-step process to solve the problem (see Figure 6.6). The first step is determining that a problem exists and making a commitment to try to find a solution. You know the problem is that you are failing English. But what else do you know? The issues are that you have not started the research paper and you had made very low test grades. So what do you do about that?

To answer this question, you generate possible solutions. What are the possible solutions? You could drop your English class. You could seek assistance from a tutor to write the paper or you could visit with your English professor to get advice. Now you have a list of possible solutions. Next, you evaluate the pros and cons of each solution.

The pro for dropping the class would be that the pressure and anxiety would be relieved. You could start fresh next semester. The con would be that you wasted money on the class and you would be further behind in graduation (and your parents would not be happy). The pro for getting tutoring would be that you would have support in completing the paper. The con would be that it would cost you extra money. When you consider visiting your professor, you realize that you do not want to tell the professor that you have not started the assignment. However, you think that maybe the professor could provide more structure to the assignment, so that you would know where to begin. You also believe that the professor might tell you that it is too late to start the paper. You decide to combine your choices. First, you will visit the professor and then begin tutoring if the professor believes that you can finish the class successfully.

So now you do what you decided to do. You visit the professor who tells you that you can finish the paper. The professor even helps you write an outline. You begin tutoring two nights a week. Even though you have to avoid the local pub on weekdays for two months, you do complete the paper and pass the English class.

Finally, you evaluate the results. How did it work out? Did you achieve your goal? The answer in this situation is that yes, you passed the class and therefore your solution was effective.

You can apply problem solving to any challenging situation. Even when problems seem overwhelming, you can follow the steps to make it more manageable. You can also find someone, such as a therapist or friend, to help you walk through the steps and provide encouragement for following through on your solution.

From the Teacher

With my older students I like to help them work on their "self-talk" to help themselves learn to self-coach and self-praise. "Like counting dance steps in your head," I tell my class as I sing one, two, three, one, two, three, and I waltz around the room. Then I repeat something that can be academic self-talk like, "Books, backpack, push in my chair—good job cha cha cha."

From the Counselor

Cognitive-behavioral interventions are my first choice for individuals with ADHD. Even though ADHD is a biological disorder that responds well to psychostimulant medication, I believe that individuals need coping skills. Using cognitive-behavioral interventions, I believe that I can teach individuals new skills that will last a lifetime. The old saying fits well here: "If you give a man a fish, he eats for a day; but if you teach a man to fish, he eats for a lifetime."

TO SUM UP

Behavioral and cognitive-behavioral interventions are effective with individuals with ADHD in conjunction with psychostimulant medications or when used by individuals who do not want to or cannot take medication. In this chapter, we stress positive interventions over punishment; however, we are not implying that negative consequences should never occur with ADHD. At times, negative consequences are unavoidable. For instance, if your teenager with ADHD drives recklessly, a natural consequence would be for you to not let the adolescent drive without an adult; or if the adolescent received a traffic ticket, he goes to traffic school or pays extra for insurance. All of which would be preferable to an accident.

Although alternative remedies are available, there is little scientific evidence for effectiveness. The best interventions are behavioral and cognitive-behavioral strategies. Behavioral interventions are known to be effective with children with ADHD. Cognitive-behavioral interventions help adolescents and adults learn coping strategies for areas in their lives affected by ADHD.

WHAT'S NEXT?

In the next chapter, we will present strategies that you can use as a parent to help your child with ADHD maximize his potential, increase positive behaviors, and learn new behaviors. These strategies will not only help your child, but will also help you be positive with your child and yourself, create the structure that your child needs, and avoid **the increased stress often experienced by parents of children with ADHD**.

PART THREE

Managing ADHD from Childhood through Adulthood

7

Interventions That Strengthen Family Relationships

Strategies for Parents

As you read in Chapter Eight, parenting a child with ADHD is sometimes very challenging. While the impact on the family might seem all doom and gloom, awareness helps parents avoid falling into potential traps. Parents of children and adolescents with ADHD experience a great deal of stress, frustration, and low self-esteem. Adding more stress to the busy lifestyles that many lead in today's society can create increased tension within the personal relationships of parents.[1] Disagreements are often about parenting style and discipline. The good news is that researchers have found effective parenting strategies that can alleviate the disagreement about the correct way to manage the child's behavior if everyone involved agrees to use the prescribed techniques.[2] In addition, using effective parenting strategies and being aware of your feelings and self-talk can help you avoid negative reactions to day-to-day stressors.

As a parent of a child with ADHD, you have taken the first step to help your child by reading this book and using the strategies described. One note of caution: you may recall from previous chapters that ADHD is genetic.[3] If you as a parent or your significant other have ADHD or suspect that you have ADHD or feel hopeless or sad, following through with the recommended parenting strategies might be challenging. We strongly encourage you to acknowledge your strengths and challenges and not only use the strategies described in this book, but consult with a professional, such as a physician, psychologist, or therapist, with expertise in adult ADHD and depression. Even if you or your significant other do not have symptoms of ADHD or depression, you may need additional support or direct face-to-face instruction in each strategy. As we have stressed, seeking professional assistance is not a sign that you are a poor parent, but that you are willing to take the necessary action to help your family and your child.

One goal for parents of children with ADHD is to parent with an eye toward positive long-term outcomes. Remember that as frustrating and challenging as parenting a child with ADHD might be, the ultimate goal of your hard work is for your child to become a healthy, well-functioning, happy, and successful adult. As parents, sometimes we forget our goal during the day-to-day hassles. To increase the likelihood of achieving this goal, techniques are included in this chapter to increase (1) positive interactions, (2) consistent discipline, and (3) involvement and monitoring.[4]

Parenting strategies are listed in Figure 7.1 and described in detail here, including (1) Triple-A parent-child interactions, (affection, positive attention, and affirmation); (2) consistent discipline (giving effective directions, determining and teaching clear expectations for behavior, enforcing and teaching rules through precorrection and negative and positive consequences; and (3) monitoring friendships, risk-taking behaviors, and medication. Several of these parenting strategies will look similar to the strategies that we recommended for teachers to use in classrooms in Chapter Six. This similarity exists, as behavior is often the same across environments.

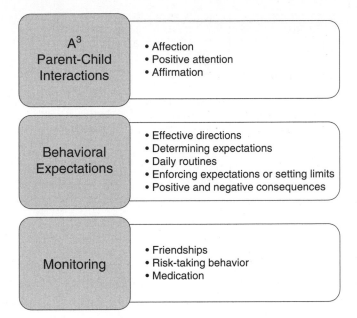

Figure 7.1. Effective Parenting

PARENT-CHILD (A³PC) INTERACTIONS

To encourage positive interactions between yourself and your child with ADHD, begin with a focus on *affection* and positive *attention* and *affirmation* (see Figure 7.2). Parents often interact with children without giving much thought to what is said or done; they typically parent the way they were parented. However, parenting is truly a skill and new strategies can be learned. Evidence suggests that positive interactions are the most effective. Therefore, making a cognitive effort to follow the suggestions in the following section will help you develop a happy and nurturing relationship with your child.

All children need **affection** from their parents, especially children and adolescents with ADHD who typically experience an abundance of negative attention and interactions with both adults and peers. At times, you may find it difficult to express

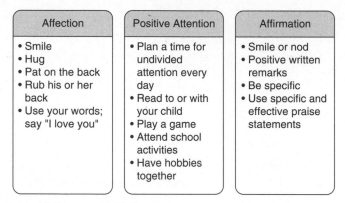

Affection	Positive Attention	Affirmation
• Smile • Hug • Pat on the back • Rub his or her back • Use your words; say "I love you"	• Plan a time for undivided attention every day • Read to or with your child • Play a game • Attend school activities • Have hobbies together	• Smile or nod • Positive written remarks • Be specific • Use specific and effective praise statements

Figure 7.2. A³ Parent-Child Interactions

affection for your child as his behavior might not seem to engender positive feelings. Have you ever found yourself so totally frustrated that the thought of being affectionate is difficult? At those moments, tell yourself that your child has ADHD and is not intentionally trying to drive you insane! Remember that if your child was blind, you would not withhold affection because he made a mistake because he could not see. Make sure that each day you express your love to your child in whatever manner is appropriate and acceptable within your family. Do you hug your child? Do you tell your child that you love him or her? What other ways do you express affection for your child? Be aware of when you do and do not say or do these things and attempt to increase the rate of affection that your child receives from you. Make a list of the ways you find appropriate to show affection and monitor your own behavior to assure that your child is receiving affection from you on a daily basis.

Positive attention is similar to affection, but includes more planned activities that are pleasant bonding experiences. Children who have a positive connection with their parents and receive positive attention tend to have higher self-esteem, be more confident, and are less likely to take part in risky behavior than those who do not feel positively connected to parents.[5] Ten to twenty minutes a day of your undivided attention is the beginning of your child's positive attitude toward his or her relationship with you. During this time, allow your child to pick the activity or teach negotiation skills so that you and your child are able to agree on an activity enjoyable to both of you. Do not lecture, point out weaknesses, or talk about things that are not of interest to the child. The concept is simply for you to enjoy your time together . . . both of you.

Give your child an abundance of positive *affirmation*. Affirm your child's worth with specific praise statements. Although most parents say key phrases such as "good job" or "awesome" after a child has done something that pleases the parent, do you ever stop and think about the praise from the child's perspective? Did the child know what he did to receive the praise? Specific components of effective praise can be used to increase the likelihood that the child will repeat the behavior. Components include the praise statement ("great job") followed by a description of the appropriate behavior ("you went to bed without being told"), skill labeling ("that shows great responsibility on your part"), and a rationale and consequence ("in the morning you will feel rested and get up on time"). When Josie comes home from school and begins her homework without her father having to remind her, using effective praise, her father would say, "Awesome, Josie, you just showed maturity and responsibility by completing your homework without a reminder, you will have time to do what you want this afternoon after you finish your homework, and your grades will certainly reflect the effort." Although it might feel a bit awkward to speak to your child in this fashion in the beginning, with time both you and your child will appreciate the change.

BEHAVIORAL EXPECTATIONS

Along with the basics of A³PC, effective parenting includes establishing expectations and setting limits. Most parents can tell you the expectations they have for their child and these are probably similar to the expectations the parents' own parents had for them. However, when parenting a child with ADHD, much thought is needed to determine which expectations are important.

Determining, Teaching, and Reinforcing Clear Expectations

Children with ADHD need to understand and be reminded of parental expectations for appropriate behavior. Along with behavioral expectations, children with ADHD need and thrive in an organized and predictable home environment with established routines. Parents often assume that children only need to be told the expectation once; however, children with ADHD often misunderstand or forget about our expectations. For this reason, it is important to teach the child the behavior that you expect, reteach the behavior, and reinforce the appropriate behavior until the child's behavior demonstrates that he or she understands the expectations consistently.

Determining Expectations   Thoughtfully consider your expectations for your child and, if another individual will be enforcing the expectations with you, select expectations together. With all children, but especially children with ADHD, expectations should be clearly stated and understood and consistently enforced. Parental expectations for behavior are influenced by several factors, such as culture, education, beliefs, and socioeconomic status. Regardless of the factors that influence your expectations, it is important to share your expectations with others who will help shape your child's behavior through rewards and consequences. Figure 7.3 can be used to develop a list of expectations in a cooperative manner. As a group all individuals with input (you and your significant other, or grandparents) can brainstorm expectations and select rules to be taught to your child. Some

Your expectations	"Rule"	Following the rule looks like:	Not following the rule looks like:	REMEMBER
I want my child not to lie to me.	We tell the truth regardless of the consequences	"Mom I spilled juice in my closet and I covered it up with the dirty clothes to hide it".	"I don't know who spilled the juice." OR Not telling anyone about a mistake or an accident or a bad decision and hoping you don't get caught.	If the consequences for telling the truth are more severe than lying, you will not encourage telling the truth
Attitude is important to me, and when I was a kid, if I yelled at my parents I would have been punished. I don't want my kids talking back.	Use an "inside voice" to express disagreement. Ask first to discuss or negotiate, if the answer is no. Walk away and come back later.	Dad says, son go do your homework.... Son says "ok?" Or Son says, "can we discuss it?"	Son says, "why don't you let me do what I want?" Or "you never understand what is important to me."	As children get older they need more power and control over their environment. Structure and consistency promote compliance. Calm repeating of directions avoids argument.

Figure 7.3. Brainstorm and Develop a List of Expectations in a Cooperative Manner

behaviors to be considered within your list of expectations are honesty, respect for others (that is, no arguing, ask before using others' things, no verbal or physical aggression, being kind and thoughtful to others), following directions, and asking permission.[6] Examples are provided in Figure 7.3. Using the chart, write down your expectations for your child, the specific rule, examples of following the rule, and examples of not following the rule. On a daily basis teach these expectations to your child through modeling (exhibiting the expected behavior for your child), verbal interactions, and the positive and negative consequences that your child receives for following or not following the expectations.

Consider Essie. Essie tells her children verbally that she expects them to always be honest. One night Essie's oldest daughter, Caitlyn, tells her that she is going to a party at Patti's house, but instead goes on a date with James. When Essie discovers that Caitlyn did not go to Patti's house, she verbally reprimands her and takes away her driving privileges for one week. However, the next week when Caitlyn wants to buy a miniskirt, her mother agrees, but reminds Caitlyn that her father does not approve. Essie tells Caitlyn to take the skirt in her bag and change clothes at her friend's house to avoid a confrontation with her father. While Essie verbally tells Caitlyn to be honest, her behavior actually is teaching Caitlyn that dishonesty is acceptable. Verbally describing and modeling incompatible or conflicting behaviors confuses children and actually teaches different lessons than intended.

From the Counselor

Many parents have told me that creating structure with consistent expectations and routines is a very difficult task. I have continually stressed that parents must reward themselves, as well as their child, when they are consistent. While it seems like a simple task, establishing the degree of structure that children with ADHD need is sometimes very difficult. As parents, we can remember to forgive and encourage ourselves when we fall short and reward ourselves when we meet the goal!

Daily Routines Parental expectations are embedded in daily routines. Children with ADHD function better when routines are consistent from day to day. When and where do you eat meals? When is bedtime? When and where does your child study? When do you spend quality time with your child? Do you have a daily routine that is the same from day to day? Routines are taught to children. Remember that consistently following routines is not always possible or easy and therefore the routines should be convenient and reinforcing for everyone involved. Potential daily routines are morning activities (such as getting ready for school), homework, chores, mealtimes, hygiene (bath and teeth brushing), privileges (such as computer and television time), and bedtime.

Enforcing Expectations Once expectations and routines are established, children with ADHD (and those without) often challenge expectations or "test the limits." The steps to enforcing expectations, or setting limits, are listed in Figure 7.4. When your child challenges your expectations, begin by stating the limit verbally.

Effective Directions Giving directions is an important parenting skill. Parents often do not give much thought to the process of giving directions. It may seem amazing, but verbal directions should include the ten components listed in Figure 7.5. Considering that children with ADHD have a difficult time

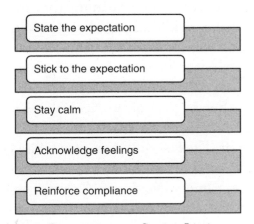

Figure 7.4. Enforcing Expectations or Setting Limits

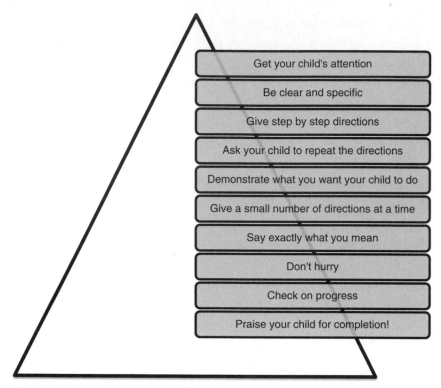

Figure 7.5. Components of Effective Directions

focusing and are easily distracted, following verbal directions can be a challenge; therefore, parents can use the ten steps to giving directions to assure that the direction is clearly understood. Verbal directions might not be enough; we encourage you to write down directions to tasks or chores that you want the child to complete.

Consider Arthur, a 4-year-old with ADHD. Arthur frequently runs through the living room, stands on his head on the couch, and kicks the wall. The first time Arthur exhibited this behavior, his parents were shocked and actually thought the behavior was funny and was a fine example of Arthur's agility. However, because they knew the behavior was dangerous and socially unacceptable, they began by enforcing expectations or setting the limit that walking in the house is expected and couches are for sitting and not for standing on your head. Arthur's mother got his attention by saying his name, was clear and specific with the limit or expectation, and stated the limit by giving the direction. She said, "Arthur, you need to walk in the house and sit on the couch." Then she asked Arthur to repeat the expectation and practiced walking through the living room and sitting on the couch with Arthur (models and practices the behavior). Arthur's mother and father stuck to the limit and addressed the behavior, remaining calm every time it occurred. Sometimes, Arthur's father found it difficult to remain calm and wanted to yell at him to get his attention, but he maintained his own composure, thus modeling appropriate behavior for Arthur. When Arthur said, "It's really fun to stand on my head on the couch" or "No, Daddy, couches are for standing on my head," Arthur's father acknowledged his feelings and said, "I understand that you think that it is fun to stand on your head on the couch, but I expect you to walk in the house and sit on the couch." Every time Arthur walked into the living room and sat on the couch, his parents praised his behavior. When Arthur demonstrated the unacceptable behavior, his mother or father modeled and practiced the appropriate behavior with Arthur and praised his efforts.

Precorrection and Consequences   You can increase compliance with behavioral expectations or limits through the use of *precorrection and positive and negative consequences*. Prior to using any of these techniques, you must evaluate the behavior. First, determine the problem behavior (behavior), what happens before the behavior (antecedent), and what happens after the behavior (consequence; see Figure 7.6).

Abigail, a 14-year-old with ADHD, refused to get up in the morning to go to school (the problem behavior). Her parents discovered that Abigail played on the computer each night until

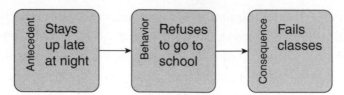

Figure 7.6. Antecedent-Behavior-Consequence (A-B-C)

2 AM (antecedent) and began to fail many of her classes (consequence). To decrease the problem behavior, Abigail's parents have a choice of using precorrection, modifying the antecedent, or modifying the consequence of the behavior. Changing the antecedent would mean that Abigail would go to bed at an earlier time. Abigail's parents cannot change the consequence of failing classes, but can add additional positive and negative consequences for making good choices, and, if necessary, save Abigail from herself by removing access to the computer by using parental control settings available on the computer, the Internet, or software; by password-protecting the computer; or, as a last resort, by taking the power cord.

From the Teacher

Precorrection is the best technique that I learned. Explaining what is expected to children before the activity not only helps the child remember, but also helps me remember the expectations. I have used this technique as a parent, also. Every time I go to the grocery store, I tell my child what he can and cannot purchase. This eliminates much, though not all, of the demands or even whining in the checkout line.

Precorrection is the use of reminders prior to situations in which you know that the problem behavior is likely to occur. Using precorrection, Abigail's parents tell her at 9:30 that she is expected to be in bed by 10:00. Another common example is the dreaded grocery store checkout line with a six-year-old with ADHD. Shopping with young children can be challenging and sometimes treacherous with a child with ADHD. Using precorrection, the parent tells the child the expectation *prior* to going into the store and *prior* to the checkout line. "When we get to the checkout line, you may select one piece of candy. If you choose to ask for more, you will not be able to get that piece."

Parents can also **modify the antecedent** to problem behavior. When you observe the problem behavior, you might determine that the only time a certain behavior occurs is when a specific event happens first. Abigail's parents modified the antecedent to the problem behavior by establishing the expectation for an earlier bedtime. Another example is determining antecedents that increase hyperactive or inattentive behavior. Randy noticed that Jo becomes extremely hyperactive when she is required to sit still for more than 10 minutes. Randy modifies the antecedent by giving Jo a break to walk around after 5 minutes. Yaya noticed that Juanita has a difficult time paying attention after 30 minutes of schoolwork. Yaya encourages Juanita to take a 5-minute break after 20 minutes and then come back and finish.

Just as modifying *antecedents* involves changing what happens *before* the behavior, modifying *consequences* involves changing what happens *after* the behavior. **Consequences** follow the behavior. The term "consequence" is often associated with a negative action; however, consider consequences of appropriate behavior. If an individual goes to work every day and does a good job (appropriate behavior), then a paycheck follows (consequence). Selecting an effective consequence for a child or adolescent with ADHD is not always easy. As mentioned throughout this book, problem behaviors demonstrated by these youth are associated with a biological disorder and thus are much more difficult to change than learned behavior. As noted in Chapter 2, problem behaviors are associated with the core symptoms of ADHD. In addition, such behaviors might represent the need for activity and stimulation. Therefore, the concept of positive and negative consequences with youth with ADHD is to encourage the use of new coping skills and to discourage inappropriate behaviors.

Positive consequences are referred to as positive reinforcement, which is something that increases the likelihood of the desired behavior (the new skill). Positive reinforcers can be social, activity, tangible, or token. Social reinforcers are praise from parents, teachers, peers, and others, such as a pat on the back, a smile, or "good job!" Activity reinforcers are being able to participate in preferred activities, such as playing a game, going for a walk with a parent, or visiting a friend. Tangible reinforcers are items that are reinforcing to the child (for example, a new book or toy). Token reinforcement is giving the youth points or tokens (secondary reinforcers) that can be exchanged for other reinforcers (primary reinforcers). We will discuss token reinforcers in detail in the following section. Remember that the selected reinforcers must be reinforcing to the child. Using spinach as a positive reinforcer would not work unless the child is truly motivated by and wants spinach.

We often hear adults say that they will not use positive reinforcement because it is simply bribing the child. This is not true. We all work for positive reinforcement. Without some form of reinforcement, whether it comes from within or from others, it would be difficult for most of us to continue to do many things. The important distinction is that a bribe is something that is unacceptable and inappropriate, and often illegal. Bribing occurs to persuade someone to do something or stop doing something they are already engaged in. Reinforcement is set up beforehand. The following is an example of a bribe: Jolene runs through the store hiding under clothes racks; after several unsuccessful utterances of "stop that," Mom says, "Jolene honey, if you will stop hiding under the racks and come out I will buy you a smoothie"— that is a bribe. Here is a reinforcement. Jolene has a sticker chart and for following the rules when shopping (stay with mommy, hands to ourselves, pockets on the chair) Jolene gets stickers at

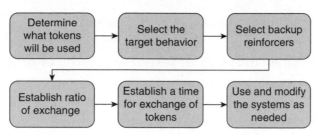

Figure 7.7. Procedural Steps for Token Economy Systems

the end of shopping. After Jolene has earned a prespecified number of stickers, she is allowed to do something that she really likes, such as go to the playground.

Token Economy Systems *Token economy systems* are effective for teaching and reinforcing the desired behavior. Token economy systems are systematic programs in which the individual receives a token when the desirable target behavior is demonstrated; tokens are exchanged at a later time for a reinforcer. Establishing a home behavior chart involves six steps (see Figure 7.7). First, determine what tokens you are going to use, such as marbles in a jar or checkmarks on a chart or any other tangible way of indicating that the child demonstrated the desired behavior. Second, determine the target behavior, which is the desired behavior that you want to see in place of the maladaptive behavior. Third, select the backup reinforcers, which are the rewards that the child will earn when he "trades in" his tokens. Fourth, establish the ratio of exchange. How many tokens does it take to earn the reward? When you first begin using the token economy, the child should earn the reward quickly and frequently. You can fade the reinforcers to extended periods of time and require more tokens when the child begins to consistently demonstrate the desired behavior. Fifth, establish when the child can exchange the tokens for the backup reinforcer. Daily? Weekly? Finally, try it for a while and see if the child's behavior improves. If not, then readjust your token system. Most important, make sure that the reward is reinforcing to the child. If not, select another. It is helpful to allow the child to participate in the development of the system by suggesting rewards.

Home Behavior Charts and Daily Behavior Report Cards   Home behavior charts and daily behavior report cards are token economy systems that are effective with youth with ADHD. Home behavior charts are used to monitor and reinforce the child or adolescent's behavior at home. Daily behavior report cards are used as communication between the parent and the school to reinforce the youth's behavior at school.

Home behavior charts are popular techniques to establish and reinforce your expectations at home and can be used as a way for a child, adolescent, or even adult to self monitor his/her own behavior. You have probably seen home behavior charts (see Figure 7.8) advertised for sale or used on the television show, *Supernanny*. You can create your own home behavior chart with your child to increase the child's buy-in. This chart includes a list of behaviors that you expect from your child and can include

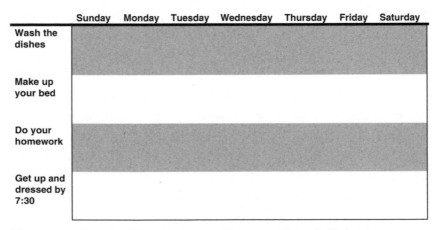

Figure 7.8. Sample Home Behavior Chart for Multiple Behaviors

chores, such as washing dishes, taking out the trash, or other specific behaviors (for example, getting up on time or completing homework without being told). The list of target behaviors should not include more than three or four and should be worded positively. For example, if you want to decrease the behavior of refusing to follow directions, you would list "following directions" on the chart. On the chart is a designated area to place a marker showing that the child has completed the task or demonstrated the behavior. The marker can be as simple as a checkmark made with an ink pen or more complex such as a magnetic or Velcro® strip. Home behavior charts can also be constructed to represent one behavior (see Figure 7.9). For example, a path could be drawn from a "start" position to a "finish" position with numbers along the way. Each time the

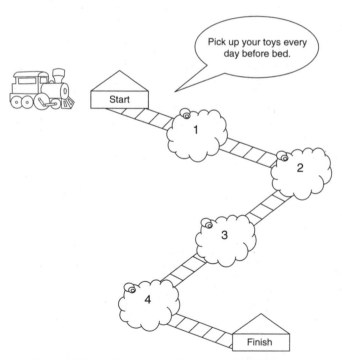

Figure 7.9. Sample Home Behavior Chart for One Behavior

child demonstrates the behavior, he can move his marker to a new number. If you want your 5-year-old to follow your verbal direction the first time, you could draw a train track. You could write "start" at one train station, with three stops along the way to the "finish" train station. Place a piece of Velcro® on the back of a train and another on each of the numbers. When you give a direction and your child follows the direction, the child can move his train along the train track. When the child gets to the "finish" train station, he earns the reinforcer.

Daily Behavior Report Card (DBRC) is a means of communicating behavioral progress between the school and the home. The steps to using a DBRC are listed in Figure 7.10. The teacher marks the student's progress towards a pre-specified goal on the card and sends it home to the parent. If the student reaches the goal then the parent provides a reinforcer at home, or the teacher provides a reinforcer at school, or both. Reinforcers can be daily, weekly, or both. Parents review the DBRC daily and discuss progress with the child. An example of the DBRC is provided in Figure 7.11. DBRCs include specific goals for improved behavior, such as "complete 80% of assignments" or "follow rules on the playground with less than two violations." The goals are individually designed to meet the needs of the ·

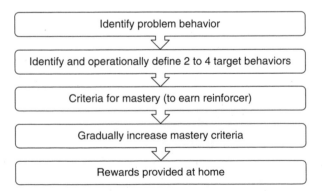

Figure 7.10. Procedural Steps for Daily Behavior Report Card

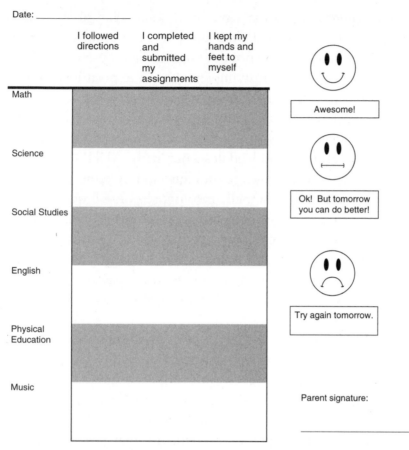

Figure 7.11. Sample Elementary DBRC

student. Criteria for improvement should be attainable and can change as the child reaches his own goal(s). The effectiveness of the DBRC is dependent on the level of parental involvement and the level of use at school.[7] Therefore, we encourage parents to consistently check the DBRC daily and provide reinforcement consistently. Teachers are encouraged to use the DBRC throughout the day. One of our coauthors (KJV) is the also the coauthor[8] of the electronic-DBRC (e-DBRC) that is available free to teachers at http://d2k.tamu.edu/products/e-dbrc.php after a training with the staff.

Planned Ignoring, Response Cost, and Time Out from Positive Reinforcement So what do you do when the child engages in the problem behavior and not the target or appropriate behavior when you have consistently implemented the positive systems? First, ensure that the child does not receive reinforcement for the inappropriate behavior. At times, mild negative consequences for inappropriate behavior are needed to increase appropriate behavior in children and adolescents with ADHD.[9] In conjunction with the positive reinforcers and systems previously discussed, you can use planned ignoring, response cost, and time out from positive reinforcement to decrease the problem behavior. Response cost can be used as a component of a token economy system. However, it is vital that positive responses to child and adolescent behavior are more frequent than negative responses. Specifically, try to maintain a 4:1 ratio of positive to negative remarks and actions.

Planned ignoring is the process of providing absolutely no attention to the maladaptive behavior. Planned ignoring is only an effective strategy for decreasing minor behaviors with the purpose of attaining adult attention. Parents have to pay great attention to the concept of "giving attention." Simply not verbally responding to inappropriate behavior may not be enough. For example, if a child continually interrupts you to get your attention when you are on the phone, planned ignoring would include not verbally or physically responding to the behavior. No eye contact, physical gestures, or verbal comments would be made. At times, it is difficult to avoid looking at your child when he or she starts talking to you. Planned ignoring requires a great deal of concentration on the part of the parent! On the other hand, if a child with ADHD consistently taps a pencil on the table as a result of hyperactivity (whether an adult is present or not), planned ignoring will not decrease the behavior. Planned ignoring should only be used when the child or adolescent has been taught the needed skill. For example, the child that interrupts the parent on the phone should be taught how to ask for assistance or to wait until the parent is off the phone to talk. Once the skill is taught and mastered then planned ignoring would be appropriate if the purpose of the behavior is adult attention.

Response cost and time out from positive reinforcement (loss of privileges) can be included in token economy systems. *Response cost* is the loss of privileges or reinforcers or the loss of tokens in a token economy system. You can take away tokens earned within a token economy system, but criteria for removal need to be established and explained explicitly so that the child understands which inappropriate behavior would result in the loss of tokens, and how many tokens would be removed. Again, we must stress that removing all of the tokens or removing more tokens than have been earned (leaving the child "in the red") is not effective. The child must feel motivated to demonstrate the target behavior. You can use response cost without having a structured token economy system; removing privileges is response cost. If your child has a scheduled time to use the computer or drive the car, then these are privileges that could be "lost."

In addition to response cost, time out from positive reinforcement can be used in conjunction with a positive reinforcement system. Most people are familiar with the term "time out" and have seen it used or used it themselves in numerous settings. The true label for "time out" is "time out from positive reinforcement"—that is, when you have a child go to "time out," you are actually temporarily removing the opportunity for or access to positive reinforcement. Time out is effective with children with ADHD.[10] Time outs are only effective in decreasing behavior if the environment from which the child is being removed is reinforcing. For example, if a child does not like to clean the kitchen and argues with his mother every night about doing dishes, then sending him to time out when the kitchen is being cleaned is not "time out from positive reinforcement" and

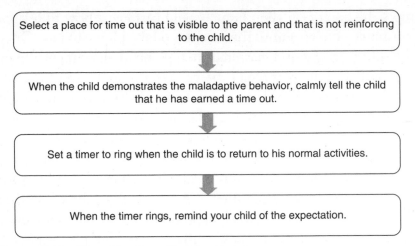

Figure 7.12. Time Out from Positive Reinforcement

is in fact negative reinforcement (removal of an aversive). Time out also must be immediate and consistent. It is not effective to wait to send the child to time out or to send the child to time out one time for a specific behavior, and then use planned ignoring the next time the child demonstrates the same behavior. A child should only receive time out from positive reinforcement for a short period of time. Typically, parents and teachers are instructed to use the rule of one minute for each year of age to set the length of a time out (that is, an 11-year-old's time outs last 11 minutes). Figure 7.12 provides a list of procedural steps for time out from positive reinforcement.

MONITORING

As parents we monitor the behavior and actions of our children in several ways. In this section, we present ideas about encouraging and teaching friendship skills and monitoring the friendships and risk-taking behavior of your child through listening and talking, knowing the important information, and knowing your child's location at all times.

Encouraging and Teaching Friendship Skills

Children and adolescents with ADHD have difficulties making and maintaining friendships.[11] Adolescents with ADHD are rejected by peers more than others.[12] Peers who do not have ADHD (and sometimes even those who do) are often annoyed by the overactivity and impulsivity of individuals with ADHD. Constant movement and overreaction often interfere with play activities and conversations. Individuals with ADHD are often blunt or overly frank with friends, appearing rude. Unstructured cooperative activities, such as outdoor play, are difficult for individuals with ADHD because sharing, cooperating, and taking turns is necessary. Making and keeping friends requires inhibiting responses and maintaining emotional self-control, both deficits associated with ADHD. Individuals with ADHD have a deficit in working memory, and so they might often forget agreements with friends. Making matters worse, individuals with ADHD do not typically respond to long-term consequences or understand cause-and-effect relationships.[13] When friendships gradually begin to fade, they do not always make the connection between their personal behavior and the friendship dissolving.

Parents can gently encourage and teach friendship skills. Be aware of your child's feelings, as this is a sensitive area, and avoid criticism. Children and adolescents who already feel rejected by peers will not respond well to criticism from adults. As a parent you can encourage the use of effective friendship skills by involving your child in group activities and arranging play dates and home visits with children of the same age. In addition, carefully select one or two activities for your child to be involved in without completely filling all of his free time. Choose group activities that are not competitive to avoid disagreements and encourage cooperation. In addition, you can involve your child in professionally led friendship groups for systematic social learning experiences.

Within these activities, monitor your child's behavior and model and teach appropriate friendship skills. Children with ADHD need to learn and practice the skills of how to join a group without being intrusive or overpowering, being positive with others and helping and encouraging friends, sharing, conversation and listening, showing interest in what others are saying, and problem solving as alternatives to fighting and arguing.

Monitoring Friendships and Risk-Taking Behavior

Risk-taking behaviors are evident in most children with ADHD. Monitoring the behavior of a young child with ADHD requires constant supervision and guidance. Recently, one author (JH) heard a parent of a young child with ADHD comment, "I don't understand it! My friend can let her four-year-old play in her room for hours without fear of the child hurting herself or tearing something up. If I let my child play alone for five minutes someone is hurt or something is broken!" Although this level of monitoring is often exhausting, parents can share the responsibility and use the time spent supervising to teach appropriate behavior. Monitoring your young child's behavior is the beginning of many years of monitoring. At this stage, monitoring can be done in such a way that the child begins to learn that you are interested in his activities and sets the stage for the expectation of continuous monitoring throughout adolescence.

The consequences of risk-taking behavior increase in adolescence, and monitoring adolescent behavior is of a different level and type. Adolescents with ADHD are at a higher risk for smoking tobacco, drinking alcohol, and using and abusing substances.[14] In addition, adolescents with ADHD are more likely to interact with deviant peer groups and respond to negative influences within those groups to a greater degree than others.[15]

To avoid these negative behaviors and associations, parents of adolescents with ADHD must closely monitor and observe friendships without being intrusive. The good news is that research indicates that monitoring adolescent behavior decreases the risk of premature sexual behavior, smoking cigarettes, drinking alcohol, physical aggression, and truancy.[16] However, monitoring is not an easy task, as adolescence is a stage when individuals are attempting to become independent and often respond negatively to parents who attempt to intervene with interpersonal relationships. The key is maintaining an open and nonjudgmental relationship beginning with A³PC during early childhood and used consistently throughout the child's life.

Monitoring your adolescent's behavior includes making a point to know all of the important information about your adolescent's activities, establishing a positive relationship with your adolescent, setting clear expectations, monitoring activities, and consistently providing positive and negative consequences.

Listen and Talk Listening and talking to your adolescent increases the likelihood that you will know what is going on with him or her. Adolescents who have positive relationships with parents are more willing to openly and honestly talk to them. Ask open-ended questions about your child's feelings, friends, and activities—and listen! Without lecturing, talk to your child about making safe choices, and make sure that your child knows how to contact you at any time and feels comfortable doing so.

Make a Point to Know the Important Information Make clear to your adolescent that the expectation is that before he will be out of your immediate supervision, you will know who he is going to be with, where he will be, what he will be doing, when he plans to return, and how to reach him. Get to know your child's friends and their parents. Prior to allowing your child to visit at a friend's house, ask if an adult will be there. As we discussed earlier, clear and consistent expectations are essential. Ensure that your child knows your expectations for his behavior even when he is away from you.

Monitor Your Child's Activity   Monitor your child's activity when he or she is with you or away from you. While this is often challenging and sometimes feels a little like detective work, it is necessary to decrease the likelihood of risk-taking behaviors. Your child will ask you to trust him and the answer is that trust is a process and does not just happen automatically. Verifying that your child is following your expectations when he is away from you will increase your trust in his decisions. A few ways to monitor your child's activities are listening to what others say, watching how and when he spends money, observing his Internet activity, and being aware of any mood changes. Although adolescence is a time of severe mood changes, mood changes can also be an indication that something is wrong or different. If you discover activities or behaviors that concern you or that you believe need to be changed, talk about your findings with your child and find a resolution that will make you feel more comfortable and help you keep your child safe.

As mentioned earlier, consistently enforce your expectations with positive and negative consequences using the techniques described in this chapter. For adolescents participating in activities away from the home, specific expectations need to be established—with everyone who will be monitoring the expectations. What time is your child expected to be home? Where is your child allowed to go and not go? Who is your child allowed to be with? Once you establish the expectations, the previously described procedures for positive and negative consequences can be used.

MANAGING MEDICATION

One parental responsibility is to monitor and manage the medication if your child is prescribed medications. Medication management includes having prescriptions filled in a timely manner, the child taking the medication as prescribed, monitoring the effectiveness and any side effects, and scheduling and participating in medication checks with the physician.

Inform your child's teachers and other caregivers of any changes in medication and ask them to help you monitor the effects of the medication. It is helpful to keep written charts to show to the physician at the next visit. Important information to chart includes any change in behavior, such as focus, activity level, school performance, appetite, and sleeping habits. Report such information to your physician from home and school to assist the doctor in determining the right medication and dose. Be patient, as this is a process; all children and adolescents are different and the doctor must adjust the medication and dose to match your child's needs.

TO SUM UP

Although parenting a child with ADHD is difficult, research provides evidence of effective parenting strategies. In this chapter, we described in detail, with examples, the use of parenting strategies to develop positive interactions with your child and to establish, teach, and reinforce behavioral expectations—strategies that can help children with ADHD to maximize the associated strengths and cope with weaknesses. In addition, because having ADHD increases the chances for association with deviant populations and engaging in risk-taking behaviors, we discussed strategies for monitoring friendships and risky behaviors. We also stressed the need to manage your child's medication regime; though medication has been found to be effective, finding the right medication and dose is a process that involves close collaboration with your child's physician.

WHAT'S NEXT?

In the next chapter, we will discuss interventions that can be used in the school and in the classroom with children and adolescents with ADHD and the rights afforded to your child as a child with a disability. In addition, we will present ways in which you can effectively collaborate with your child's school and his or her teachers.

8

Helping Students with ADHD Succeed at School

Strategies for Teachers

As a neuropsychologist, counselor, and teacher, as well as parents and researchers, we have often heard teachers describe students with ADHD as "very capable, but not reaching full potential academically." Our goal in this chapter is to provide effective behavioral and academic interventions for educators to use to help children and adolescents learn and master concepts taught at school and to then "reach full potential."

A circular relationship exists between behavior and academic interventions. A circular relationship is one of "which came first, the chicken or the egg?"—that is, "does the behavior cause the academic problems or do the academic problems cause the behavior?" For example, Mark, a 16-year-old with ADHD, is inattentive during classroom lectures, often missing important information. When given a test on the material presented in class, Mark becomes frustrated and leaves the classroom. In this example, Mark's inattention interfered with learning and resulted in additional problem behaviors.

As a parent, you will find in this chapter intervention information to share with your child's teacher when collaborating to select appropriate services and interventions that you can use at home when your child is studying or doing homework. As a teacher, you will find interventions to implement in your class-room to decrease the impact of inattention, hyperactivity, and impulsivity on learning and functioning socially at school. Given that 25% of youth with ADHD are served by programs for youth with learning disorders,[1] it is vitally important that teachers and parents become aware of, and understand, implementation pro-cedures in order to encourage the positive characteristics of ADHD and decrease its negative impact.

We begin with considerations and actions to be taken prior to selecting effective interventions in the classroom, or at home to increase learning. As individuals with ADHD are all different, it is essential to select the best intervention by using data to determine which problems should be targeted and to be able to measure how well the intervention increases child and adolescent motivation. It is important to match the intervention to the developmental stage of the individual with ADHD.

We will next describe classroom management strategies, instructional strategies, specific skills training, collaborative interventions between home and school, and multimodal inter-ventions implemented across skills areas and environments.

BEFORE SELECTING INTERVENTIONS

As you are selecting academic and behavioral interventions to increase the learning of students with ADHD, consider strategies to enhance data-based decision making, motivation, and matu-rity and development.

Using Data to Select and Monitor Interventions

While ADHD is the diagnosis, your goal is to modify specific behaviors, either by increasing, decreasing, eliminating, or replacing the behavior. Behaviors are changed through interven-

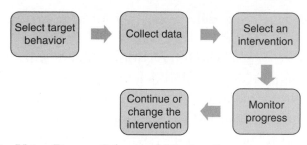

Figure 8.1. Using Data to Select and Monitor Interventions

tion. In order to select or design a strategy or intervention, you have to identify an observable behavior that is interfering with the child's progress (see Figure 8.1). Sometimes, you might say that you want to change your child's "poor attitude." However, poor attitude cannot be measured, so you cannot really measure how much the attitude has changed. Therefore, you must describe internal states (such as poor attitude or happiness) in terms that can be measured. Observable behaviors are those that can be seen and measured: you can see (observe) a child walk into the classroom with all materials (or without them); you can count (measure) the number of times that he has his completed homework (or does not). Thus, the first step is to define the behavior in observable and measurable terms. For example, Jaime brings completed assignments to class, throws books on the desk, and says "no" when told to begin his assignment. Next, you need to know "how often" or "how long" the behavior is currently occurring so that you can measure the impact of the intervention on the behavior. For instance, when starting a weight loss program, we weigh first to see where we are starting from and measure the extent of the problem. Our ADHD example is about schoolwork. Let's say you notice that Christy does not bring her books to class, so you collect some data to determine the number of times that Christy did and didn't bring her books to class for a period of time long enough to be an accurate reflection. One day may not be enough but, conversely, every day for a month is probably overkill.

The next step in the intervention process is to determine whether the problem is a skill deficit or a performance deficit. Ask yourself the following kinds of questions. Have you seen the child do the correct behaviors sometimes? That would indicate they "can do it" but they just aren't consistent. If the answer is never, then we might assume that this is a skill deficit and not a performance deficit. They might not have the skill yet and therefore need to be taught how to engage in the appropriate behavior. For example, does Cannon know what to do to get help? Or that the expectation is to wait to be called on before talking in class? If not, then it would help Cannon for the teacher to specifically and explicitly teach, model, and rehearse these expectations. Does Clint understand the behaviors associated with paying attention or the behavioral indicators that he is not paying attention (for example, looking out the window, texting a friend)? If not, then Clint needs to be taught the skill of paying attention.

After you implement the intervention, then you monitor progress by collecting data to determine whether the behavior is getting better. If you find that the behavior is getting better, you continue the intervention. You will find that if you stop the intervention too early, the behavior will return. With students who have ADHD, interventions need to be implemented for long periods of time. If the behavior is not getting better, you want to select another intervention. But do not give up too early. Make sure that you have tried the intervention for a week or two before trying another one.

When your data show that the behavior has improved to the point that you want, then you can slowly decrease use of the intervention until you are not using it anymore. However, if the behavior returns, you will want to start the intervention again.

Motivating Children and Adolescents

Before implementing an intervention, the individual with ADHD must be motivated to change the behavior. As adults, we often decide that a child's behavior needs to change and then select a strategy to change that behavior without ever discussing the behavior or the strategy with the child. However, the likelihood of intervention success is minimal if the child or adolescent is not motivated to use his personal strengths to decrease weaknesses. To motivate the student, it is important that he or she: (1) recognize the personal strengths to be built upon and understand his or her problem behavior, (2) understand the intervention, and (3) believe the intervention will help.

Have you noticed that when you begin discussing a behavior with individuals who have ADHD, they often tell you that they do not have a problem? This is because they do not always recognize their true weaknesses, which can be a result of "a positive illusory bias," one of the many unique characteristics of many individuals with ADHD. Students with positive illusory bias overestimate their strengths, have inflated self-esteem, and do not often recognize their own shortcomings.[2] In fact, children and adolescents with ADHD often view their weakest areas as their strengths. For example, Lorelei is a 14-year-old with ADHD. Although she completes only about 50% of her mathematics homework and struggles with tests, Lorelei often tells her teacher, friends, and family that she is a "math whiz."

Aside from being a completely intriguing phenomenon, understanding the positive illusory bias begs the question, "What do I do to motivate a student who believes there is not a problem?" The answer is in the data collected prior to intervention implementation. Begin by selecting target behaviors based on direct observation of behavior and on the concerns of significant individuals involved in the lives of these children. Second, once data exist to identify a problem behavior, begin by discussing the student's strengths, then share concrete information (the data collected) about the problem, discuss options for intervention, and explain to the student what he or she will gain from changing the behavior. Remember to discuss the behavior and not the student as a person and place emphasis on the student's true strengths. Do not present the information to the student as all doom and gloom, but as an opportunity to maximize on strengths or become more successful. Avoid the "argument" and move on to discuss the plan for improvement—regardless of agreement or not from the child.

For example, Lorelei's teacher can print a copy of her classroom grades and select a time to have a one-on-one conversation with her. She could say, "Lorelei, you really enjoy your math class and I totally appreciate your participation; however, I am concerned about your grades. You have completed 5 out of 10 homework assignments and made three low test grades. At this time, your failing math grade is going to keep you from marching at the football game on Friday night. Since math seems to be a subject that you like, I have a good strategy to help you remember to turn in your assignments and bring up your test grades." The teacher then would describe the intervention and continue by saying, "If this strategy works, then your grade will be much better and you will be able to march with the band on Friday night instead of sitting out."

Selecting Developmentally Appropriate Interventions

When selecting interventions, consider the maturity and development of the individual; the interventions must match the developmental level of the student. As individuals grow and mature from childhood to adulthood, they progress through different *developmental stages* marked by specific characteristics. Behaviors associated with ADHD are different at each developmental stage and thus interventions should match the characteristics of the child. In the following sections, we discuss developmental characteristics and associated difficulties created by ADHD in preschool, elementary, middle and high school, and in adult learners. Although this chapter is focused on classroom and school interventions, young adults are included, as ADHD has an impact on postsecondary school and work, and the young adult in each of those environments can use some interventions discussed here as self-help strategies, or some may be used by professors as accommodations.

Preschool　Preschool children do not understand or even see the perceptions of others. They view their own behavior from a "needs and wants" perspective. At this age, the child is most influenced by the actions of the parents or guardians who are responsible for shaping and directing the child's behavior. Typically, preschoolers with ADHD are very overactive, day-dream, have problems listening and focusing, fidget and talk excessively, blurt and interrupt, and have trouble taking turns. Change is driven completely by external agents, such as parents and preschool teachers. Preschool-appropriate strategies are those based on immediate, "touchable," and frequent positive reinforcers and consequences.

Elementary School　Children in elementary school are character-ized by concrete thinking and are beginning to understand that others have feelings and perceptions about them. Symptoms that define ADHD (hyperactivity, impulsivity, and inattention) are all characteristic of young children. In fact, the criteria were developed for young children. Therefore, as children enter ele-mentary school, focus on intervention includes teacher- and parent-directed intervention and teaching skills for academic achievement, developing friendships, and social functioning, with a slow transition to self-directed interventions as the child matures.

Middle and High School   Adolescence is characterized by a change from total dependence on adults to more independence. However, this is a gradual change and you will often see the adolescent fluctuate back and forth. Middle school is the time when individuals begin to experience increased demands in the academic environment and pressure to "fit in" with peers. Adolescents are focused on being independent, are influenced more by their peer group than are younger children, and have a tendency to engage in risk-taking behaviors. As children with ADHD move into adolescence and middle and high school, demands of school and friends often seem almost opposite to the characteristics of ADHD. The focus of intervention in middle and high school includes teaching skills, such as organizational and communication skills. Thus intervention selection should include the individual and address academic achievement, communication, and decreasing impulsive behavior associated with risk taking.

Adult Learners   As adolescents move from high school to postsecondary education (college or university) or work environments, expectations change dramatically. Early adulthood is characterized by the development of independence and competence.[3] Young adults are expected to move toward and achieve financial, residential, and emotional independence. Within academic and work environments, young adults are expected to use analytical and comprehensive thought, be self-disciplined, listen and communicate, and manage emotions. Such expectations represent a difficult transition for young adults with ADHD. Although their hyperactivity appears to decline, inattention and impulsivity remain constant or increase.

As the focus of this chapter is on school- and classroom-based interventions, consider the impact of behaviors associated with inattention and impulsivity on the expectations just described. What do you think the impact of impulsivity is on being self-disciplined? The two are polar opposites. Similar to the situation in high school, inattention and impulsivity affect the young adult's ability to arrive at class on time, follow directions, organize and complete academic tasks, manage time, listen and concentrate, and attend to details. Different from high school, the supports provided by parents and others are removed and are expected to come from the young adult. More about this topic is presented in Chapter Ten.

INTERVENTIONS

In this section, we will describe classroom management strategies, instructional strategies, skills training, collaborative interventions between home and school, and multimodal treatment programs.

Classroom Management

Typically, elementary and special education teachers tend to have more training in classroom management than middle and high school teachers. Therefore, as a teacher, the interventions described in this chapter may seem familiar or foreign to you. As a parent, you might have wondered why some classrooms "run like a clock" and others appear and feel chaotic and disorganized. The key to creating an environment that is helpful to learning is systematic, well-planned classroom management—which does not just happen. Effective teachers plan classroom management in the same manner that they plan academic lessons. Effective classroom management is essential for students with ADHD, regardless of age, and consists of creating an accepting and supportive climate; structure, rules and routines; and an organized plan for behavior management (see Figure 8.2).

Climate An effective classroom management plan begins with an accepting and supportive classroom climate, which is

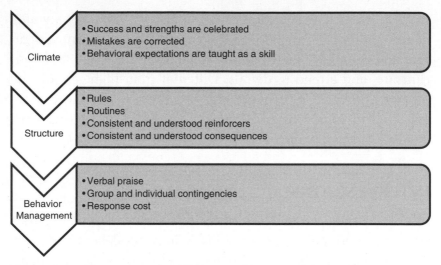

Figure 8.2. Characteristics of Effective Classroom Management

important for academic success and self-esteem for students with ADHD. Student success and strengths are celebrated and reinforced. Mistakes, inabilities, and inappropriate behavior are privately discussed and corrected through rewards, consequences, and teaching of new skills. Expected behavior is taught and modeled by the teacher. Teacher behavior reflects the core values of equality, respect, responsibility, and acceptance. Teachers are consistent and predictable. Students know what is expected and what the teacher's response will be to appropriate and inappropriate behavior. Inappropriate behavior is just that . . . inappropriate *behavior*, not inappropriate *children*. Behavior is thought of as a skill set, similar to academic knowledge. Behavior is not character or personality; social behavior in school and home is learned and therefore no child is "beyond help."

Structure   Effective classroom management begins with structure. Individuals with ADHD can thrive in highly structured environments because such environments are optimal for learning and for effective intervention. Creating a structured classroom includes **rules, routines, reinforcers**, and **consequences**. Rules and routines are thoroughly thought out, taught, and retaught until mastered by all students in the class. All students, including those with ADHD, can describe what is expected in the classroom and the reinforcers and consequences for following or not following the established rules and routines.

Rules　Three to five solid rules are established prior to the first day of school. On the first day of school and for many days after, examples of following the rules are described, modeled, and practiced. Non-examples are also described to students for clarification. Rules should be taught until all students can describe and model the rule. As a teacher, you might not have given much thought to how rules are selected and written. As a parent, you might not have given any thought to how teachers select the rules for their classroom. The following sections will help you as a parent teach your children and adolescents rules that are important in classrooms and at home. With consistent expectations across home and school, students are more likely to be successful.

When classroom rules are taught, practiced, and modeled with students (see Figure 8.3), you are creating a structured

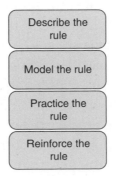

Figure 8.3. **Teaching Rules and Expectations**

learning environment that is essential for the success of not only students with ADHD, but for all students. Rules and expectations are necessary in all classrooms and homes. We often hear high school teachers say that adolescents have been in school long enough to know the expectations. However, the reality is that expectations are and should be different at different ages and between different teachers and schools. Teaching the expectations in the same manner that you teach academic subject matter is necessary for all students at all ages to have similar opportunities to learn.

We encourage you to write rules based on knowledge of common problem behaviors demonstrated by students in classrooms and behaviors that often result in students being removed from the learning environment for office referrals and subsequent consequences; rules will be different in elementary, middle, and high school classrooms. Our research[4] has established the most common problem behaviors in general education classrooms, and others have discovered the most common reasons for discipline referrals.[5] It is interesting that the most common problem behaviors at the classroom level are very similar to behaviors demonstrated by children and adolescents with ADHD. Therefore, it is essential that rules be taught and retaught until students with ADHD can demonstrate mastery of the skill of following the rules. Based on this knowledge, we have developed the sample rules in Figure 8.4; the following paragraphs describe the problem behaviors addressed by these rules in elementary, middle, and high school classrooms.

Teaching rules includes describing the rule, modeling the rule, practicing the rule, and reinforcing the rule (see Figure 8.3). First, tell the student about the rule, and then provide examples and non-examples. Next, practice the rule and provide reinforcement to students who follow the rule correctly. After the students have mastered following the rule, then you must provide further reinforcement. This is often described as "catching them being

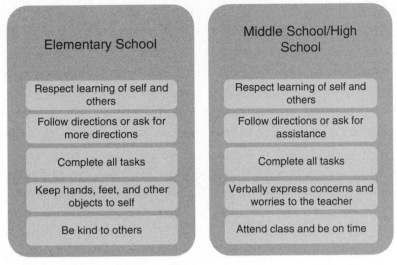

Figure 8.4. Example Rules and Expectations

good." On a daily basis, when you see a student following the rule, then verbally praise the student or the group.

Common problem behaviors in elementary school classrooms are distraction from task, being off task, and not following directions,[6] and the most common reasons for discipline referrals in elementary schools are fighting and defiance.[7] Five rules for elementary students are established in Figure 8.4 based on these common behaviors.

The most common problem behaviors at the middle school and high school are distractibility and lack of concentration (excessive movement or silliness); not following directions; behaviors associated with worrying, self-doubt, and concern about what others think; and trying to be perfect. The most common reasons for office discipline referrals in middle school are defiance and disruption and in high school are tardiness, skipping, and leaving the building.

Routines   Routines are a sequential set of independent behaviors that lead to a desired outcome for actions that occur on a regular basis in classrooms. Students with ADHD need to have a thorough understanding of the procedures in each classroom routine and be able to demonstrate the routine. Routines help students remember and follow through with expectations without ongoing teacher direction. For example, students sharpen pencils, go to the restroom, get a drink of water, and submit completed assignments to be graded. Teaching routines to students is structured in the same format as teaching an academic skill, such as addition—the concept is introduced, modeled, and practiced. The routine is reinforced until each student has mastered the skill. When mastery of the skills is not evident, then the skill is retaught. Routines are taught to students at all levels from preschool to university classrooms. Teachers can develop and teach routines for anything that happens in a classroom on a consistent basis. Some specific routines that assist students with ADHD are (1) preparing to learn, (2) getting out of and returning to seat, (3) recording assignments, and (4) submitting assignments.

Every day, students enter the classroom and are expected to be prepared to learn when the teacher begins instruction. But how often do teachers teach this as a skill? As a parent, ask your child or adolescent what it means to be prepared to learn at the beginning of class. As a teacher, think about how students with ADHD often enter the class. We would expect the answer to be loudly, with papers and supplies either missing or in disarray, unless the teacher has taught the skill. This routine should be taught to all students in all classes. The routine may differ by teacher, but similar steps are typically expected. Students are to walk into the classroom quietly, take a seat, and take out completed homework, paper, pencil, books, and notebooks within a specified time. Behaviors specific to individual classrooms should be added to this list. In middle and high school, this routine usually occurs between the ringing of the first bell and the tardy bell. In elementary school and in university settings, this typically occurs between the time the students enter the class and the teacher begins teaching. To assist students with ADHD, a step that includes writing daily assignments and homework in an agenda book or on an assignment sheet can be included. Once needed supplies are gathered, students can copy the daily work and/or homework from a marker board, Smartboard, or chalkboard. Students should understand the exact amount of time allotted for this routine.

During an academic day, students get out of their seats many times; sometimes appropriately and sometimes not. Students sharpen pencils, go to the restroom, get water, turn in assignments, request help from the teacher, and work in cooperative learning groups. Students with ADHD often get out of their seat without permission or at inappropriate times, such as during the teacher's lecture. During a recent observation of a student with ADHD in a high school classroom while the teacher was lecturing using a PowerPoint presentation, the student was doodling with colored pencils. Each time he wanted to use a different colored pencil, he got out of his seat and went to the front of the classroom to find the pencil. This might seem like a minor behavior problem; however, while the student was walking to the front of the class, he was not focused on the lecture or taking notes and the focus of the other students shifted from the teacher's lecture to the student's behavior. Although this behavior could have been eliminated by including getting all necessary supplies during the preparing-to-learn routine, a routine for getting out of seat would let the student know that to get out of his seat, he would need to raise his hand and ask for permission, or wait until the lecture was complete. Such a routine could include raising a hand to ask for permission and discussing appropriate times for asking for permission and times when permission is not needed.

Students with ADHD often forget directions and assignments to be completed. A routine for recording assignments provides the student with a written reminder of what is due and when. This routine can occur at the beginning or end of class. The assignment can be recorded in an agenda book or on assignment sheets. Students are expected to write the assignment and the due date. Students should be taught to note assignments with enough detail so that the assignment can be completed without asking for further directions. In addition, the routine should include provisions for long-term assignments or studying for tests at later dates, if either is applicable to the class.

As teachers, we have seen students frantically search through disorganized backpacks and binders for completed assignments. As a parent, you probably know the frustration of helping your child complete an assignment only to find out that the child received a zero, because he could not find it. Teachers, ask yourselves whether your students know when assignments are due and where to put the assignments. If you do not have a routine for submitting assignments, ask a student with ADHD when an assignment is due and where it should be turned in. We suspect that the answer will be "I don't know." Teachers often ask students to submit assignments in different methods. For students with ADHD, it is vitally important for assignment submission—when and where to turn in papers—to become a routine.

Behavior Management   So what happens if students (especially those with ADHD) **do or do not** follow the rules and routines once taught and mastered? For optimal success, children and adolescents with ADHD know the answer to this question. The reinforcers and consequences are established in the school and classwide behavior management plan. The plan is similar to a contract between a business and a client. The plan includes classroom rules and routines, as described earlier, and reinforcers and consequences for following and not following rules and routines. We often see behavior management plans with only negative consequences, but it is important that positive consequences also be included. Students often understand or at least have read or been told what will happen when they DO NOT follow the rules, but do they know what will happen if they DO follow the rules?

When developing a behavior management plan for a classroom or for an individual student, you consider the characteristics of individual students. Students with ADHD respond differently than other children to rewards and consequences. The impact of consequences should be considered. Consequences provide three positive effects for children and adolescents with ADHD: (1) positive or negative social effects, (2) feedback about correct and incorrect behavior, and (3) stimulation.[8] Although rewards are designed to increase behavior and negative consequences are designed to decrease behavior, children with ADHD may be more interested in the degree of stimulation from the adult response. For example, when adults respond with high emotion or loud voices, the behavior might increase because the adult response was actually stimulating and not punishing to the child.[9]

Verbal Praise Verbal praise is an important component of all behavior management plans. Students, as well as adults, respond to specific verbal praise; it is especially important for students with ADHD, because frequent negative comments about their behavior impacts their self-esteem and productivity. If you spend much time in an elementary class, you will notice that the teacher often makes comments such as "good job" or "awesome." However, specific verbal praise includes explaining to the student what he or she is doing correctly—that is, it includes a description of the appropriate behavior and "skill labeling." For instance, when Cannon raises his hand to ask a question in class instead of interrupting the teacher, then the teacher would say, "Good job. You just raised your hand showing me that you understand how to politely ask me a question." Be careful to make sure that your verbal praise, as a parent or a teacher, is developmentally appropriate. Praising adolescents sounds different from praising children. If Cannon was in high school, a better praise statement would be, "Good job. Thanks for raising your hand and being considerate to your classmates."

Group and Individual Contingencies   Behavior management plans include group and individual contingencies. Group and individual contingencies are effective with students with ADHD when implemented consistently for extended periods of time.[10] Contingencies can be thought of as "if-then" statements that the students understand. Group contingencies are based on the behavior of the entire group and the entire group receives the reward. Individual contingencies, on the other hand, are based on the behavior of the individual student.

For example, Mrs. Harvey has a group contingency program in her class. If all students complete and turn in their assignments each week, then all students are allowed to watch a short movie on Friday. If all students do not complete the assignments, then the time that would have been spent watching a movie is spent completing assignments. In addition, one of Mrs. Harvey's students, Zoe, has severe ADHD and often loses her completed assignments. Mrs. Harvey created an individual contingency management plan for Zoe within a multimodal intervention program. If Zoe submits her assignments complete, then Zoe is allowed to be the leader during movie time, passing out popcorn and controlling the remote control.

Response Cost   Response cost is a negative consequence, similar to a "fine," often included in effective behavior management plans when combined with positive consequences. Response cost is the loss of a reward or reinforcing activity that occurs when the student displays an inappropriate behavior. For example, Mrs. King gives her students tokens (marbles in a jar) randomly when she notices the student following a classroom rule. When she notices that the student did not follow the classroom rule, then she takes a token out of the jar. Mrs. King is very careful to make sure that her students receive more tokens than they lose. If the students do not, then the system becomes more punishing than rewarding and will not continue to be effective.

From the Teacher

Classroom management is the most important part of my day; without it learning is difficult. My organizational skills have to be top-notch to get 30 students of differing abilities on the same page for hours and hours in a day. You can never get enough practice at classroom management no matter how good you are.

Instructional Strategies

As a teacher, you probably have noticed that students with ADHD learn more when you present material in different ways and include interest and choice in assignments. This is because specific instructional strategies are more effective with students with ADHD. Instructional strategies are techniques used by teachers when teaching content to students to increase the likelihood that the student will learn the material. Students with ADHD learn best when instruction involves the six components listed in Figure 8.5.

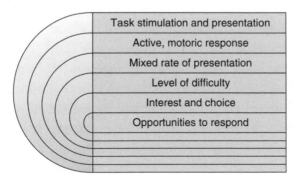

Figure 8.5. Instructional Strategies

Task and Presentation Stimulation   Individuals with ADHD are often drawn to tasks or activities that are "stimulating." You probably have noticed the student with ADHD paying attention to objects or activities in the environment that "catch their attention" instead of monotonous tasks, such as long worksheets or writing assignments. Students with ADHD pay more attention to activities or lessons that are bigger, brighter, more intense, or louder.[11] Teachers can use this trait to their advantage by making lessons or activities more stimulating for the student; however, it is important to make sure that the classroom and other students are not more stimulating than the activity, task, or assignment. Students with ADHD often learn material presented in a novel fashion as opposed to typical lecture-style teaching. For example, books can be played on tape for the entire class or students can be allowed to listen to the books with headphones, and lectures can include demonstrations and activities.

Mixed Rate of Presentation, Active Response, and Opportunities to Respond   Teachers will find that students with ADHD respond best when lessons are presented at a mixed rate of instruction. A mixed rate of instruction involves presenting the material to the students at a brisk rate when the students appear to understand and then slowing the rate when the students are struggling to grasp the content. In addition, during the instruction, students with ADHD maintain attention better when given ample opportunities to respond to teacher questions and respond in an active manner. For instance, Mrs. Danese has several students in her class with ADHD. While teaching lessons, she encourages all students to respond to questions throughout the lesson and allows them to respond with hand signals or individual whiteboards. With modern technology, Mrs. Danese can use student engagement tools called "clickers" that are attached to her Smartboard. Therefore, when she asks the entire class a question, each and every student provides a response assuring that students are actively engaged in the lesson. This activity level helps students with ADHD pay attention and maintain focus.

Level of Difficulty, Interests, and Choice   Teachers strategically select assignments and tasks for students with ADHD. Though other students often complete and submit all assignments given by the teacher, students with ADHD often DO NOT. This can be for multiple reasons, such as being disorganized and not being able to find the completed assignment, or forgetting to complete the assignment. But it can also be because the assignment is not of interest to them. Students with ADHD are more likely to complete assignments that are not too easy and not too difficult for them, are interesting, and involve choice by the students themselves.

For example, Mrs. Cloth creates assignments for her English class based on these criteria. First she ensures that assignments are matched to the academic level of the students. Next, she uses an interest inventory that she gave to her students at the beginning of the year on which they answered questions about their interests. Therefore, Mrs. Cloth knows that Tommy, a

From the Teacher

When I was receiving training as a teacher these principles sounded straightforward enough: "provide choice," "use student interest," "make sure the material is on grade level," but so many times these things were just not feasible or practical. A room with 30 students didn't allow me opportunity or time to do what I wanted to do; there was not enough prep time or resources to create the materials choices and difficulty levels for everyone. But what I could do was help a student find his or her own ways to make choices and get help and locate an interest within a general assignment. This took some time but it was doable for me as a fallback plan. I would ask, "What is interesting about this assignment?" Then I would wait and endure some silence until the student would help me by self-identifying something interesting. This helped me with the burden of individualizing and helped a student recognize a strategy for working.

student with ADHD, is interested in joining the army. When assigning reading tasks, she is careful to select several interesting articles about the army and allows Tommy to select the article that he wants to read.

Skills Training

Skills training is needed when skills are not developed to allow the individual with ADHD to function successfully in school. The skills we refer to here are communication, time management, organization, note taking, problem solving, and self-management skills—that is, more general skills, rather than "math computation" or "vocabulary." When a child continues to experience skill deficits after the core symptoms of ADHD (inattention, hyperactivity, and impulsivity) have been alleviated, then skills training is necessary. As mentioned earlier, interventions for ADHD are long-term and should not be discontinued immediately after symptoms begin to subside. Individuals will continue to use the learned coping strategies throughout their lifetime and may need "refreshers" or "boosters" in the form of instruction from time to time.

Interpersonal Communication   Individuals with ADHD may have problems communicating effectively with others. As a parent, you may be saying, "Oh no, my child with ADHD communicates *all* of the time." And this is true. However, the communication style often contradicts *effective* communication. Individuals with ADHD communicate in an impulsive, hyperactive, and inattentive manner, reflecting ADHS core symptoms. Have you noticed that your child or others with ADHD interrupts, talks constantly, and does not pay attention to what others are saying? This communication style interferes with interpersonal relationships with peers, friends, and adults. In addition to verbal communication and listening, communication involves body language.

The individual with ADHD might appear to respond physically to others without thinking and sometimes this response is not socially appropriate, such as making a grimace or twinge or walking away when someone is speaking. Nonverbal cues from others can be missed or misinterpreted. Teaching interpersonal communication skills will help the individual function effectively in all areas.

Note Taking Have you ever looked at the notes taken by an adolescent or young university student with ADHD during a lecture-format class? Because individuals with ADHD experience problems attending during lectures and organizing information, classroom notes are either nonexistent or totally disorganized. Note taking is a very important skill, for notes serve two purposes: (1) the physical act of writing down content helps to increase concentration, and (2) notes are valuable study aids. Note taking is an essential skill for success in secondary schools and universities and is a skill that must be taught to individuals with ADHD[12]—doing so requires not only teaching students to take notes, but to prepare to take notes, and to study using the notes after the lecture.

Individuals with ADHD can be assisted to take accurate notes with the use of guided notes and taught note-taking skills with direct note-taking activities. Guided notes are teacher-prepared student handouts that include an outline or map of the important ideas and facts included in a lecture, with blanks to be filled in by the student. Blanks represent the key concepts, definitions, facts, and other important information. As discussed, students with ADHD stay focused better when teaching includes activity; in this case, students will stay focused in order to complete the handout. Teachers should review or even grade the guided notes to ensure that students are staying focused and completing the notes correctly; successful completion should be rewarded.

Using guided notes helps students to focus and gather all of the important information in a lecture; however, because students will not always have guided notes, they must learn note-taking skills. Teachers can teach students to take good notes through direct note-taking activities. Instruction typically takes place at the beginning of a school year in lecture-format classes, but some students will need extended instruction or booster sessions throughout the year. Direct teaching activities involve gradual learning procedures. First, the teacher provides the students with a handout of her own notes. As the teacher lectures, she models note taking in a visual manner using a whiteboard or overhead projector. As she writes down the notes, she explains the rationale behind what she writes. Students are taught to divide the notes provided by the teacher into main ideas and details in an outline format. With each lecture, the teacher gives the students less information on the handout, but continues to prompt the students to write down specific information as she explains why the information should be recorded in the notes. Teachers gradually fade the intervention until the students have mastered the activity. Teachers continue to check notes taken by students to ensure that they are gathering the important information.

Time Management   Individuals with ADHD have problems with time management; however, this is a skill that can be taught by parents or counselors. Individuals with ADHD often have difficulties arriving at school or appointments on time and gauging the amount of time that an activity will take. Time management becomes more and more important in adolescence and adulthood. Teaching time management involves teaching individuals to use a planner, prioritize activities, plan ahead on a daily basis, and use external cues to prompt activity changes. When using a planner, students are taught to record the time of an appointment, the time required to prepare to leave, and the time required to get to the appointment on time. A compensating strategy for the inability to gauge time is to consider doubling the amount of time you think is required to get to the appointment. When you teach the individual to plan ahead, include preparation activities that can be done the night before. Are clothes and materials ready? Are keys or transportation needs lined up? For a school-age person, are all assignments in a binder and in a backpack? Is the backpack placed in a preestablished place every night? Teach the individual to set an alarm clock to wake up and, to fade from parent reminders, consider using a list or a timer to signal changing activities. For example, James is always late for appointments. His counselor teaches him to set an alarm on his cell phone to signal that it is time to leave for his appointment.

Organizational Skills How would you describe the organizational skills of the individual that you know with ADHD? Some might describe it as horrifying or atrocious. Have you ever heard individuals describe people as "very organized" or "completely disorganized?" It seems as if we consider organization to be a character trait and not a skill that can be learned. The fact is that some individuals are more organized than others; however, organization can be taught and is important. Ask the individual with ADHD if he enjoys being unorganized. Ask what the impact is on his life. If you are talking to an older adolescent or adult, the response will probably be that being disorganized creates frustration and a great deal of wasted time. If you are talking to a child or adolescent, chances are that he does not recognize that he is not organized or is not aware of the impact on his life. Therefore, it is important to teach the student about organization and how to be organized as early as possible.

Individuals with ADHD can be taught organizational skills at home, at work, or at school. As the focus of this chapter is on school-based interventions, we will describe organizational skills at school that increase learning. The focus of organization at school with children and adolescents at schools is on the binder, book bag, and locker.[13] These are the areas where missing assignments and missing clothing tend to hide. Students can be systematically taught to organize each area. First, the teacher and student retrieve all assignments from the student's locker and book bag. Next, the student and teacher together organize the binder with dividers for each subject, place work behind the appropriate dividers, and designate binder folders for completed and incomplete assignments. Next, the teacher checks the binder on a regular basis and provides a reinforcer for binder organization. A checklist can be used to monitor the percentage of binder, locker, and book bag organization.[14] Organization should be monitored for an extended period of time until organization seems to be a habit and then less frequently. However, periodic book bag, binder, and locker checks should continue throughout the school year with reteaching and reorganizing as needed.

In addition, using the seven steps to self-management in Figure 6.5 in Chapter Six, middle and high school students can be taught to self-manage and self-reinforce organization. Although the target behavior can still be organization of book bags, binders, and lockers as mentioned above, we recommend that students include self-manage classroom preparation as an outcome of organization.[15] With successful organization and time management, students will be prepared for class by being on time and having paper, pencil, notebook, completed homework, and any other required materials for the class.

Self-Management   The most effective strategy to teach students the skills needed for successful academic performance involves self-monitoring, self-reinforcement, and self-evaluation.[16] Self-monitoring was described extensively in Chapter Four; however, the importance of students self-monitoring performance at school is stressed here. After learning any or all of the skills needed for successful academic performance, students are taught to self-monitor use of these skill and the outcomes associated with the skill, and to self-reinforce. For example, if the teacher taught Randy to manage his time effectively, he can be taught to self-monitor arriving at class or appointments on time. If Randy meets a prespecified criteria (such as arriving on time to class 9 out of 10 times), he will allow himself 30 extra minutes of sleep on Saturday morning.

Collaborative Interventions Between Home and School

For optimal student outcomes, parents and teachers work collaboratively to increase appropriate behavior and learning. As a parent you can collaborate with the school in several ways. Open lines of communication between home and school are best; you can stay engaged and monitor your child's progress by talking to and meeting with the teacher frequently, reading to and with your child, helping with homework, attending school meetings and functions, and rewarding your child for acceptable academic progress. If your child receives special education services, then individualized education program (IEP) meetings are held at least once a year. Prepare for, attend, and be an active participant in all IEP meetings. Remember that you can request that strategies (such as those mentioned in this chapter) be included in your child's IEP. Chapter Ten provides more information about your rights as a parent and working with the school to assure that your child's IEP is appropriate.

One systematic method of increasing collaboration and parent engagement is through the use of a daily report card or daily behavior report card (DBRC).[17] DBRCs are progress reports sent home to parents on a daily basis that specify the target behavior (either the inappropriate behavior or the replacement behavior), goal for decreasing or increasing the replacement behavior, and daily progress on the frequency or duration of the target behavior. The purposes of DBRCs are to identify, monitor, and modify target behaviors; to increase goal attainment; to increase communication between home and school; and to reinforce changes in behavior.[18] Before using the DBRC, the teacher meets with the parent and explains the process; parents agree to provide a positive or negative consequence for progress towards the student's goal on the DBRC.

To create a DBRC, the teacher identifies the target behavior, which can either be the maladaptive behavior or the replacement behavior that he or she would like the student to demonstrate. For instance, if Cam typically completes one out of five assignments per week, then his replacement behavior could be to turn in five out of five assignments per week. After the target behavior is identified, behavioral indicators are identified, such as behaviors that represent letter grades. So if Cam turned in two assignments, he could get a D for the day; turning in three assignments earns a C; four assignments a B; and five assignments an A. Once the behavioral indicators are identified, the teacher determines when he or she will monitor the student's progress. In Cam's case, monitoring would be once a day; however, if you were using a DBRC to monitor getting out of seat, the teacher would want to monitor more frequently during the day. Next, the teacher begins monitoring student progress every day, and the DBRC is sent home to the parent daily.

From the Teacher

Communication with parents is sometimes intimidating. You never know how a parent or caregiver will respond to information about a student's performance in school. Will they think it is all my responsibility? Will they punish a child at home for problems at school? If I have conflict with a student, whose side will they be on? Most parents want to know what is going on and want to know what to do to support my efforts and help, and I feel the same. The more communication we have the better I can do my job.

Multimodal Treatment Programs

The gold standard of ADHD intervention is multimodal treatment, which is a combination of two or more interventions used to teach the individual to self-regulate with effective coping strategies. A combination of the interventions described in this chapter could be considered multimodal intervention; however, multimodal treatment programs are well-coordinated treatments that usually involve collaboration with different professionals and include interventions that fit into three categories: (1) parenting skills (described in Chapter Seven); (2) cognitive behavioral interventions (teaching and learning coping strategies described in this chapter and in Chapter Five); and (3) medication (discussed in Chapter Three).

While medication is beyond the scope of school-based interventions, several multimodal school-based or summer treatment programs are currently under way for children and adolescents with ADHD. However, a majority of schools do not have multimodal treatment programs per se available. While you can create a pseudo-individualized multimodal treatment program for your child by combining interventions, collaboration between the teachers and practitioners implementing the interventions is essential. For example, if your child is on medication, receives counseling from a private counselor, your child's teacher implements interventions described, and you attend parenting classes, this program would appear to be multimodal. The key component of this multimodal treatment plan would be collaboration between the child's physician, counselor, parenting instruction, and you.

We are aware of three evidence-based, organized multimodal treatment programs continually being evaluated for ADHD, the Summer Treatment Program (STP),[19] the Challenging Horizons Program (CHP),[20] and Youth Experiencing Success in Schools (YESS).[21] The CHP and YESS are currently being evaluated by researchers at Ohio University where one author of this book (JRH) is a clinical research scientist.

The STP is an eight-week summer program for children and adolescents with ADHD (grades 1–6) in New York. The components of the STP are reward and response-cost programs; training in group problem solving; social, negotiating, and contracting skills; training in strategies to overcome learning deficits and increase concentration, task completion, and self-concept; time out; and daily feedback. Treatment plans are written for both groups and individuals. More information can be found at http://ccf.buffalo.edu/STP.php.

The CHP is an after-school program for middle school students with ADHD. CHP is implemented by research staff and school psychologists with expertise in ADHD and school-based mental health interventions. CHP includes 15 specific interventions that target interpersonal skills, recreation, educational skill training (including those discussed in this chapter), and family support. For more information about CHP in Ohio, see http://oucirs.org/research/chp, and in South Carolina see http://www.scstudentexcellence.org/CHP.html.

The YESS program is a classroom-based program for elementary students with ADHD or oppositional defiance disorder currently being evaluated by researchers at Ohio University. Components of YESS include classroom-based behavioral programs, individual parent support programs, parenting groups, individual and group counseling for students, DBRC, and teacher in-service and consultation.

TO SUM UP

In addition to medication, school- and classroom-based interventions are the most important interventions for learners with ADHD from preschool to graduate school. Interventions designed to teach coping strategies to individuals with ADHD to their increase success and learning throughout their lifetimes. Interventions discussed in this chapter can be implemented by teachers and counselors in classrooms, by parents at home, and by individuals as self-help strategies. We began this chapter with a discussion of considerations to be taken prior to implementing any intervention. Interventions should be data driven, developmentally appropriate, and care should be given to motivate the individual to use personal strengths to work on weaknesses. Next we described classroom management strategies, instructional strategies, and specific skills training, and then strategies for increasing collaboration between home and school. Finally, we discussed multimodal treatment programs. Effective implementation of these interventions will increase the likelihood of maximizing the strengths of individuals with ADHD and decreasing the weaknesses.

WHAT'S NEXT?

In the next chapter we explore the special education process and laws. We start with what happens after you inform your child's school initially that he has ADHD and then take you through the entire process.

9

A Crash Course in Special Education and Section 504

To anyone who works with individuals vulnerable to discrimination, the law is something we hold onto like a life jacket. Knowledge of special education law, the Individuals with Disabilities Education Improvement Act (IDEIA), and Section 504 of the Rehabilitation Act of 1973[1] arm you as a parent or educator to protect the rights of your child, your student, or yourself with the skill to work side by side with schoolteachers and other professionals in the schools. The Americans with Disabilities Act (ADA),[2] which provides a basis for legal protection of workers beyond school when your child grows beyond K–12 education and education law provisions no longer apply, is presented in the next chapter. Individuals with ADHD in elementary and secondary schools may or may not be identified for services available through Section 504 or IDEIA.[3] Understanding the difference in eligibility criteria, services, and procedural safeguards available under each law is a start in learning the rights entitled to you and your child—and to ensuring that a child with ADHD receives a free, appropriate public education (often abbreviated as FAPE) as dictated under federal law. This chapter will overview federal law pertaining to individuals with disabilities, including those with ADHD, in schools and will provide

From the Teacher

The law can protect you or your child from discrimination based on the disability but it will not "fix it." That takes more than knowledge—that takes work. Work to learn compensatory strategies and work to consider all methods of assistance.

references for where to go if you are looking for more information. The authors of this book are not lawyers, nor should this information be construed as legal advice.

AFTER DIAGNOSIS OF ADHD

If you, or a person you care about or care for, has received a diagnosis of ADHD, you have a variety of protections under the law. In this chapter, we will talk about your rights in public schools as provided by Section 504 and IDEIA. In a K–12 education setting, a free and appropriate public education or FAPE is guaranteed to you under federal law and is guaranteed to be provided in the least restrictive environment (LRE). We will discuss each concept further in this chapter. This right cannot be denied without due process. If anyone suggests denying your child a FAPE, you have a right to contest the decision through legal processes.

The constitutional underpinnings of establishing public schools for the creation of citizens began early in our history and are credited mostly to work by Horace Mann in the early and mid-1800s. Horace Mann, a member of Congress and the secretary of the Massachusetts State Board of Education, advocated for a universal public education. In 1896, Lightner Witmer, often called the father of both school psychology and of clinical psychology, opened a laboratory at the University of Pennsylvania to teach children with cognitive and behavioral disabilities,[4] frequently referred to as the first "experimental school for backwards children." Elizabeth Farrell and the New York Board of Education are credited with the beginnings of special education in public schools. Elizabeth Farrell taught the first public school special education class and organized the Council for Exceptional Children (CEC) in 1922. Today, CEC is an international organization with 37,652 members "dedicated to improving the educational success of individuals with disabilities and/or gifts and talents. CEC advocates for appropriate governmental policies, sets professional standards, provides professional development, advocates for individuals with exceptionalities, and helps professionals obtain conditions and resources necessary for effective professional practice."[5]

However, before 1975 when the first special education law (PL 94-142) was passed, children with disabilities could be excluded from schools if they were determined "not to benefit" from education or would be disruptive to others. In some states, it was a crime even to attempt to enroll a student with disabilities in public school![6]

In 1954, a landmark civil rights decision in Brown v. Board of Education[7] set the stage for inclusive education practices. When the U.S. Supreme court found that there was "no place in the field of public education" for segregated schools with regard to children who were African American, parents of children with disabilities argued that segregation for their children was likewise a denial of the benefits of an education. Thus began the road to Public Law 94-142, known as The Education for All Handicapped Children Act, which has been reauthorized four times, most recently in 2004 when it was renamed Individuals with Disabilities Education Improvement Act (IDEIA).

In addition, Section 504 of the Rehabilitation Act of 1973 is an overarching law that protects individuals with disabilities (see Figure 9.1). While your child with ADHD may or may not be eligible for Special Education Services under IDEIA, he remains protected by Section 504, a civil rights law—if you inform the school that he has ADHD (it's best to give the school written documentation from your psychologist or physician) and if ADHD substantially limits one or more of his major life

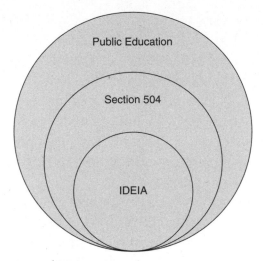

Figure 9.1. ADHD and Education

activities, such as learning. In fact, Section 504 is considered the "umbrella" law protecting students with disabilities, whether served by general or special education. If you decide to share with your school that your child has ADHD, you should begin a notebook or file where you keep copies of all the information and correspondence between yourself and the school. It is not uncommon for parents to forget what was discussed; maintaining careful records allows you to review information and services proposed or provided for your child.

You will find it helpful to understand the distinction between IDEIA and Section 504 eligibility criteria, because the school, in collaboration with you and with information from other professionals, will make decisions based on each law regarding services provided to your child. The identification criteria for defining a "disability," procedural safeguards, and potential services are different for section 504 and IDEIA. This is at first confusing to many parents, but the funding of these two laws is different and the schools must distinguish which type of services they are providing—specialized accommodations under 504 to facilitate obtaining a FAPE or special education services (typically a higher-level, more intensive service) under IDEIA.

SECTION 504

Section 504 is a federal law designed to eliminate discrimination based on disability (as defined by Section 504), including disabilities of students in educational settings, and is enforced by the U.S. Office of Civil Rights (OCR). Section 504 actually applies to all individuals in all settings, but the emphasis in this chapter is on the application in schools. Section 504 is considered a general education mandate as federal funds are not used. Section 504 requires that students identified with disabilities (according to 504 criteria) receive services designed to meet individual needs to the same extent as individuals without disabilities. The purpose of Section 504 is to "level the playing field" in order for individuals with disabilities to have the same opportunity for full inclusion in the general education curriculum as their typically developing peers. The concept is that students receive services, such as classroom and assessment accommodations and related services, that "accommodate" the impact of the disability. A student is considered eligible for protection under Section 504 if he: (1) has "a physical or mental impairment that substantially limits one or more major life activities including learning and behavior" and (2) "has a record of having such an impairment or be regarded as having such an impairment." More than likely, the symptoms of ADHD impact your child's learning, and learning is considered a "major life activity." The key is in the term "substantially limits." Section 504 does not define "substantially limits." To determine if your child's learning is substantially impacted, the 504 committee (a group made up of you, your child, your child's 504 coordinator [a designated professional at the school who coordinates 504 plans], and the section 504 coordinator) will review evidence of academic and behavioral performance at school such as grades, achievement scores, attendance, and discipline referrals. Interestingly, if your child's ADHD symptoms and impairment are significantly decreased by medication (considered a mitigating measure), your child may still be eligible for Section 504 accommodations. The key is whether or not accommodations or other services are needed to ensure that his educational needs are adequately met in comparison to others without disabilities.

From the Counselor

As educators, we are very comfortable with our own professional language (or jargon) used in meetings, such as Section 504 committee meetings. However, at times we forget that parents are not always as familiar with the terminology. Though parents are often reluctant to ask for clarification, when they do it reminds us that it is our responsibility to make sure that parents have sufficient information to participate in their child's education. I want to encourage you to ask questions and not be anxious about educational procedures. It is our fault and not yours if you do not understand what we are doing or planning to do for your child. Always ask for explanations of anything unclear to you. Otherwise, you cannot make clear, informed decisions about your child's accommodations or a special education plan.

Procedural Safeguards

Once your child is determined to be eligible for services under Section 504, you should receive a written document from the school that describes the procedural safeguards that protect you and your child. Read this information carefully and ask questions if you do not understand. If you do not receive this information in writing, ask for it.

Section 504 procedural safeguards assure that your child receives a FAPE. Procedural safeguards are a list of requirements to ensure that children with disabilities are provided FAPE. The school will give you a copy of your procedural safeguards.

Section 504 includes the following procedural safeguards. You must receive notice: (1) when your child is being considered for identification as a child with a disability under Section 504, and (2) when the school will review all pertinent information, or conduct an assessment, or both. You have a right to a copy of the Section 504 report delineating all services in your child's 504 plan. In addition, all information should be provided to you in your native language. Notices should include the name and contact information of an educator that can explain the written information upon your request. You have a right to review and have copies of all educational documentation in your child's school file. Simply ask the school for the information that you need or write a letter requesting the information; some schools might require you to pay for the copies. In addition, the procedural safeguards document should contain information regarding procedures for filing a grievance (if you cannot resolve differences at the local level) including names, addresses, and telephone numbers of administrators in your district and the contact person at the Office of Civil Rights (OCR).

Evaluations

Evaluation procedures for Section 504 are far less formal than those required for special education services through IDEIA (described in the next section). The school will review information from a variety of sources (including all of your child's educational records and any outside information that you provide to them). For this reason, it is vitally important that you provide information from the professional who diagnosed your child with ADHD. This statement should indicate the diagnosis and any relevant information that was gathered to make that diagnosis. In addition, the professional should state how your child's learning is impacted by the symptoms of ADHD. Just having ADHD is not enough to receive 504 accommodations at school or elsewhere—your child's symptoms of ADHD must limit one or more major life activity. If you spend a great deal of time helping your child with homework or studying for tests, you should document the time and effort that is required on your part. At times, as parents, we spend numerous hours a day helping our children be successful in school. We consider this simply part of being a good parent. However, if it is taking a majority of your free time at home or interfering with your other responsibilities, it is important that you provide enough information for the educators to understand that without your supplemental instruction your child might not be successful. For the evaluation, the school might ask you to complete rating scales or conduct some formal evaluations of your child's achievement. A formal comprehensive evaluation is not necessary for Section 504 eligibility to be determined and services granted.

Plan

Your child's Section 504 plan is usually completed on a form developed by the state or local education agency to assure compliance with the law and includes statements (1) that your child will receive an appropriate education that is comparable to those without disabilities in the general education classroom, (2) of your child's strengths, (3) that your child was diagnosed with ADHD, (4) of how ADHD affects your child's major life activities, (5) accommodations that were selected by the 504 committee that your child will receive, and (6) other services that your child will receive at school. The format will be different depending on your state and district requirements. Figure 9.2 is an example of a completed Section 504 plan.

Accommodations are changes that focus on antecedents to problem behavior, provide a greater benefit to students with disabilities than to those without[8] to moderate the impact of a student's disability, do not change the skills and knowledge that are taught to all students, and provide equal access to programs,

ADHD CITY SCHOOLS
Section 504 Plan

Student ID: _15018_   Date: _5/21/11_

Student Name: _Cassidy King_

Student D.O.B: _2/11/1996_   Student Grade: _9_

School: _ADHD High School_

Next Review: _5/30/12_

Section 504 Committee:

Name	Position
James Berry	Principal
Deborah Johnson	Counselor
Allison Biederma	School Psychologist
Rob King	Parent
Cassidy King	Student
Sheila Hartwick	Teacher
	Teacher
	Other:
	Other:

The Section 504 Team concludes that _Cassidy King_

has a disability, as defined by Section 504 of the Rehabilitative Act of 1973.

(Yes)

No

Disability: _Attention Deficit Hyperactivity Disorder_

Student Strengths: _Memorization, math calculation, reading fluency_

Figure 9.2. Example of Section 504 Plan (*continued*)

IMPACT OF THE DISABILITY ON A MAJOR LIFE ACTIVITY:

Impacts learning

INSTRUCTIONAL ACCOMMODATIONS:

Provide activity between tasks.
Provide exams on computer.
Provide computerized flashcards.
Seat Cassidy in area of the room that is distraction-free.
Small group as needed.
Allow frequent breaks.
Allow multiple days for extended assignments and tests.

Accommodation(s) for State Wide Testing: *Small group, frequent breaks,*

multiple day assessment

SECTION 504 COMMITTEE PARTICIPANTS:

Signature	Position	Date
James Berry	*Principal*	*5/21/11*
Deborah Johnson	*Counselor*	*5/21/11*
Allison Biederma	*School Psychologist*	*5/21/11*
Rob King	*Parent*	*5/21/11*
Cassidy King	*Student*	*5/21/11*
Sheila Hartwick	*Teacher*	*5/21/11*

Figure 9.2. (*continued*)

activities, and services in general education inclusive environments. Therefore, accommodations are not changes to the curriculum, and assignments completed with accommodations are graded the same as for other students. Accommodations are changes in (1) how your child responds to academic instruction, (2) the classroom setting, (3) the way the teacher presents the content, and (4) the timing or scheduling of academic tasks. For example, an accommodation for a student with ADHD might be to divide a long assignment into several sections to be submitted each day. Students can self-advocate by requesting specific accommodations.

As such, accommodations for students with ADHD, while not as clear as with physical disabilities or some learning disabilities (for example, a book in Braille for a student who is blind or books on audio listening devices for students with dyslexia), assist the student in learning the same content as their typically developing peers and "accommodate" for the deficits created by ADHD. An important note here is that accommodations are not required to be based on scientific evidence of effectiveness. Therefore, as parents and educators, it is important to be vigilant in determining whether your child's accommodations are actually a benefit to your child. If an accommodation is not beneficial to your child, then it is not necessary. We believe that accommodations are needed at times, but are not a replacement for interventions that will teach your child skills necessary to be successful in the long term. For example, one accommodation might be that your child's teacher checks your child's notebook or book bag each day to ensure that the necessary materials are included to complete any homework. This will be helpful on a day-to-day basis. However, our long-term goal would be for your child to learn to organize his own notebook daily.

Some accommodations typically provided on Section 504 plans for students with ADHD follow. In a structured classroom, students with ADHD can be seated in an area of the classroom that decreases the possibility for distraction and is away from temptations. For example, seating Emma, a fourth grader with ADHD, next to the fish tank is probably not the best idea. Emma would do better seated in an area of the classroom with minimal distractions. Students with ADHD are drawn to tasks with highly attractive stimuli that are bigger, brighter, and more intense.[9] Thus, as discussed in Chapter Eight, tasks and assignments can be designed to maximize these characteristics. Activity level and type of activities can be varied during the class, thus increasing the amount of activity involved and decreasing repetitions. For instance, Ali pays attention for longer periods of time if she completes part of a math worksheet, plays a math game on the computer, and uses manipulatives during a class period. Ali's teacher rotates these activities every 10 minutes. Tests can be completed over several days so that the student completes shorter components of the test each day instead of an entire test in one day. Additional accommodations are listed Figure 9.3. Remember that different accommodations are helpful for different students. We have listed several potential accommodations, but not all accommodations are effective for all children. Teachers and parents should carefully monitor student progress to be sure that the student is learning the content being taught with the accommodations. Simply "passing" the assignment is not sufficient evidence that the accommodation is effective.

Some accommodations that may seem logical for students with ADHD are in fact not effective. For instance, many believe that students with ADHD need extended time on assignments and tests. Though students with ADHD have a deficit in time management, some research has provided initial support for extended time for students with ADHD, but additional research is needed.[10] As inattention is a hallmark of ADHD, extending the time on a task might require that focus be maintained for longer periods of time. Adding frequent breaks to extended time might be necessary for optimal benefit. In addition, because students with ADHD often forget homework or cannot find completed assignments, many teachers do not assign homework to this population. Again, this is not effective accommodation. Appropriate homework is designed for needed practice. Without this practice, the student could fall behind his peers. However, parents can use accommodations at home to increase homework

Activities	•Allow the student to be active between tasks. •Use manipulatives during independent seat work. •Use motor games and activities during instruction.
Organization	•Check the student's binder daily to assure all homework and needed materials are included. •Write down the student's homeworks asignments daily.
Computer Assistance	•Allow the student to take exams on the computer. •Allow the student to type written assignments instead of writing. •Allow the student to participate in computerized lessons. •Allow the student to study for exams using computer flash flash cards or other types of study aids.
Interest and Choice	•Allow the student to do one of two or three equivalent tasks. •Allow the student to select reading material of personal interest. •Present information during instruction that connects the material taught to familiar content.
Background Music	•Add background music that helps the student. •Decrease background conversations.
Distraction-Free Environment	•Seat the child in an area of the room that is distraction free. •Encourage students to work quietly during independent work. •Allow the student to work in small groups during assessment.
Shortened Assignments	•Shorten assignments and tests. •Divide long assignments into multiple shorter assignments.
Audio Presentation	•Allow the student to listen to books on tape.
Highlight Relevant Information	•Highlight important words in the directions. •Highlight main ideas.
Frequent Breaks	•Allow the student to take frequent breaks during assignments.

Figure 9.3. Accommodations That Might Be Beneficial

compliance, such as seating in a distraction-free environment and frequent breaks.

When taking various classroom and standardized tests at school, accommodations designed to obtain more accurate results for a student with ADHD also can be requested. These will vary depending upon each student's needs. It is also important to note that the College Entrance Examination Board (CEEB) and the Educational Testing Service (ETS), the company that administers the SAT, GRE, and many other college admissions tests, also makes available accommodations for improved accuracy of test results for individuals with ADHD. However, strict rules apply to these accommodations and application for them must be made in advance. The CEEB lists their requirements and provides an application online at: http://sat.collegeboard.com/register /for-students-with-disabilities. This process needs to be initiated well in advance and the CEEB recommends that applications for accommodations be made the year prior to the first such test a person will take. Other admissions testing programs also offer accommodations. For example, for those contemplating medical school, the American Association of Medical Colleges indicates that examinees with disabilities or medical conditions who feel adjustments are necessary to the testing environment are encouraged to apply for accommodated testing. You need to apply for accommodations if you have a condition or disability that results in a deviation from the standard testing environment. For example, presentation of testing materials in large print, extra testing time, a separate testing room, or an authorization to bring in an inhaler, water, or hard candy all constitute accommodated testing. Please be advised that having been diagnosed with a condition(s) or impairment will not automatically result in an accommodation (https://www.aamc.org/students/applying/mcat /accommodations/). You can easily search on the website for any college or graduate or professional school admissions testing program to determine the methods of applying for accommodations. However, we cannot stress enough that you must begin this process well in advance, preferably a full year, in case appeals are needed or any specialized examinations are required.

Related services might be included on a Section 504 plan if they are needed for the student to have equal access to the curriculum. Though related services are not always needed for students with ADHD, some students might benefit from the services of the school psychologist, counselor, or behavior intervention specialist. One important service these professionals might provide is consultation to teachers. Mental health professionals at the school have tremendous knowledge of services needed by students with ADHD in schools. Helping the teachers learn and implement effective teaching strategies and the accommodations listed on your student's 504 plan might be beneficial to your child. In addition, students with ADHD might benefit from an understanding mentorship with school-based mental health professionals.

Grievance and Appeals

If you disagree with the school's decisions regarding your child's 504 services including eligibility, evaluation, placement, or accommodation plan, you can file a grievance. Although we recommend attempting to work collaboratively with the school to resolve any issues, we recognize that at times, it is necessary to seek resolution through a nonbiased entity. For this reason, Section 504 has designated procedures to resolve such issues. First, attempt to reach a resolution through informal complaints (written grievance) following the school district chain of command (for example: from teacher to assistant principal, principal, assistant superintendent, superintendent, school board). Ask the principal or counselor at the school for the administrative chain of command. Typically, the principal or other designee will meet with you to discuss your disagreement. Prior to the meeting, spend some time putting your concerns and disagreements in writing. Mail the letter to the principal in advance of the meeting to give him sufficient time to investigate your concerns and potential solutions (and make sure that he receives it). If you have evidence that the current program is not meeting your child's needs, include that with the letter (for example, graded assignments and tests). Also, ask even before you attempt an informal resolution specifically if there is a formal appeal process in place in your school district. There will be such a process in all schools, and you should be aware of the requirements of this process at the local level. The schools are required to give you this information in writing. Knowing this in advance helps you prepare during the informal process and alerts you to information to be collecting and organizing.

If you do not reach resolution through this process, you can elect to begin the formal grievance process. Exhibit 9.1 contains a list of helpful resources.

THE INDIVIDUALS WITH DISABILITIES EDUCATION ACT: SPECIAL EDUCATION

Special Education Services are enforced by the U.S. Department of Education's Office of Special Education Programs (OSEP) and Office of Special Education and Rehabilitative Services (OSERS) and are provided to students who (1) meet the disability criteria established by IDEIA and (2) demonstrate educational need. Specific categories of disability are designated under IDEIA as autism, deaf-blindness, deafness, hearing impairment, cognitive impairment, multiple disabilities, orthopedic impairments, other health impairment, emotional disturbance, specific learning disability, speech or language impairment, traumatic brain injury, and visual impairment, including blindness (See Exhibit 9.2).

Although ADHD is not a specific category, this was considered in 1990. In 1991, eligibility for special education for

---

Exhibit 9.1: Helpful Section 504 Resources

Office of Civil Rights Frequently Asked Questions	http://www2.ed.gov/about/offices/list/ocr/504faq.html
OCR Fact Sheet	http://www.hhs.gov/ocr/civilrights/resources/factsheets/504.pdf
OCR Hotline	1-800-368-1019
OCR E-mail	ocrmail@hhs.gov
OCR Website	http://www.hhs.gov/ocr
National Resource Center on ADHD	http://www.help4adhd.org/en/education/rights/504
Office of Special Education and Rehabilitative Services	http://www2.ed.gov/about/offices/list/osers/index.html
Office of Special Education Programs	http://www2.ed.gov/about/offices/list/osers/osep/index.html
Advocates for Special Education	http://advocatesforspecialeducation.com/
Children and Adults with Attention-Deficit/Hyperactivity Disorder (CHADD)	http://www.chadd.org/

---

students with ADHD was explained in a memorandum from the United States Department of Education (USDOE) to the chief state school officers stating that students with ADHD might qualify for special education under the categories of other health impairment (OHI), specific learning disability (SLD or LD), emotional disturbance (ED), or developmental delay depending on the unique learning needs and characteristics of the individual. All special education eligibility categories are described

---

Exhibit 9.2: NICHCY Definitions of Special Education Categories

NICHCY *National Dissemination Center for Children with Disabilities* provides a wealth of information including the following definitions of special education categories, and on their web page, hot links to additional resources. (http://www.nichcy.org/Disabilities/Categories/Pages/Default.aspx)

1. Autism . . .

. . . means a developmental disability significantly affecting verbal and nonverbal communication and social interaction, generally evident before age three, that adversely affects a child's educational performance. Other characteristics often associated with autism are engaging in repetitive activities and stereotyped movements, resistance to environmental change or change in daily routines, and unusual responses to sensory experiences. The term *autism* does not apply if the child's educational performance is adversely affected primarily because the child has an emotional disturbance, as defined in #5 below.

A child who shows the characteristics of autism after age 3 could be diagnosed as having autism if the criteria above are satisfied.

2. Deaf-Blindness . . .

. . . means concomitant [simultaneous] hearing and visual impairments, the combination of which causes such severe communication and other developmental and educational needs such that they cannot be accommodated in special education programs solely for children with deafness or children with blindness.

3. Deafness . . .

. . . means a hearing impairment so severe that a child is impaired in processing linguistic information through hearing, with or without amplification, and that adversely affects a child's educational performance.

4. Developmental Delay . . .

. . . for children from birth to age three (under IDEA Part C) and children from ages three through nine (under IDEA Part B), the term developmental delay, as defined by each State, means a delay in one or more of the following areas: physical development; cognitive development; communication; social or emotional development; or adaptive [behavioral] development.

5. Emotional Disturbance . . .

. . . means a condition exhibiting one or more of the following characteristics over a long period of time and to a marked degree that adversely affects a child's educational performance:

(a) An inability to learn that cannot be explained by intellectual, sensory, or health factors.

(b) An inability to build or maintain satisfactory interpersonal relationships with peers and teachers.

(c) Inappropriate types of behavior or feelings under normal circumstances.

(d) A general pervasive mood of unhappiness or depression.

(e) A tendency to develop physical symptoms or fears associated with personal or school problems.

The term includes schizophrenia. The term does not apply to children who are socially maladjusted, unless it is determined that they have an emotional disturbance.

6. Hearing Impairment . . .

. . . means an impairment in hearing, whether permanent or fluctuating, that adversely affects a child's educational performance but is not included under the definition of "deafness."

(continued)

7. Mental Retardation . . .

. . . means significantly subaverage general intellectual functioning, existing concurrently [at the same time] with deficits in adaptive behavior and manifested during the developmental period, that adversely affects a child's educational performance.

(Note: *Mental Retardation* is the term found in the law since passage of the original legislation in 1975. In 2008, the American Association on Intellectual and Developmental Disabilities (AAIDD) (formerly the American Association on Mental Retardation, AAMR) and members of the community recommended use of the term *Intellectual Disability*. For changes in language to be made in the regulations, Congress must first change it in the legislation. Until such action occurs, we provide the existing language from IDEA.)

8. Multiple Disabilities . . .

. . . means concomitant [simultaneous] impairments (such as mental retardation-blindness, mental retardation-orthopedic impairment, etc.), the combination of which causes such severe educational needs such that they cannot be accommodated in a special education program solely for one of the impairments. The term does not include deaf-blindness.

9. Orthopedic Impairment . . .

. . . means a severe orthopedic impairment that adversely affects a child's educational performance. The term includes impairments caused by a congenital anomaly, impairments caused by disease (e.g., poliomyelitis, bone tuberculosis), and impairments from other causes (e.g., *cerebral palsy*, amputations, and fractures or burns that cause contractures).

10. Other Health Impairment . . .

. . . means having limited strength, vitality, or alertness, including a heightened alertness to environmental stimuli, that results in limited alertness with respect to the educational environment, that—

(a) is due to chronic or acute health problems such as asthma, *attention-deficit disorder or attention-deficit hyperactivity disorder*, diabetes, epilepsy, a heart condition, hemophilia, lead poisoning, leukemia, nephritis, rheumatic fever, sickle cell anemia, and Tourette's syndrome; and

(b) adversely affects a child's educational performance.

11. Specific Learning Disability . . .

. . . means a disorder in one or more of the basic psychological processes involved in understanding or in using language, spoken or written, that may manifest itself in the imperfect ability to listen, think, speak, read, write, spell, or to do mathematical calculations. The term includes such conditions as perceptual disabilities, brain injury, minimal brain dysfunction, dyslexia, and developmental aphasia. The term does not include learning problems that are primarily the result of visual, hearing, or motor disabilities; of mental retardation; of emotional disturbance; or of environmental, cultural, or economic disadvantage.

12. Speech or Language Impairment . . .

. . . means a communication disorder such as stuttering, impaired articulation, a language impairment, or a voice impairment that adversely affects a child's educational performance.

13. Traumatic Brain Injury . . .

. . . means an acquired injury to the brain caused by an external physical force, resulting in total or partial functional disability or psychosocial impairment, or both, that adversely affects a child's educational performance. The term applies to open or closed head injuries resulting in impairments in one or more areas, such as cognition; language; memory; attention; reasoning; abstract thinking; judgment; problem solving; sensory, perceptual, and motor abilities; psychosocial behavior; physical functions; information processing; and speech.

(continued)

The term does not apply to brain injuries that are congenital or degenerative, or to brain injuries induced by birth trauma.

14. Visual Impairment Including Blindness . . .

. . . means an impairment in vision that, even with correction, adversely affects a child's educational performance. The term includes both partial sight and blindness.

Considering the Meaning of "Adversely Affects"

You may have noticed that the phrase "adversely affects educational performance" appears in most of the disability definitions. This does not mean, however, that a child must be failing in school to receive special education and related services. According to IDEA, states must make a free appropriate public education available to "any individual child with a disability who needs special education and related services, even if the child has not failed or been retained in a course or grade, and is advancing from grade to grade." [§300.101(c)(1)][11]

in Exhibit 9.2. Special education is defined as "specially designed instruction, at no charge to the parents or guardians, to meet the unique needs of a child with a disability."[12] The ultimate purpose of special education is to ensure that a student with a disability receives a FAPE, with an emphasis on the A for appropriate. Individuals with ADHD are most often served as students with disabilities under the educational eligibility categories of Other Health Impairment (OHI), learning disability (LD), or emotional disturbance (ED).[13] Nearly half of students with ADHD qualify for special education services with half of those served as ED and another quarter receiving services under the category of LD.

If your child is determined to be eligible for special education services, do not be alarmed by the eligibility category that is given to him/her by the school. In order for your child to receive special education services, he/she must meet specific eligibility criteria for one of the educational disability categories specified in the law. A multidisciplinary team made up of individuals that know your child well (i.e., you, your child, special education and general education teachers, principals, school psychologists, and others with pertinent information) will determine which eligibility category matches your child's academic and behavioral characteristics. Ask for any information that you need from the school to feel more confident in that decision.

You have the right to dispute the category by following the procedures outlined in the due process information given to you by the school and discussed below, but think seriously about the implications of the category. The significance of the "label" given to children has been debated for years. Some believe that the "label" might make your child feel differently about him/ herself; others believe that teachers might treat your child differently based on the label, and you might have certain emotional reactions or feelings related to the label. You are the best judge of the true impact. You know your child and your child's teacher(s). Remember that you know that your child has ADHD and regardless of the special education category, all children served by special education have the right to services deemed necessary by the child's Individual Education Program (IEP) team. The category of disability is just the gateway into special education to assure that children with true disabilities receive services.

When discussing special education services with educators, you might hear different terminology and acronyms. We list some of the acronyms in Exhibit 9.3; however, if language is used that you do not understand, ask for clarification. You have a right to be a full member of the IEP committee that makes decisions about your child's education. Understanding the language or asking for clarification is your responsibility as your child's best

Exhibit 9.3: Important Acronyms

FAPE	Free Appropriate Public Education
IEP	Individualize Education Plan
LRE	Least Restrictive Environment
LD	Learning Disability
ED	Emotional Disturbance
AT	Assistive Technology
BD	Behavior Disorder (not IDEIA language)
EBD	Emotional and Behavioral Disorders (not IDEIA language)
ESY	Extended School Year
FBA	Functional Behavioral Assessment
BIP	Behavior Intervention Plan
OHI	Other Health Impaired
IDEIA	Individuals with Disabilities Education Improvement Act
IEP	Individualized Education Program
AYP	Adequate Yearly Progress
CHADD	Children and Adults with Attention-Deficit Hyperactivity Disorder
RtI	Response to Intervention
SEA	State Education Agency
LEA	Local Education Agency
SPED	Special Education
NCLB	No Child Left Behind
PBIS or PBS	Positive Behavior Intervention and Supports/ Positive Behavior Supports
FIE	Full and Individual Evaluation

advocate. Too often, educators and other specialists in various disabilities will inadvertently intimidate parents with all of the special language or jargon used at meetings you will attend, and parents often leave such meetings frustrated or afraid they do not understand what is happening with their child. The best ways to avoid these problems and to ensure the proper services are obtained for your child is to ask questions frequently and repeatedly until you are satisfied that you understand what is happening.

Special education operates on several principles of which you should be aware. We will list them here and then briefly talk about them in relationship to ADHD. These principles include zero reject, nondiscriminatory evaluation and identification, free appropriate public education (FAPE), least restrictive environment (LRE), procedural safeguards, student participation, assistive technology, and personnel development. These are not "separate" components of the law but rather a way of negotiating a rather complex set of procedures.

Zero Reject

Zero reject means that all children have a right to a free appropriate public education (FAPE). Even if your child's ADHD severely affects his education, he cannot be denied the right to an education. Once your child has been assessed and special education services are deemed necessary, there is no threshold for saying, "Well, in this case, the child is just too severe." All means all. In addition, it is the responsibility of the school to locate and identify students who need services. If and when a school district suspects or becomes aware of a disability, evaluation for the need for services is expected. This takes us to the next principle, nondiscriminatory evaluation and identification.

Nondiscriminatory Evaluation and Identification

Identification and evaluation tenets of IDEIA ensure a fair and accurate assessment and identification process. This means objectivity, multiple sources, good tests with strong reliability scores and good validity. Assessments (tests) cannot be discriminatory. Professionals should be appropriately certified, licensed, and/or trained to give the assessments and interpret their scores and able to follow protocols for administration accurately. Either parents or the school may begin the evaluation process. If you think your child would benefit from special education services, you can request an evaluation in writing. School districts have 60 days from the time of receiving consent (you will be asked to provide consent for the assessment) to determine eligibility (unless the child is unavailable).

Prior to evaluating your child formally for special education services, if your child has recognized academic or behavioral problems that are interfering with educational progress, teachers are required to provide documentation that **prereferral interventions** (alternative academic or behavioral strategies) were identified, developed, and implemented before a special education referral for special education. The purpose of prereferral strategies is to determine if what are called evidence-based and effective teaching strategies (teaching strategies that actually have existing research evidence proving they work for most students) can remediate your child's academic or behavior problems. However, these prereferral interventions cannot, by law, interfere with the 60-day time line for determining the need for special education—the clock continues to tick during this time.

While it's important to remember that a child with ADHD can qualify for special education as a child with an OHI or with ED, we also note that children with ADHD often have learning disabilities (LD). The procedures of prereferral and identification of LD changed a great deal with the reauthorization of IDEA in

2004. Schools were given the option to use a **response to intervention (RtI)** model to determine if a child had a learning disability (LD) instead of the previously used "achievement gap" method. Prior to 2004, to determine whether your child had a learning disability in addition to ADHD, an educator with expertise in assessment (typically an educational diagnostician or a school psychologist) would have administered individual standardized achievement and IQ tests. The professional would then compare the results of the IQ test to the achievement test to determine if a "gap" existed (achievement below IQ), thus indicating that your child was not achieving at the level expected of children with this level of IQ or academic potential.

However, in 2004, the option to use RtI as a method of identifying a learning disability was given to school districts. School districts have the option to choose either method and many are selecting RtI. The basic premise behind RtI is that research-based interventions including high quality instruction are implemented with your child to determine if your child "responds" to the intervention without special education services. Typically three tiers of interventions are implemented, moving from less to more intensive interventions. Interventions at tier 1 are effective schoolwide core instruction, strategies, and teaching methods used in the classroom. Interventions at tier 2 are core instruction **plus targeted** interventions that focus directly on the academic problems being experienced (for example, poor reading fluency). For example, many districts have adopted extra small group instruction or computer-assisted instruction for Tier 2 interventions. Tier 3 is either a referral to special education or more **intensive** individualized instruction depending on the model that your school district has adopted. As your child "moves through the tiers," he will continue to be involved in general education instruction. Interventions received in each tier are *in addition* to current instruction. Throughout the process your child's teacher(s) will monitor his progress (similar to progress monitoring within PBIS described in Chapter Eleven) and make data-based decisions regarding the need for more intensive interventions at the next level. The concept is that if data collected during the RtI process indicates that your child does not respond to the evidence-based interventions, then he should be evaluated for a learning disability. However, the evaluation that follows this decision varies according to the state and school district. Some districts will administer an IQ and achievement test and others are using more specific tests, such as tests of only reading or another subject matter content area, and may not be comprehensive in their approach. Many school districts across the United States have adopted RtI for LD identification; the procedures for implementing RtI and determining if a child responds to intervention are still being developed and evaluated by researchers. However, in January of 2011, the U.S. Office of Special Education and Rehabilitation Services (OSERS) issued a memo clarifying that RtI cannot be allowed to delay an assessment for determination of a disability once such an assessment has been requested formally by a parent.

Once prereferral activities are complete (and your child did not respond to a series of evidence-based interventions, as mentioned previously), the **initial evaluation** will be completed at no cost to you. Your district will ask you to give written consent for your child to be evaluated. The consent form may include the name of the tests that are going to be administered to your child. If you have questions about the tests, again, feel confident in asking for more information. Prior to beginning psychoeducational testing, your school will complete hearing and vision tests to make sure that neither are interfering with your child's academic progress. If your child is 12 years old or older, a vocational assessment also will be administered to determine your child's strengths and aptitude for future employment and independent living skills.

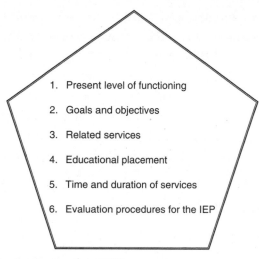

Figure 9.4. Components of an IEP

Once the evaluation is complete, you will receive a notice of an **individualized education program** (IEP) meeting. The purpose of the first or "admission" IEP meeting is to review the evaluation and develop an IEP. At the heart of special education is the concept of an IEP. The program developed by the IEP team is based on your child's individual strengths and weaknesses. The components of an IEP are listed in Figure 9.4. Your child's present level of functioning will be included along with goals and objectives to be taught within the school year. Any related services that your child will receive will be included along with the frequency and length of each service. Your child's educational placement will be included. It is important to assure that placement is decided based on the goals and objectives and should be in the LRE. Placement is not determined prior to determining the services that are needed. The IEP should include evaluation procedures for determining mastery of the included goals and objectives.

Prior to the meeting, you will receive a copy of the evaluation report. Read it and ask questions. Be prepared for the first meeting, as your child's strengths and weaknesses will be discussed openly among the members of the IEP team. The IEP team that reviews the evaluation and determines eligibility consists of you, your child's general education teacher, a special education teacher, a person who serves as an administrator (who has the right to approve fiscal decisions), a person knowledgeable in the area of the suspected disability and who has knowledge about your child, the meaning of the evaluation results, and placement options.

Free Appropriate Public Education (FAPE)

A FAPE means that circumstances and services are created that allow a student with a disability to receive the same benefits from participation in schooling as they would have received if no disability existed, at least to the extent possible. There are limits to the degree of normalization that we are able to provide to students with particularly severe disabilities, but it should be provided to the extent a student with a disability can receive the benefits of education available to students without a disability; the concept of a FAPE requires that all reasonable efforts be made to achieve this goal. FAPE includes meaningful participation by parents and child in the educational process and covers the ages of 3 to 21. Free includes service provisions that are related and services provided in other locations if the local public school does not have the appropriate services (determined by an IEP team or committee) on their campus. For example, if a student is "placed" in another district (the district sends the child to another district), the financial responsibility for education remains with the original school district. This includes transportation to the other district. Service provision different from or more than that which is provided to a typical student is directed by your child's Individual Education Plan (IEP). The school district is held responsible for that which is authorized in the IEP. IEPs are yearlong documents and should be reviewed annually.

Least Restrictive Environment (LRE)

In addition to being free, schooling must be most like the school experienced by non-disabled or non-ADHD students. That is, a student with a disability must be educated in a manner that most resembles the educational experience of students without a disability to the extent possible and to which a FAPE can be provided to the student with a disability. This is called the LRE. The LRE principle may operate like this: A student with ADHD could go to a special education room and learn language arts or the student could go to a general education (typical) language arts classroom. Some families may want a small classroom setting or some schools may say the student "needs" a setting with less distraction. However, the choice is made on the principle of LRE in which the student can be successful or receive a FAPE, and only if this is unsuccessful would the child be moved to a more restrictive, smaller class setting. Most likely your child would receive services in the general education classroom with accommodations or modifications needed to meet the needs of your child. Accommodations and modifications are different from each other. Accommodations are services or strategies provided to your child that allows him or her to progress in the general education classroom without changing the knowledge and skills taught. In other words, your child will learn the same thing as all of the students. However, if your child's skills are below the "norm," he or she might need modifications.

Modifications include changes to the general education curriculum (or what is taught). All accommodations and modifications that your child will receive will be listed on his or her IEP. For example, accommodations for a student with ADHD might include a "quiet area" for test taking, an area that is distraction free for completing assignments, or the IEP may allow for an iPod playing white noise during seat time assignments to block out distractions. We discuss accommodations and modifications in more depth in a later section.

When a disability interferes with education in the general education setting, the least restrictive environment for a student may be a separate class, a separate school, or a separate campus (separate meaning not typical). This is called a "continuum of placements" and is another underpinning of special education law. The full continuum could range from full-time residential placement (hospitals, home services) to general education classrooms. Some of the classroom arrangements that fall in between include special classes, pull-out services (your child would leave the general education class for part of a class to receive individualized or small-group services), coteaching (a special education teacher would teach along with a general education teacher in the general education classroom), and resource classrooms (typically content is taught on your child's academic level and not on grade level), to name a few (most states have their own names for the arrangements). If you or the school believes that your child's placement needs to change, an IEP team must convene to make the decision. All decisions made in IEP meetings should be based on data. In the case of placement, you or your school should have sufficient data to warrant a change in placement. Progress monitoring systems, assessments, class records, and direct observations may all serve as data for these meetings. When in discussion about placement a "stay put" rule applies; this says that if a school or parent wants to move a student to a more restrictive placement or the least restrictive placement, while the decisions is being made, the student "stays put" (that is, remains where he or she is currently receiving services). Changes were made to the "stay put" rule in IDEIA 2004. Before 2004, during any disagreement about which placement was the most appropriate for a student, the student remained in the original setting; changes made in 2004 require the child to be moved to an alternative education program for violations of the student code of conduct that involves illegal drugs, serious bodily injury, or a weapon. Under these circumstances, "stay put" does not apply. If your child is removed to a disciplinary setting, the child should continue to receive special education services to assure that he is receiving FAPE.

Procedural Safeguards

Procedural safeguards cover the rights of your child with ADHD, once involved in the evaluation procedures for special education, and your rights as a parent of a child with a disability. Procedural safeguards contain requirements such as those listed in Exhibit 9.4. Most importantly and the overarching safeguard is that you have the right for your child to have FAPE. All remaining procedural safeguards are in place to assure that this right is never denied. The school will request your permission to evaluate your child. Along with this consent should be an explanation of any evaluations that will be conducted. This same evaluation should be done every three years unless an IEP team (with you as a member) determines that an evaluation is not needed. You can request an Independent Educational Evaluation (IEE). An IEE is completed by a professional that is not directly associated with the school. You can request that the school pay for an IEE or you can pay for one yourself. The school may or may not agree to pay for the evaluation. As with any disagreement you have with the school regarding special education services, you can request due process procedures to resolve the issue. However, if you elect to pay for the evaluation yourself, the school must consider the findings in an IEP meeting. The school will send you written notice before: (1) any IEP meeting, (2) your child is identified for special education or a decision is made that your child no longer needs special education services, (3) evaluation, or (4) placement decision. All notices sent to you should be in your native language. You have the right to fully participate

Exhibit 9.4: Procedural Safeguards for IDEIA

1. You have a right for your child to have a free appropriate public education (FAPE).

2. You have a right to give or deny informed consent before the school conducts an evaluation of your child or initially provides special education services to your child.

3. You have a right for your child to have a full and individual (FIE) evaluation before initial placement in special education.

4. You have a right for your child to be reevaluated every three years unless an IEP team determines that an evaluation is not needed.

5. You have a right to request an independent educational evaluation (IEE); however, the school may initiate a due process hearing prior to paying for an IEE. If you or the school pays for the IEE, the IEP team must consider the results.

6. You have a right to receive written notice when the school proposes to change your child's program including identification, evaluation, and placement.

7. You have a right to be informed of your rights under IDEIA in your native language.

8. You have a right to participate in meetings regarding decisions about identification, evaluation, and placement.

9. You have a right for your child to be educated in the Least Restrictive Environment (LRE) to the maximum extent appropriate to your child's educational needs.

10. You have a right to pursue due process if you feel your child has been denied FAPE.

in all IEP meetings regarding your child's special education services.

Within discussions in IEP meetings, all members will collaboratively focus on ensuring that your child is educated in the Least Restrictive Environment (LRE). If you disagree with the decision of the IEP team, you have a right to due process. Within the procedural safeguard document there will be phone numbers and addresses that you can use to request due process. We encourage you to try to resolve issues with the school before requesting due process; however, if all attempts have been made with no resolution, you have the right to request outside assistance.

From the Counselor

I have participated in many hundreds of IEP meetings and I always try to remember what it feels like to be the parent in these meetings. Typically, there are at least four educators in the meeting and sometimes there are many more. It can be an intimidating experience. However, that is not the intention. As a parent, remember that you know your child better than anyone else in the room. While educators have the expertise to discuss educational services, you are the "expert" on your child. Be prepared. Read anything that you can prior to the meeting and walk into the meeting as an equal collaborator. Everyone's intention should be to develop an appropriate individual education program for your child and YOU are your child's best advocate.

Student Participation

Both you and your child are participating members of the team that plans and develops your child's IEP. We encourage you to ask that your child be taught to participate in the IEP meeting in a meaningful way. Preparation is the key to active and effective participation. IEP team meetings can be intimidating to children with disabilities, but with sufficient preparation your child can be comfortable in advocating for his own education. Specifically, your child can be taught to inventory his own strengths and areas of need and be assertive (and not aggressive) in requesting services to meet his needs. Several programs are available to teach your child to participate in IEP meetings, such as The Self-Directed IEP instructional program.[14] To fully participate in an IEP meeting, your child will need to be prepared to listen to the discussion and understand that at times this discussion will focus on behaviors that he may feel are very difficult to manage. For instance, the discussion may focus on his inability to maintain attention or to remain still for long extended periods of time. He will hear candid discussions of his educational level which may or may not be below that of his peers. With preparation, your child can participate in these meetings without feeling criticized. In addition, discuss the length of the IEP meeting with the committee members prior to the meeting. For your child with ADHD to participate fully, the meeting may need to occur across several short meetings. Expecting him to sit through very long meetings might be unreasonable.

From the Counselor

I was participating in an IEP team meeting many years ago with a student with ADHD. The child was in the meeting when a psychological evaluation was reviewed, including the eligibility criteria for emotional disturbance (ED). The multidisciplinary team determined that the child had an ED and the school psychologist reported this to the committee. The student became very upset. With prior preparation, the significance of this decision could have been discussed with the student prior to the meeting to prepare him for the results. I encourage everyone involved in IEP meetings to make sure that students are well informed prior to the meeting.

Assistive Technology

Assistive technology (AT) must be considered in your child's IEP meeting. IDEIA defines assistive technology as any item, piece of equipment, or product system, whether acquired commercially off the shelf, modified, or customized, that is used to increase, maintain, or improve the functional capabilities of a child with a disability. IDEIA does not list specific AT devices. Some assistive technology devices that might be beneficial to your child include self-monitoring and time management "beepers," noise-cancelling headphones, computer-assisted instruction, memory aids, or PDAs. An expert in assistive technology can complete an AT evaluation for your child. However, minimal research is available to support the effectiveness of AT devices for individuals with ADHD.

Personnel Development

Section 662 of IDEIA requires that Institutes of Higher Education training pre-service teachers and LEAs and SEAs employing in-service teachers provide personnel development for teachers who will teach or currently teach students with disabilities to ensure the teachers have (1) the skills and knowledge necessary to improve academic achievement and functional performance of students with disabilities, and (2) the skills and knowledge to implement scientifically based instructional practices. As a parent, you can encourage your school district to prepare and train your child's teachers to most effectively teach your child and other children with ADHD.

Implementation of Special Education

After your child's initial IEP meeting, special education services begin. You should expect that your child will receive all services agreed on and included in the IEP. The IEP will be implemented in the setting that you agreed on in the ARD meeting and your child should receive all services included. Check in with your child consistently to be sure that services are being provided. Ask your child if he feels like the services are helping. If the IEP lists specific accommodations, then the accommodations should occur. You should be able to see evidence on his assignments and tests. Talk to your child about accommodations. Are the accommodations helping him? Are they interfering instead of providing assistance? You will attend an IEP meeting every year to discuss your child's progress, update goals and objectives, and select new goals and objectives for the school year. Be honest with the IEP team. Report your child's and your perspective of the effectiveness of services being provided. Your child should continue to make educational progress. You will receive the scores that your child earns on state mandated assessments on a yearly basis. Watch the scores carefully. If your child is not mastering the tested standards, request an IEP meeting to discuss supplemental services, such as tutoring or strategy training (such as study skills, test taking skills, organizational skills) that might help your child master the standards. Remember that it is your right to request an IEP meeting at any time.

TO SUM UP

In this chapter, we provided essential knowledge regarding additional services that your child can receive at school through Section 504 or special education. The processes and procedures may seem overwhelming at times, but these mandates assure that all children with disabilities receive a free appropriate public education in the least restrictive environment. You may recall that there was a time when children with disabilities were not even allowed to attend school. The goal is to make sure that no child is ever denied the right to an education. We began the chapter with a brief discussion of the history of special education law and of the people and organizations instrumental in establishing the need for and development of these mandates. We explored Section 504 as an umbrella for all students with disabilities and IDEIA, the nation's special education law, and discussed seven basic principles of special education: zero reject, nondiscriminatory evaluation and identification, free appropriate public education (FAPE), least restrictive environment (LRE), procedural safeguards, student participation, assistive technology, and personnel development. Armed with the knowledge in this chapter, we support you in being a full participant in your child's education, working with educators and advocating for your child as an equal partner throughout the process.

WHAT'S NEXT?

In this chapter, you learned about ADHD and Section 504 and IDEIA. Though not all children with ADHD need services provided by each of these mandates, some do. We encourage you to be an active participant in your child's education by collaborating with educators and advocating for your rights under the law. In the next chapter, we will discuss the rights of adults with ADHD in postsecondary education programs or employment.

10

Practical Strategies for College and the Workplace

Have you ever heard anyone say, "You can give him all of the accommodations you want in high school, but when he gets into the 'real' world, he will be expected to do the same tasks the same way as everyone else?" The reality is that individuals with ADHD have a right to accommodations in colleges and workplaces[1] and throughout the "real world" of the United States. We have stressed throughout this book that ADHD often continues into adulthood and has the potential to affect employment or postsecondary education (higher education) negatively. The amendments of 2008 to the Americans with Disabilities Act (ADAA) ensure that reasonable accommodations are available for individuals with disabilities, including those with neurobiologically based disorders, due to associated impairment that substantially limits major life activities.[2] ADHD is one of the most common chronic mental health disorders in the United States[3] and one of the many disorders intended to be covered under the ADAA. If you are an adult with ADHD, you may not have recognized the symptoms in yourself until your child was diagnosed, and may have experienced a life of development without requesting or receiving any accommodations for your relevant ADHD symptoms. This is not unexpected as 9 million adults between the ages of 18 and 44 years old are estimated to have ADHD[4] but fewer than one in four recognize their own symptoms[5] until after their child has been diagnosed.[6]

After graduation from high school, we were all faced with making a decision about our future. Some decide to go to work or enroll in some form of higher education, such as a technical school, junior college, or a university. This is a personal choice based on what the individual and significant others believe is the best option, the resources available, and how best to meet long-term goals. When making this decision as an adult with ADHD, understanding the skills and supports that you need in coping with ADHD either in the workplace or at the university is important. Knowing which accommodations are most likely to be helpful for you—and that are considered reasonable and thus available to you—can be life-changing in many positive ways. You may find that for you hyperactivity and impulsivity are less severe in adulthood, but inattention continues.[7] Also, you may be surprised to find a sense of self-restlessness and active avoidance of sedentary activities within yourself.[8] Some adults with ADHD experience failures in social, academic, or occupational pursuits adding to feelings of underachievement, frustration, disappointment, and disillusionment.[9] Understanding that ADHD is a neurobiological disorder and that you have options available to help you is important and assists you in counteracting these negative emotions. Though individuals with ADHD are a heterogeneous group with differing strengths and weaknesses, areas in which you might find a need for support (either through accommodations or assistance in increasing your skill level) are time management, memory, concentration, organizing and prioritizing, social skills, activity level, refraining from impulsive actions, multitasking, and paperwork. Each of these deficits can interfere with success in the workplace or in pursuit of a degree, but their impact can be lessened considerably in a supportive environment with adequate resources and reasonable accommodations, thus enhancing the probability of your success.[10]

The strengths of individuals with ADHD, such as the ability to function well in fast-paced, busy, and hectic environments[11] and to be highly creative, are often a good fit for certain vocations, with great benefit to the employer. In fact, some contend that individuals with ADHD can easily become workaholics.[12] Creating a supportive environment not only helps the employee in maximizing strengths and minimizing challenging areas, but assists the employer in decreasing the impact of ADHD on the return of the investment of the employer. The estimated cost of absenteeism and nonproductive attendance at work by individuals with ADHD is estimated to be a loss of $19.6 billion for employees with ADHD across the United States.[13]

The transition from high school to a university or to employment can be difficult for anyone. Typically, these environments require some degree of independence, involve less structured time (especially at colleges and universities), more distraction, greater responsibilities, and new social situations—all without the

From the Counselor

I have known many high school students with ADHD who made good grades and achieved academically without having to study much for exams. They simply learned the material during the class period. All excited about bright futures, these students entered the university world with high expectations, only to find that they lacked the necessary study skills to be successful in this more demanding environment. After a huge blow to the ego, many scrambled and found a tutor, or asked a friend to teach them to study, or visited their university's counseling center, where they asked for and received accommodations and training in study skills. This training allowed them to be quite successful in higher learning and to continue learning at an improved rate throughout life.

support of parents or teachers that was received in high school. In addition, young adults might not have the necessary coping strategies and may experience more task-interfering intrusive thoughts and more depressive symptoms. Accommodations, including instruction in coping strategies and other skills, are often needed to bridge the transition successfully.

You might be surprised to find that individuals with ADHD qualify for accommodations under the Americans with Disabilities Act (ADA, amended in 2008, and referred to as the ADAA) and that employers and institutes of higher education have a legal obligation to provide reasonable accommodations to individuals with ADHD.[14] Accommodations are designed to "level the playing field" between individuals with disabilities and those without, allowing qualifying individuals to pursue their goals without fear of being held back by disability-associated problems that are easily remedied by making reasonable changes in the work or educational environment. Appropriate accommodations should be beneficial to the individual with ADHD, allowing him or her to demonstrate knowledge and skills without the interference of an ultimately irrelevant impairment. People without expertise in this area often associate the ADA and most recently the ADAA with the mandate for employers, businesses, public transportation, or institutions of higher education to make accommodations only for individuals with physical disabilities and limited mobility, such as wheelchair ramps, restroom accommodations, or elevators. However, the ADA was originally written (and amended in 2008 to clarify its original purpose) to ensure that individuals with physical or *mental* impairments are not subjected to discriminatory practices, and that reasonable accommodations are provided to them to allow them to compete and succeed on equal grounds with their peers without disabilities. Different from modifications which change the content, accommodations are alterations of environment, format, or equipment to allow equal access.

The following sections contain a brief history and description of the Americans with Disabilities Act of 1990 (ADA) and the Americans with Disabilities Act Amendments of 2008 (ADAA). Next, we follow with practical descriptions of accommodations that might be appropriate for individuals with ADHD in the workplace, postsecondary educational environments, and high stakes testing, such as college entrance exams, graduate entrance exams, and licensing exams. An overview of requirements for psychological evaluations used to support the need for accommodations in high stakes testing is included, as this is the setting with the most frequently requested accommodations. Throughout the following sections, we will refer to "you" as the adult with ADHD. However, if you are reading this book to learn more about ADHD in your child, your spouse, or others, you can use the information to assist the individual in requesting ADA accommodations or learning coping strategies to use in the workplace or university settings.

Potential accommodations discussed in this chapter are those most frequently recommended or requested; however, accommodations should be selected based on individual needs and outcomes. Accommodations described here might be helpful to adults in postsecondary or workplace environments struggling with deficits associated with ADHD. The accommodations are logical and most are fairly inexpensive and can be requested from an employer or you can use the accommodations as coping strategies.

Research indicates that accommodations help to level the playing field so that these individuals may demonstrate their ability rather than their disability. As in all areas of science, future studies may shed light on how to tailor accommodations more specifically to each individual's needs. Because individuals with ADHD are a heterogeneous group, no "one size fits all" accommodation is available; accommodations should be selected based on the individual's strengths and weaknesses.

AMERICANS WITH DISABILITIES ACT (ADA)

What Are the ADA and the ADAA?

The ADA originally became a law in 1990. Three "titles" are included. Title 1 requires that private and public employers with 15 or more employees make reasonable accommodations for individuals with disabilities who ask for assistance. Title II applies to public entities, such as state and local governments (including state funded universities), and Title III addresses places of public accommodations (that is, anywhere the public is welcome). Title 1 and II are applicable to this chapter.

The purpose of the law is to prevent discrimination against persons with disabilities and provide **equal access** to housing, education, public transportation, recreation, health services, voting, and public services. Equal access means not just being allowed to be present. It means making accommodations that increase the likelihood of success when barriers are removed that impeded the individual with a disability from demonstrating and being judged on his or her abilities. Remember, barriers are not just physical features like stairs and curbs—they can be far more ethereal. For example, a college professor may give a pop quiz periodically to encourage students to keep up with their reading assignments. She makes the quizzes short, and so only allows 10 minutes for the students to complete the quiz. The purpose of the quiz is to demonstrate they have acquired adequate knowledge from the reading assignment. For nearly everyone, 10 minutes is a generous time allocation—but Andre, who has ADHD and whose primary symptom is his level of distractibility, needs 15 minutes to work through the quiz properly. This gives him no advantage over the others, but the failure to allow him these few extra minutes means the quiz is measuring not his knowledge of the assigned readings, but his level of distractibility in the classroom that day—which is unfair and subverts the intent of the exam. Allowing Andre these extra

An individual with a disability is defined by the ADA as a person who has a **physical or mental impairment** that **substantially limits one or more major life activities**, a person who has a **history or record of such an impairment**, or a person who is **perceived by others as having such an impairment**.

Figure 10.1. Definition of Individual with Disability According to ADA

minutes actually gives the professor a more accurate appraisal of Andre's knowledge of the assigned reading material.

One of the most important aspects of the ADA is the definition provided for "an individual with a disability" (see Figure 10.1). The clinical and legal definitions of a disability are different and the ADA does not provide a list of disabilities, such as the Individuals with Disabilities Education Improvement Act (IDEIA), but instead provides three specific criteria that must be met. Having a diagnosis of ADHD is the first step to receiving accommodations for ADHD. The ADA recognizes that an individual has a disability if the person (1) has a **physical or mental impairment** (2) that **substantially limits one or more major life activities**, (3) has a **history or record of such an impairment**, or is **perceived by others as having such an impairment**.

As the ADA was amended in 2008 to ensure that it does address mental as well as physical impairment, several of the core symptoms of ADHD create mental impairment that substantially limits one or more life activities. Two court cases address this issue. Brown v. Cox Medical Centers[15] and Gagliardo v. Connaught Laboratories, Inc.[16] found that "the ability to perform cognitive functions" and "concentrating and remembering (more generally cognitive function)" are major life activities.

The Americans with Disabilities Act Amendments in 2008 that are relevant to ADHD are (a) a change in the interpretation of disability and (b) definition of major life activities. In 1990, the law stated that if "mitigating measures" (for example, medication, hearing aids, and prosthetics) eliminated the impact of the disability on major life activities, then the individual did not qualify for protection. Therefore, if an individual was prescribed psychotropic medication that was effective in decreasing the core symptoms of ADHD, then the individual would not be protected. However, in the ADA amendments of 2008, this clause was removed and replaced. The amendment in 2008 states that the "determination of whether an impairment substantially limits a major life activity shall be made without regard to the ameliorative effects of mitigating measures." As stated by Representative George Miller from California to the House Education and Labor Committee in 2008, "an individual with an impairment that substantially limits a major life activity should not be penalized when seeking protection under the ADA simply because he or she managed their own adaptive strategies or received informal or undocumented accommodations that have the effect of lessening the deleterious impacts of their disability"[17] (transcript available on the Yale Center for Dyslexia and Creativity website at http://dyslexia.yale.edu /Policy_StarkComments.html).

In addition, the amendments of 2008 expanded the definition of major life activities to include caring for oneself, performing manual tasks, seeing, hearing, eating, sleeping, walking, standing, lifting, bending, speaking, breathing, **learning**, reading, **concentrating**, **thinking**, communicating, working, and the operation of a major bodily function," such as "the immune system, normal cell growth, digestive, bowel, bladder,

neurological, brain, respiratory, circulatory, endocrine, and reproductive functions."[18]

ACCOMMODATIONS

Requesting and Selecting Accommodations

The ADA mandates that accommodations are provided to individuals with disabilities, including in schools, on examinations, and in the workplace. The following section details potential accommodations for high stakes testing, and discusses helpful documentation to provide when requesting accommodations.

Questions to guide the selection of accommodations (for the workplace or higher education) are listed in Figure 10.2. First, define the limitations and the degree of impact on job or academic performance. Second, decide which specific work or academic tasks are impacted and how the impairment interferes. Third, brainstorm potential accommodations that would reduce or eliminate the problematic nature of that task. Fourth, decide

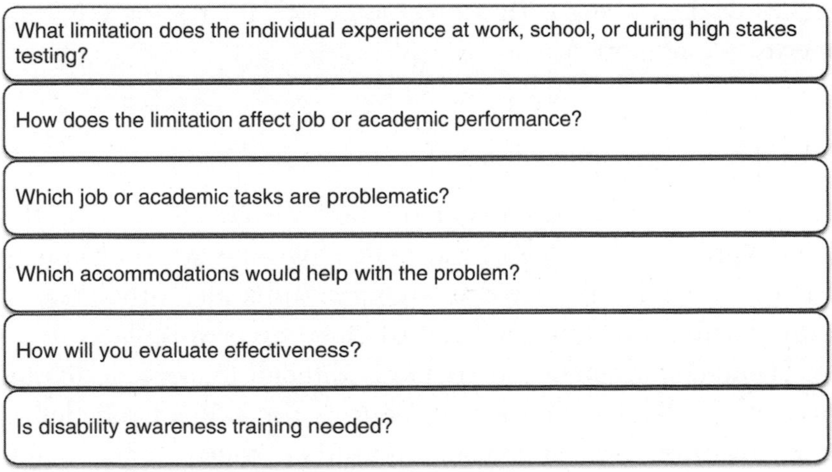

What limitation does the individual experience at work, school, or during high stakes testing?

How does the limitation affect job or academic performance?

Which job or academic tasks are problematic?

Which accommodations would help with the problem?

How will you evaluate effectiveness?

Is disability awareness training needed?

Figure 10.2. Questions to Select Accommodations

how and when you will determine whether the accommodation is beneficial to the student. Finally, after using the accommodation, determine if it is effective or if another accommodation might be more beneficial. In the workplace, if other employees are involved and might question the accommodations or have to work closely with the individual, it might be helpful to have training on disability awareness. The employee and employer would agree that this would be helpful prior to conducting the training.

The following sections include potential accommodations in the workplace, in higher education institutions, and on high stakes testing. As work environments vary widely from entirely outdoor jobs to indoor office jobs that require an individual to sit at a desk for extended periods of time, workplace accommodations are described in "areas of impairment," such as time management and memory problems that often interfere with production (see Figure 10.3). As higher education environments often have similar tasks, accommodations will be described in relation to tasks, such as studying and completing assignments. Specific requirements for requesting accommodation(s) on high stakes testing, along with accommodations for testing environments, are presented.

Workplace Accommodations

Requested specific accommodations are individualized to the person and the demands of the work environment. As you read each of the following accommodations, think about the areas of impairment being impacted and what fits your workplace.

Time management is particularly difficult for some individuals with ADHD. Time management is the skill of scheduling and organizing time (a valuable resource) efficiently to accomplish designated tasks and projects. Organizational strategies to increase the efficient use of time include creating a checklist of

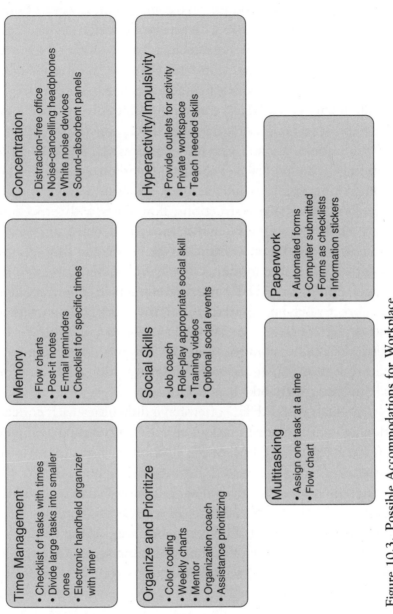

Figure 10.3. Possible Accommodations for Workplace

tasks and writing task due dates on a wall calendar. In addition, when the task is complete, the employee can place a check beside the task and thus self-monitor task completion. Large tasks can be divided into smaller tasks with separate due dates. During the day, a kitchen timer, a timer on an electronic handheld organizer, or a timer on a cell phone can be set to cue the individual to change tasks or to attend a scheduled meeting.

Individuals with ADHD often report difficulties with **memory** manifested at work as forgetting instructions, appointments, and other important items and activities. Prompts and cues are helpful to remind the individual to begin and complete specific tasks or attend specific activities and meetings. Prompts and cues can be in the form of written instructions, flowcharts with procedural steps, post it notes, e-mail reminders, or a checklist of items to be completed by the end of the day or at specific time periods during the day (in the morning, at the end of the workday). For example, Alison has ADHD and often forgets to submit required paperwork to her boss at the end of the week. Alison sets an alarm on her phone to go off on Friday two hours before the paperwork is to be submitted and her boss sets up an automatic e-mail that goes to Alison every Friday morning to remind her to submit the paperwork.

Individuals with ADHD often have difficulties with **concentration** at work. Concentration means maintaining complete attention over time. Concentration is often disrupted in work environments by noise-related distractions, such as office traffic, chatter between other employees, telephone calls, individuals "dropping by" the office, and noises from office equipment. In addition, with current technology, employees using computers might be distracted by e-mails or instant messages. Distractions can be reduced in several ways. In office environments, individuals with ADHD can be placed in a distraction-free office away from the typical noise. In other work environments, this might be more difficult, but every attempt can be made to reduce distractions naturally. In fact, we recently read where one adult with ADHD found that working from home on tasks that lend themselves to individual work was the most helpful accommodation.[19] When reducing distracting noises cannot naturally occur, the individual can wear noise-cancelling headphones, or sound-absorbent panels, or white noise devices can be used.

Visual distractions are sometimes a problem for individuals with ADHD. Again, these can be naturally avoided by working in a space that does not have a lot of visually distracting stimuli. Most important, the individual with ADHD must identify which stimuli are most distracting. For example, some individuals with ADHD are distracted by activities outside when the window is open and others might be distracted by workplace traffic.

Some jobs or positions require the individual to **multitask**. This is an area that is particularly individualized with ADHD. Some are excellent at multitasking and others absolutely cannot multi-task. For those with difficulties multitasking, employers can attempt to assign one task at a time. When this is not a possibility, assisting the individual in creating a flowchart of activities that are to be completed simultaneously could be beneficial. The flowchart could assist the individual in identifying tasks that are to be completed at the same time and those that are to be performed individually. When completing simultaneous tasks, most individuals with ADHD will need a thorough understanding of the expected performance standards, such as completion time and accuracy rates.

Some individuals with ADHD have trouble **organizing** and **prioritizing**, and helping adults with ADHD organize and prioritize in the workplace is often a needed accommodation. Organizational systems can include color coding and weekly charts with daily tasks. In addition, a mentor, organization coach, or professional organizer can assist in teaching the employee organizational skills. However, though teaching organizational skills can help, it is not always enough. Assistance is often needed to follow through with the organizational systems. In addition, supervisors can agree to prioritize tasks for the employee and only assign one project at a time instead of giving long lists.

Along the same lines as organization, individuals with ADHD often have problems **completing and submitting paperwork**. As mentioned several times in this book, doing boring, monotonous (but often necessary) tasks is not typically a strength of the individual with ADHD. Paperwork often falls into this category and requires organization to maintain any system for completion and submittal. A friend of ours with ADHD often proclaims that she is a "paper hoarder" because she has a filing cabinet full of papers in no specific order—and never discards of any of them. The reality is that she has organizational difficulties with paperwork.

To assist the individual with ADHD to accommodate for (or cope with) weaknesses in paperwork management, forms can be automated to create electronic files that can be completed on the computer and submitted. In addition, with secure data-encrypted systems, forms can be completed and stored on the Internet for easy retrieval by the next person. Possibly some information can be completed by someone else prior to the individual with ADHD using them, or preprinted stickers can be supplied for specific information. Forms can be created as checklists instead of requiring a lot of narrative writing. At the very least, the supervisor can assure that the individual with ADHD has a large quantity of the forms that are frequently used in an easy-to-access location.

On the one hand, **hyperactivity** and **impulsivity** may create difficulties for some adults with ADHD in some work environments. On the other hand, hyperactivity may actually help individuals be more productive in some fields. For example, for individuals in positions where they are required to sit through long meetings or work for long periods on monotonous tasks, hyperactivity would definitely interfere, whether the hyperactivity is manifested as actual body movement or rapid thoughts. But individuals working in fast-moving environments (for example, coaches, car wash attendants) might benefit from overactivity. Possible accommodations include teaching the individual skills to reduce impulsivity or hyperactivity, or providing outlets for activity. For instance, a job coach can be hired or the employer can provide frequent structured breaks to allow the individual to move around. In addition, if the activity level of the individual interferes with the work of others, he or she can be allowed to work from home or in a private work space.

Probably one of the most difficult areas of impairment to accommodate for in the workplace is a lack of **social skills**. Social skills are the skills needed to effectively interact with people and perform in group activities. Individuals with ADHD often demonstrate a deficit in social skill performance. The individual can tell you the appropriate social skill, but does not often demonstrates behaviors associated with the skill. For example, Aaron knows that interrupting others who are speaking in meetings is inappropriate, but he continues to interrupt. Some suggest that an appropriate accommodation would be a job coach to teach social cues, role-playing appropriate social skills with the employee, or training videos that model appropriate behavior in the workplace. One accommodation is to allow individuals to exercise choice in group project participation. Employers can provide individual tasks with minimal social requirements. Employers can also lead meetings and other work tasks with interactions in ways that maximize structure and prevent or minimize open-ended social interaction. We have addressed accommodations for eight potential areas of weakness demonstrated by individuals in the workplace. We must stress again that people with ADHD are all individuals demonstrating differing characteristics and degrees of impairment. The accommodations will differ widely across individuals; some can be used by the individual without assistance from the employer and others will

From the Counselor

It is important to help teenagers see that learning coping strategies for ADHD can improve the transition between high school and after high school. If a teenager believes ADHD is something related to school and something simply to outgrow, he or she might not take the opportunity to learn these compensatory strategies.

Many believe that going to work at a hands-on outdoor-type job without the requirements of sitting at a desk in a school building, completing boring assignments, and taking tests will make life simpler and help them feel more successful. However, this is not often true. For example, the same adolescent who had difficulty completing work and getting along with peers will often return to visit and report numerous job changes since high school. Ask them why and they'll tell you because they couldn't get along with their coworkers or boss and did not finish projects. Many accommodations might benefit these individuals—seeking out a job that requires much physical work is not the answer to employment issues for individuals with ADHD and such recommendations deny them the rights to apply for and be successful at the same jobs as their peers.

need to be requested formally through the ADA policies and procedures of the company. We encourage employers to be understanding and accommodate individuals as much as possible to maximize their potential in the workplace. This is simply a win-win situation for both the employee and the employer.

Higher Education Accommodations

Many of the accommodations that might be effective in the workplace are also appropriate for college and university students, and some additional tailored accommodations might be helpful. Although policies and procedures may vary widely across universities and colleges, they must adhere to the ADA and ADAA.[20] Many universities have an Office of Disability Support Services and this would be your starting point for accommodations. If your university does not have a designated disability office, then you could begin with admissions or the registrar to determine where you should report your disability or possibly the university student counseling center/service. Your university will have procedures for you to register as a student with a disability and request appropriate accommodations. The personnel in this office can tell you the documentation that you will need to proceed. Do not assume that just because you had accommodations in high school that you will qualify for accommodations at the university—some will accept this "transfer" and some will not. Accommodations in high schools fall within the scope of the IDEIA and in universities under the ADA and "rights" are not always transferred from one to the other. Also, if you are moving from an undergraduate school (where you had accommodations) to graduate school, you might have to provide additional documentation. Colleges or universities might request additional documentation that may require you to get further documentation of your diagnosis and the degree to which ADHD interferes with your major life activities. Be sure to ask specifically what should be in the report, as potentially each university requires different information and you will need to ensure that the professional writing the report includes all needed information. Along with other required information, the documentation that you present will need to specify accommodations that are directly related to the areas of impairment that you experience. If you received accommodations in high school or in your undergraduate school that were helpful, tell the professional (for example, the psychologist) that is documenting your disability.

Along with some of the accommodations that are mentioned in the previous section on workplace accommodations, we will discuss additional accommodations that might be of assistance

Exhibit 10.1: Possible Accommodations for Postsecondary Education Environments

In Class	Assignments and Studying	Exams
Note-taking assistance	Study skills instruction or assistance	Testing in nondistracting environments
Recorded lectures	Tutoring	Small-group exams
Guided notes	Audiotaped textbooks	Computerized tests
Printed notes	Written instructions from the professor	Break testing into multiple sessions
	Break long-term assignments into multiple components.	Extended time
	Extended time	Frequent breaks

in your pursuit of a college degree. However, we stress that the accommodations must be specific to your needs. Your clinician might request that you receive accommodations for courseload and registration, class, assignments and studying, and exams (see Exhibit 10.1). All of these are areas that have the potential to be impacted by symptoms of ADHD and related impairment.

Courseloads and Registration   Individuals with ADHD should give careful consideration to individual needs prior to registration. Priority registration can allow students to select classes that are most beneficial. When ADHD creates learning deficits, students might need to substitute classes that are a better fit for the student for courses typically included on the degree plan for the student's major course of study. Some individuals with

ADHD might benefit from a reduced courseload primarily during the freshman year when individuals are adjusting to having less support.

Class   Individuals with ADHD might have problems maintaining attention to lectures and avoiding distractions. Therefore, accommodations for class time are focused on the ultimate goal of the student attending to lectures and leaving class with all of the information that was presented in order to study and to complete assignments. To assist in focusing in class, some students benefit from front-row seating, avoiding distractions such as Internet access and cell phones, and sitting away from other students who demonstrate hyperactive behaviors, such as playing with pens, drumming on the table, and talking to other students.

Valuable accommodations to assist students in leaving class with all important information include note-taking assistance, audiotaped lectures, guided notes, and copies of the professor's own notes. In fact, with modern-day technology many professors provide copies of PowerPoint presentations, guided notes, and copies of their own notes on the Internet prior to the class to all students. This can be especially beneficial to individuals with ADHD.

Assignments, Studying, and Housing   Assignments and the amount and type of studying that is required to complete a degree are different from those in high school and students might experience much less support and should be encouraged to seek out any needed assistance. Individuals with ADHD often struggle with the transition and adapting to the different demands. Assignments are often complex and long term with a great quantity of assigned reading. Many class grades will simply be based on four or fewer tests, indicating that the amount of information and time between tests can be overwhelming.

If studying for exams is an area that is affected by ADHD, individuals can be enrolled in a study skills course or have a study coach or tutor to assist with studying. Academic coaching has some research support.[21] Coaching sessions can be peer or adult mediated and emphasize self-advocacy, time management, study skills, organizational skills, and planner use. In fact, many individuals actually accommodate themselves by finding a classmate or friend with whom to study. Strategies that teach the individual coping strategies are probably the most beneficial, as skills learned potentially can be generalized across a lifetime. Through academic coaching individuals can be taught self-awareness to identify areas of weakness, to self-manage organization and systematic approaches to tasks, to utilize calendars and agendas, and to study in an organized, clutter-free environment.

If maintaining attention while reading textbooks is a problem, the individual with ADHD might be assisted by texts that are audiorecorded. E-books on devices such as the Kindle and others can be read aloud by the device as well, enhancing access. Again, this is dependent on the individual. Some individuals are better able to focus on auditory information whereas others do not focus well when information is presented this way. For example, Brittany, a college freshman with ADHD, often finds her mind wandering to her plans for the evening when she is reading, but maintains attention when someone else reads the material aloud. Audio texts could be beneficial for Brittany. Kathy is the opposite. When attempting to listen to someone reading aloud, her mind wanders after about two minutes and thus audio texts are not helpful.

Some individuals with ADHD express difficulties with maintaining attention to all forms of studying due to housing issues. If the individual lives in a dormitory environment, finding a place to study that is conducive to maintaining attention is important. Some ask for separate housing arrangements where they do not have to share a room. This may or may not be beneficial to the student. Careful consideration to all of the positives and negatives of living alone is important. University officials might accommodate the student by carefully selecting a compatible roommate. A practical solution might be to find a quiet, nondistracting environment to study in, such as a library carrel or a designated study lounge.

Some individuals with ADHD have trouble with the long-term assignments which are very common at the university level. To accommodate this area of impairment, long-term assignments can be broken down into smaller assignments by the professor with written instructions provided for each "section" or short term component. The professor can thus monitor the student's progress by assigning due dates to each section, grading the completed work, and providing feedback on progress to the student. Students also can be taught to separate long-term assignments into multiple short-term assignments and monitor their own progress.

Many students with ADHD find that they procrastinate when long-term assignments are given. After all, it's not due for a month, right? The next thing the individual knows, it is the night before the due date and nothing has been done. Breaking the assignment down and helping the student determine the length of time that each section will reasonably take to complete is beneficial. Students can be taught to schedule time to work on

From the Counselor

I wonder about the benefit of living alone for young adults with ADHD. I understand the need for a distraction-free study environment. However, I have known many that have benefited from having a roommate. Roommates are often good sources of study skills instruction and can even be real-time social skills teachers. Social skills seem to be taught through living. Sharing a dorm room with another person might discourage disorganization and clutter as the roommate will ultimately express great frustration with the situation. The individuality of needs is evident here. Some might benefit from living alone and others might actually be harmed.

each section daily. Scheduling time and using calendar reminders (such as electronic calendars on computers and cell phones) will help the student complete each section and ultimately the entire assignment. Alarms can alert the student to begin working or to submit completed assignments.

Exams. Universities report that a majority of accommodations requested by individuals with ADHD are for exams. Extended time is the most common request. Research suggests that extended time may benefit other individuals without disabilities, but individuals with disabilities benefit to a greater degree than those without disabilities so that extended time is essential for those with some disabilities if they are to demonstrate their knowledge and ability.[22] As we have discussed, accommodations should be requested based on the benefit to the student. If extended time is beneficial to the student with ADHD then it should be requested. Frequent breaks are often combined with extended time, which increases effectiveness for some students. Also, accommodations provided for class and studying for exams will assist the student in performing well on the exam.

Distracting environments are not typically beneficial for individuals with ADHD, so one testing accommodation is a **distraction-free environment**. Students might request that exams be given in a separate classroom from the remainder of the class or with a small group. Many university classes have more than a hundred individuals enrolled, creating the opportunity for numerous distractions during testing situations, especially on the lengthy exams that are more common in college and university settings. If students have a difficult time maintaining focus on lengthy exams, an accommodation can be requested to take the exam at **multiple times** or to have **more frequent testing with smaller amounts of material**. In addition, if the individual has a specific learning disability, a common comorbid condition for students with ADHD, additional accommodations should reflect the needs associated with that comorbid condition.

High Stakes Testing Accommodations

Many individuals with ADHD request accommodations on high stakes tests or assessments. High stakes tests refer to tests that have significant consequences for the individual or others such as high school graduation exams, college and graduate school entrance exams (for example, Scholastic Assessment Test, Medical College Admissions Test, Graduate Record Exam, Law School Admissions Test), and licensing exams (such as for medicine and law).[23] High stakes assessments often demand fluent (accurate and rapid) reading and sustained attention for long periods of time under stressful circumstances. In 1999, the American Council for Education noted an increase in requests for accommodations for college entrance exams. Accommodations are not intended to modify or change the content that is measured, only to provide an alteration of environment, format, or equipment that assures that the exam truly measures what it is supposed to measure. For example, if Eddy is taking a high school graduation exam that typically takes four hours to complete, but he has ADHD and can only focus for two hours at a time, then without accommodations to address his impairment in concentration, the test might be measuring Eddy's ability to focus rather than the knowledge learned. The accommodation then makes the test a more valid assessment of what was intended, which is an outcome that should be desired by all—the makers of the test, the consumers of the results, and the test taker.

In the next section, we will provide a description of typical documentation requirements. Criteria have been established for each particular exam to assure that individuals are provided the appropriate accommodations and that the individual meets the

---

Exhibit 10.2: Sample Websites for ADA Information

Job Accommodation Network	http://askjan.org/ Search accommodations, access help, find resources
American with Disabilities Act	http://www.ada.gov/ Standards and information; regulations and assistance
United States Medical Licensing	http://www.act.org/aap/disab/policy.html Examination link to test accommodations
Florida Department of Law Enforcement Special Accommodations Manual	http://www.fdle.state.fl.us/Content /getdoc/f7422824–6085–4271 -a567–8f8e5ca2eba3/Special -Accommodations-Manual.aspx Accommodations for state law enforcement exam

---

definition of an individual with a disability according to ADA requirements. Sample websites are provided in Exhibit 10.2 that will provide some information regarding the requirements for some exams; however, as websites change with time and might be outdated and more information is available, you should contact the testing agency prior to requesting accommodations to assure that your documentation provides all of the required information.

Evaluation Reports Evaluation reports written by clinical psychologists, school and educational psychologists, and neuropsychologists provide a foundation of evidence to support that accommodations on high stakes exams are needed. When selecting a clinician to complete a required evaluation, you should consult with potential clinicians to assure expertise in ADA documentation.

Typically evaluation reports must include a diagnosis of ADHD, documentation and evidence of impairment, and recommendations for accommodations. Documentation is needed to support a **diagnosis of ADHD** with evidence that the individual demonstrates each diagnostic criterion. The clinician will establish that from prior to the age of 7 until the present, the individual demonstrated behavior that was developmentally different from peers and created impairment in major life activities. The clinician will complete a comprehensive diagnostic interview with the individual, but, if available, will also evaluate objective historical data (that is, documents from the past). You should provide evidence from your prior academic experiences. For example, if available, your previous report cards, transcripts, prior psychological or educational evaluation reports, prior standardized test reports, evidence of prior educational accommodations, and teacher comments are evidence that you demonstrated behaviors associated with ADHD at a young age that continue to create impairment in your daily functioning.

Though a narrative summary is needed, it is not sufficient. In the report, the clinician will need to document the types of information that were evaluated along with results from the interview and standardized scores on any testing that was completed. Rating scales completed by someone who knows you well or has supervised you are important. For instance, the clinician might ask your parents, spouse, coworkers, roommates, supervisors, teachers, or professors to complete a multidimensional or ADHD rating scale.

The clinician might **rule out alternative explanations** for the symptoms. Other possible reasons for behaviors associated with ADHD are other mental health disorders (such as a mood disorder or anxiety disorder) or physical injuries or illnesses (for example, head injuries or thyroid problems). Documentation in the report can include evidence that the clinician considered all other possible explanations and ruled them out.

In line with diagnostic criteria for ADHD, the clinician will provide evidence that the **magnitude of impairment** meets diagnostic cut points for ADHD. To provide evidence of impairment, the clinician will demonstrate that some impairment from inattention, impulsivity, or hyperactivity was present prior to age seven and that clinically significant impairment in social, academic, or occupational functioning is present in two or more settings.[24] World life experiences will supplement standardized evaluations given by the clinician. For example, in addition to the previously mentioned evidence you could provide the clinician with performance evaluations from jobs, military records, and narrative descriptions of your behavior from parents, spouses, teachers and professors, friends, roommates, coworkers, and supervisors.

Recommended accommodations are derived from the evaluation, including the documentation gathered. The clinician will provide **a rationale and purpose** of each requested accommodation based on the evaluation results. Drawing a direct connection between the areas of impairment and the accommodations is beneficial. For example, the clinician might recommend small-group testing if evidence from previous testing experiences demonstrates clearly that small group testing was needed to assure equal access on the exam. In most ways, psychologists who conduct comprehensive diagnostic assessments do these things routinely and according to professional standards that govern the reporting of the results of a psychological examination; however, there do remain some areas that are more specific or helpful in obtaining the needed accommodations, and that is why we recommend using a psychologist who does such "disability" or accommodation exams regularly.

Potential Testing Accommodations. The most commonly requested accommodations are extended time and tests read aloud.[25] As previously mentioned, research on extended time has found that extended time can be beneficial to many students, but is more beneficial to students with disabilities than to those without. In 2007, 2% of people who took the SAT were given extended time.[26] Contacting the disability office of the testing agency is a logical first step in obtaining the accommodations you need to be successful in demonstrating your knowledge and skills. If distractibility is a clear area of impairment, then **small-group or individual administration** might be beneficial.

Some individuals with ADHD find benefit in taking **computer-administered tests** instead of paper-based tests; however, students reported that the benefit was more in the environment than in the presentation.[27] For example, computer-based tests are often given in secluded settings, such as study carrels, whereas paper-based tests are administered to large groups of individuals in open spaces, with others close enough to distract.

TO SUM UP

In this chapter, we have provided a brief description of the Americans with Disabilities Act (ADA) in relation to accommodations for ADHD in the workplace, higher education, and high stakes testing. We encourage you to use some of the accommodations discussed as coping strategies and to request needed accommodations. Asking for assistance in the workplace or from your professors at the university is a personal choice. However, accommodations are available to you through protections provided by the ADAA. When accommodations are needed, there is no reason to be ashamed or embarrassed. Knowing and advocating for your rights when appropriate will assist you in finding success throughout your lifetime. The people and lawmakers of the United States and some other countries have determined that you should not be held back in any aspect of your life by any disability imposed by ADHD when a reasonable accommodation or change to the environment, rules, or time lines can allow you to demonstrate your ability and not your disability. To us, this seems only fair, but it is up to you to ask for what you need.

CONCLUSION

Knowledge Is Power

ADHD is real. Our goal in writing this book was to share as much of our relevant knowledge as possible within the constraints of a book that is appropriate for a nonmedical audience and easily accessible to you, a person with ADHD, or a person working with, living with, or loving someone who has ADHD. We shared information with you that will allow you or someone you care about with ADHD to maximize personal strengths and cope with the associated difficulties and, in some cases, the disabilities that ADHD can present. We addressed many of the myths and fallacies straight on; we told you the positive characteristics and strengths often associated with ADHD; we discussed interventions and strategies that work and those that do not; we covered the problems encountered and created by persons with ADHD; we shared stories from our experiences as counselors and teachers and from the point of view of a neuroscientist. We told you the truth, and we told you where facts have yet to be discovered. One of our key aims in writing this book is to empower you to deal directly with ADHD if you have it; directly with loved ones, if they have it; and directly with the medical establishment, schools, vocational agencies, and employers. We hope to empower you with the knowledge to make decisions, requests, and evaluate options far more effectively than is possible without the information in this book. Now it is up to you.

As you embark on your journey with ADHD, however it presents in your life, we encourage you to use and apply the information shared in these pages. Armed with this knowledge, you will not fall prey to myths and inaccurate information or to the quackery of instant cures, simple diets, supplements, or other magic bullets, nor should you fear discussions with your physician about whether or not medication is right for your situation. You can focus on strengths while working to address challenges.

This book has shown you that ADHD is more than just the core symptoms of impulsivity, inattention, and hyperactivity. Although these are the basic diagnostic criteria, in this book you read about other conditions often experienced by those with ADHD, such as depression and anxiety, and about areas of functional impairment associated with ADHD, such as learning and social skills deficits. You read about ADHD's impact on families, friendships, and other relationships. You have learned that medication is one option for treatment, but that a multimodal approach is known to be most effective—while medication has a role to play in many cases, it should never be the only form of treatment or intervention. Understanding how medication works on the ADHD brain will help you make informed decisions. Remember that if you decide that medication will be beneficial also, select and use the nonmedical interventions and strategies that we described to assist in the home, school, and workplace.

If you are a parent of a child with ADHD, you read about how to interact positively with your child, how to establish behavioral expectations, and how to respond when your child does or does not follow those expectations. We stressed the importance of monitoring your child's behavior and medication.

If you are an adult with ADHD, you learned how ADHD might interfere with your activities at work or in learning environments, and about strategies to help you overcome those challenges.

Whatever your role, if you have difficulty following the procedures, consider finding a professional with expertise in ADHD who can provide guidance. Advocate for your child or yourself at work or school by using the information in the chapters about Section 504, ADA, and IDEIA, but remember to consider yourself a collaborative team player and to use the strategies to teach and learn new and effective coping skills.

As we have noted, ADHD is not new, but new knowledge is being uncovered by research every day. We urge you to stay up-to-date on the latest ADHD research and to keep reading, learning, and growing with ADHD. We wish you our best with your journey and hope the information in this book has helped you along the way.

PART FOUR

Appendixes

APPENDIX A

How Positive Behavioral Intervention and Support (PBIS) Helps at School

Positive behavioral intervention and support (PBIS) is a process (we often refer to it as a "model") and a school-reform movement that started with creating school environments that encourage and teach positive behavior to children with severe disabilities and challenging behavior. As a parent, you might recognize PBIS as the disciplinary approach taken by your child's school. If so, you will notice that emphasis is placed on positive consequences (reinforcement) for appropriate behavior. Originally the work of Horner, Sugai, and others at the University of Oregon, the past two decades have seen widespread implementation and designation of a national center.[1] The National Center on Positive Behavioral Interventions and Supports is funded by the U.S. Department of Education Office of Special Education Programs (OSEP) in collaboration with the Office of Safe and Drug Free Schools, even though PBIS is considered a general education initiative. The purpose of the center is to make sure that schools, families, and communities are aware of PBIS and the center conducts research to demonstrate that PBIS is effective and feasible for implementation in schools.

The PBIS (sometimes called PBS) framework is now widely used in schools to support any and all students with behavioral challenges, including those with ADHD. PBIS focuses on understanding how the school environment, teacher practices, and student skills interact to increase or decrease student behavior problems. If your child with ADHD attends a school that has a PBIS system, you will notice that school staff address your child's behaviors in a positive, preventative, or proactive manner by teaching appropriate behavior rather than punishing inappropriate behavior a majority of the time—if this is not the case at your school, the model is not being followed or implemented properly. Also, you should notice a focus on ensuring that every reasonable attempt is made for the primary disciplinary action to be something other than removing your child from the learning environment. You will see students being assigned to in-and out-of-school suspension, which is used rarely and only for severe behavior. PBIS supports inclusive environments and least restrictive settings. PBIS is behavioral in orientation. As discussed in Chapter Five, one basic premise of a behavioral orientation includes a "function" (the purpose) of behavior (that is, all behavior serves a purpose, serves to communicate what the student does not have the words to explain, or both). Students behave in certain ways to get something or to escape something.

The PBIS model is multitiered and often illustrated on a triangle with three tiers or layers. All of the students in a school fit somewhere within the "tiers," as each tier represents a percentage of the student population. This "triangle" (See Figure A.1) was first used in medicine and health services. Primary prevention (the first tier) would be for the largest segment of the population and is at the broad base of the triangle, targeted or secondary prevention (the second tier) would address a smaller segment of the population and is further up the triangle as it narrows toward its point, and tertiary (the third tier) is for the smallest segment of the student population and is closest to the tip of the triangle. Primary prevention serves to "prevent" prob-

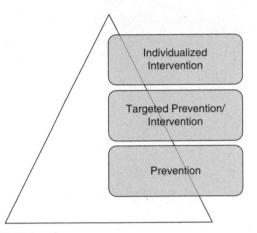

Figure A.1. PBS Triangle

lems from occurring, secondary to lessen the problem and keep it from becoming chronic, and tertiary serves to manage a chronic condition.

PBIS schools have many benefits, especially for students with behavior challenges, such as ADHD. Research indicates that PBIS increases positive behavior in both individual students and throughout the entire school. If you are in a school when PBIS is initially implemented, you will notice many changes to the "climate" of the school, both in terms of the physical environment and the actions of staff and students. Physically you will notice that positive sayings and posters appear in prominent areas such as "Respect yourself and others" and "All students at Homewood Elementary are stars." Expectations are posted in all areas including classrooms, halls, and cafeterias. We will talk more about schoolwide expectations in this chapter. In addition, PBIS makes school environments safer for students. Within the last several decades, after several highly publicized school shootings, communities have become increasingly concerned about the safety of schools. The immediate reaction to the violent actions was to become more punitive and initiate zero tolerance policies. However, educators quickly learned that

From the Neuroscientist

Zero tolerance policies have become popular in many school systems across the United States. Zero tolerance refers to a school or district policy mandating predetermined consequences for various student rule violations that removes any discretion surrounding punishment or other handling of rule violations from teachers and administrators. These policies have become quite controversial. It is essentially a one-size-fits-all approach to rule breaking and punishment that ignores students' intents and circumstances. The concept of "zero tolerance" was introduced as policy by the Drug Enforcement Administration (DEA)[2] as part of the so-called war on drugs, but was ultimately abandoned by the DEA as an unworkable, inappropriate model for law enforcement—and yet such policies proliferated in the public schools. In 2005, the American Psychological Association (APA), as part of its mission to advance health, education, and human welfare, commissioned and funded a special Zero Tolerance Task Force to examine the evidence concerning the effects of zero tolerance policies in the nation's schools, and appointed one of the authors of this book as its chair (CRR). The task force examined the assumptions that underlie zero tolerance policies and all data relevant to testing those assumptions in practice. The Zero Tolerance Task Force examined research pertaining to the effects of zero tolerance policies with respect to child development, the relationship between education and the juvenile justice system, and the effects on students, families, and communities. In an official report of the Task Force, based upon a great deal of research, which has now become a policy document of the APA, the task force concluded, among other findings: "A key assumption of zero tolerance policy is that the removal of disruptive students will result in a safer climate for others. Although the assumption is strongly intuitive, data on a number of indicators of school climate have shown the opposite effect, that is, that schools with higher rates of school suspension and expulsion appear to have less satisfactory ratings of school climate, less satisfactory school governance structures, and to spend a disproportionate amount of time on disciplinary matters. Perhaps more importantly, recent research indicates a negative relationship between the use of school suspension and expulsion and school-wide academic achievement, even when controlling for demographics such as socioeconomic status. Although such findings do not demonstrate a cause-and-effect, it becomes difficult to argue that zero tolerance creates more positive school climates when its use is associated with more negative achievement outcomes."[3] The task force went on to state that students with disabilities, including ADHD, are more likely to suffer suspensions and other harsh discipline in schools with zero tolerance policies. Zero tolerance policies were found not to be a deterrent to future behavior problems and created a school climate that was less conducive to learning. Zero tolerance policies are not the answer to maintaining good deportment in schools (or elsewhere, for that matter); rather, the answer is clear thinking, the application of common sense to disciplinary matters, and the use of positive behavioral approaches (see http://www.apa.org/releases/ZTTFReportBODR evisions5–15.pdf, p. 6). The entire 142-page report (it does contain an executive summary!) on zero tolerance policies may be viewed and downloaded at the URL given here. In our personal experience, zero tolerance policies are especially detrimental to students with ADHD.

zero tolerance frequently was not the right answer. In fact, most zero tolerance policies are ultimately harmful to the school climate and do not create safer or more positive learning environments (see sidebar).

The PBIS movement, however, has much to offer and has increased school safety.[4] Along with safety, research indicates that preventing problem behaviors at the school level decreases the number of office referrals that teachers write and the amount of time that students are removed from the learning environment.[5] Thus, the amount of learning that occurs in schools is increased when teacher time spent on discipline decreases and the climate becomes more positive. In PBIS schools, students are more engaged in learning, and much research has demonstrated across many cultures that the best predictor of student achievement is the actual amount of time spent on task, engaged in learning activities in the classroom. Within the PBIS system, students are taught appropriate behavior that might have a lifelong impact on their functioning.

In this appendix, we will discuss PBIS as a process to assist your child with problem behaviors associated with ADHD. The majority of this appendix will discuss how to ensure that the school environment in which your student is educated operates in a manner consistent with PBIS or a multitier model in order to keep ADHD problem behaviors in tier 1 rather than escalating into tier 2 or even tier 3. We emphasize that ADHD is a brain-based disorder that cannot be eliminated, only managed. Some of your child's behaviors are directly related to his symptoms of ADHD; however, some of his behaviors are learned and can be managed with tier 1 or 2 interventions. Learned maladaptive behaviors can be replaced with more positive or prosocial behaviors. In the past, your child may have received numerous office discipline referrals. You may have heard your child express feelings that all of his interactions with teachers are negative. If your child is in a PBIS school our hope, and the goal of the school, is for your child to learn adaptive behaviors to cope with the impairment associated with ADHD, receive fewer discipline referrals, and feel more positive about school. To achieve these goals, PBIS has multiple components including: PBIS tiers, progress monitoring, and problem-solving and decision-making procedures.

PBIS COMPONENTS

PBIS has several important components. In this section, we will tell you about the three tiers within PBIS, the importance of monitoring student progress, decision making, and PBIS teams.

PBIS Tiers

Within the PBIS process, the degree of risk for problem behavior or severity of problem behavior falls into what is called tier 1, 2, or 3 (see Figure A.1). We refer to the "degree of risk," as all children are at risk for developing problem behaviors. Some do and some do not, depending on various factors. This degree of risk determines which tier (and amount of support) the student would need. These tiers indicate both the level of problem and the degree of supports. Children at tier 1 often demonstrate minor problem behaviors and thus only require minimal support, and of course all children will at some time exhibit some form of emotional or behavioral upset; it is a matter of the normal course of development. On the other hand, children at tier 3 demonstrate a great deal of problem behaviors, receive multiple office referrals, and require tremendous support.

Prevention: Tier 1 As mentioned earlier, PBIS is intended to prevent problem behaviors altogether or from getting worse; thus, prevention on a PBIS campus has a few basic premises beginning with tier 1. You should, as a parent, be well aware of whether or not your school is engaged in these practices. A school campus would have very clear schoolwide expectations (this is synonymous with what we used to call school rules). Schoolwide expectations (SWE) are different from a discipline or code of conduct. SWE are positively stated behaviors in which students should engage in order to get along and do well in school. Some common SWEs are things like "Be Prepared" or "Show Respect." A school should be actively teaching and reinforcing these prosocial behaviors. Many schools will have assemblies, posters (see Figure A.2 for an example), and token reinforcement systems in widespread use. It is estimated and generally supported in research that approximately 80 to 85% of the population in a school will respond well to tier 1 behavior

Figure A.2. Example Poster of Schoolwide Expectations for the Bobcat School

Ask a teacher or student about schoolwide expectations—they should be able to recite them to you.

Look for visuals about expectations on walls in classrooms and hallways, cafeterias, bathrooms, and common areas.

Ask a teacher about how often students are "caught being good" and reinforced for performing how they ought to.

Figure A.3. Want to Check If Your School Is a PBS School?

management and require little else to be on task and perform within normal limits of student behavior.[6]

You can check to see if your child's school is a PBIS school by answering the questions in Figure A.3. Answers to these questions should be evident and obvious. The language used in PBIS reform is relatively standardized. Want to see PBIS started on your campus? Ask an administrator about starting a team that involves teachers, parents, and administrators to develop universal expectations, or get in touch with your state or the national center (http://www.pbis.org). The research and our experiences are unequivocally clear. When teachers are consistent with expectations and teach and reinforce appropriate behaviors on campus across classrooms and settings, students will perform better academically and socially and office discipline referrals will go down.

Secondary: Tier 2 Many schools screen students for social, emotional, and behavioral problems to identify students who may need additional help in these areas. This type of screening is similar philosophically to the vision and hearing screenings that happen annually in elementary schools, the physical screening for curvature of the spine/scoliosis in grade 5 or 6, or the reading and math screenings that target students who need additional help. Some schools use office discipline referrals to identify students with social, emotional, or behavioral problems through PBIS team meetings, but we find that the use of teacher referrals (through discipline referrals or teacher requests for assistance) misses students who may not demonstrate severe or chronic discipline problems, but who still need more behavioral support. A universal screener, such as a rating scale completed by the parents or teachers that detects elevated risk for social, emotional, and behavioral problems, is our preferred choice to accurately identify students who would fit in a tier 2 level of need.

Students at tier 2 are those who do not respond initially to the universal practices of having positive behavioral expectations throughout the school and reinforcing the behaviors associated with those expectations. Students identified as at risk or already in tier 2 may need a little bit more. If your child is identified for tier 2, do not be surprised. Behaviors demonstrated by children with ADHD often require more behavioral support than is provided to other students. There are common interventions at tier 2[7] and many are described in Chapter Six. Some typical interventions at tier 2 may include contingency plans, differential reinforcement of incompatible or alternative behavior, daily behavior report cards (DBRC); check in–check out[8] token economies, self-management, or the teaching of replacement skills.

A contingency plan is a technique to provide reinforcement for specific behaviors. With a contingency management plan, your child will know what behavior is expected of him and what reinforcement the teacher will provide (what he will "earn") when he demonstrates that behavior. For example when your child turns in homework, he might lead the class to lunch.

Differential reinforcement of incompatible (DRI) behavior is when a child receives reinforcement for demonstrating an appropriate behavior that cannot be done at the same time as the replacement behavior. For example, if your child frequently taps his pencil on the desk, distracting other students, the teacher might provide reinforcement when he puts his pencil inside his desk. Your child could not tap the pencil on the desk if it were inside the desk. Differential reinforcement of alternative (DRA) behavior is reinforcing a behavior that is an alternative for the maladaptive behavior. For example, if your child frequently gets out of his seat, his teacher could provide a reinforcer when your child is working on an assignment. Working on his assignment would be an alternative for walking around the classroom.

DBRC are effective techniques for changing behavior and increasing collaboration between yourself and the school. Your child will bring home a "behavioral report" on a daily basis and you can provide the reinforcer for appropriate behavior. For more information about DBRC, see Chapter Six. If your child has a DBRC, be sure to collaborate with the teacher to determine what ratings your child must achieve daily to receive the reinforcement.

Check in–check out (CICO) is another very common intervention at tier 2 intervention that is used in many schools. The child is involved in the CICO intervention and meets to "check in" and "check out." Checking in involves a review of goals and verbal encouragement. Checking out involves a review of performance and sometimes an opportunity to debrief when things go wrong or to practice new skills. The adult doing the checking is usually a homeroom teacher or a counselor. Sometimes this person is also doing the ratings. For example if your child has multiple teachers throughout the day, then he might check in at the beginning and end of class with each teacher. The teacher will rate your child's performance on following schoolwide expectations during that time period.

Token economies, another common tier 2 intervention, are systematic plans for reinforcing appropriate behavior. Typically, students receive tokens for appropriate behavior and then exchange the tokens for a larger reinforcer. Further information on token economies is included in Chapters Five and Six.

Self-management is a technique in which your child will develop a goal with the teacher and then rate his own behavior on that goal. In addition, your child might be taught replacement skills along with any of these techniques. Replacement skills are appropriate behaviors or sets of behaviors that replace inappropriate behavior. For example, Jaime, a 16-year-old with ADHD, typically interrupts the teacher by blurting out questions or answers, and sometimes random thoughts. Jaime is taught to write down these thoughts and questions for discussion at the end of the lecture. This way Jaime is not expected to "do nothing"; rather, he can channel the energy into something productive and appropriate.

Tier 2 is not special education; there are no legal provisions for supports at this level or any state or federal guidelines for developing or implementing programs. In fact, your school may not yet be implementing these types of supports. If they are, and if your child is a participant, we encourage you to join forces with the school in communication, training, and consistent delivery of any home programs. If your school does not currently have a PBIS system, we encourage you to talk to the principal about developing one. Catching a student early on, before problems become significant, is one way to prevent problems from becoming worse. Identification is not enough to ameliorate risk, however, and families can really help schools make a difference in the behavior and academic support of students.

Ask what programs the school is using. Parent training is a viable option at tier 2 and one that would be very beneficial to you as a parent. Ask about parent training either through the school or in the community. Sometimes schools will help you locate resources. Ask for specifics about where and when problems are occurring, and what skills you might be able to teach and reinforce at home. Ask if there are teachers willing to communicate daily with you by rating student behavior and sending home the rating for your signature, or check with a counselor or other front office person who might touch base each day with your child about the school's rules as a reminder for a good day. If you decide to do any of these programs, keeping track of the information about how your child is doing makes for great documentation with your physician and can help inform decisions about the use and effectiveness of medication or other treatment programs. Let's discuss data and progress monitoring.

Progress Monitoring (PM)   Your child's behavior will be monitored at tier 2. Progress monitoring in school settings is a process where teachers or other professionals keep track of how a student is doing, record it, and then graph it. For example, Lauren may need PM of her attention during instruction or Denise may need PM of impulsivity during recess. John might require PM for turning in assignments. The behavior being monitored can be just about anything you and or a teacher feel your child needs to work on. Sometimes progress monitoring occurs with a normed instrument, so that scores are standardized and can be compared to a larger population. Nationally normed and standardized progress monitoring has much to offer in the context of PBIS or multitier service delivery models. For example, the Behavior Assessment System for Children-2 Progress Monitor (BASC-2 PM)[9] is a way to monitor student progress easily after interventions have been implemented. One of the benefits of using standardized PM instruments is the ability to evaluate a broad range of students on their progress; some have software report systems to simplify the process, and some are written in multiple languages.

Using a standardized progress monitor, such as the BASC-2 PM, specific domains of behaviors can be monitored especially those relevant to individuals with ADHD, such as externalizing and ADHD problems, internalizing problems, social withdrawal, and adaptive skills. Multirater reports (behavior is rated by more than one person such as the teacher and the parent, or by multiple teachers) and progress reports ensure that behavior is monitored across settings. In addition to comparing the progress of the individual's behavior to his own behavior, the individual's behavior can be compared to a nationally representative sample of individuals his or her own age.

Progress monitoring also may occur periodically throughout the school year, such as in September, December, and March. Some behavior that is progress monitored may be subject to daily observation and recording or even multiple times per day. We will use some examples here to illustrate how progress monitoring might work at the daily progress monitoring level.

PM comes from our understanding that data-based decision making is more ideal than decisions based on hunches or guesses or even memory. Our first example is Lauren, whose teachers are

	100–75% Attention	75–50% Attention	50–25% Attention	25–0% Attention
Language Arts	✓			
Math		✓		
Science		✓		

Lauren

Figure A.4. Sample 1 Progress-Monitoring Form

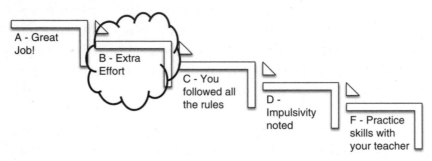

Figure A.5. Sample 2 Progress-Monitoring Form

monitoring her progress on paying attention during instruction. Lauren's teacher rates her at the end of language arts, math, and science using a "percentage of time" scale for how well Lauren is paying attention (see Figure A.4).

Lauren's teacher completes a progress monitoring form every day. At the end of the day, the teacher gives the form to Lauren to take home. In this example, the PM form becomes a home-to-school note to communicate progress. Lauren's mom can use this to praise Lauren when she gets off the bus or even to let her earn time on the iPad.

Our example for Denise was PM for impulsivity during recess. At the school she attends, Denise's recess is supervised by two on-duty teachers who rotate the supervision responsibility. Denise's primary teacher created the form in Figure A.5. Denise checks in with the on-duty teacher every day before recess, tells the teacher her goal for working on impulsivity, and then the teacher keeps the form. At the end of recess she gives Denise a "grade" by circling a letter on the form representing how she performed and Denise takes the form back to her teacher. When Denise gets an A or a B at recess she receives a high-five from the teacher; when Denise earns a C the teacher simply acknowledges the form and says, "Thank you." Earning a D or an F means that later that afternoon Denise's teacher will talk to her about what went wrong on the playground and help her develop a plan to earn an A or B the next day. If Denise continues to make D's or F's then the plan is revisited and changed. There is no punishment for impulsivity, but there is teacher attention for self-management and good performance.

After Denise gets her score at recess her teacher inputs the grade into an Excel spreadsheet on her computer. On Fridays, Denise is allowed to print out her progress, and when she has a good week, a trip to the principal's secretary is a special treat. Setting up an Excel spreadsheet is easy for progress monitoring and doing so makes graphing easy. The steps are in Exhibit A.1. Copy this figure to give to a teacher if you think it would help.

John, who does not turn in homework, was our third example. All of John's teachers at his junior high school are monitoring his progress on homework completion. John is old enough to take responsibility for his homework and the use of a progress monitor helps John have a routine that never changes, because even if there is no homework due, he is still checking in about homework. On the days he has homework due, the progress monitoring form prompts him to remember. John's parents are very busy with twins, but John knows that if he wants to play Xbox in the evening he has to show his homework monitor. Every day that he brings home the form with all the necessary signatures he gets access to his Xbox. John's form looks like Figure A.6.

Progress-monitoring data are useful for teachers, parents, and individuals for decision making. Charting and graphing these

Exhibit A.1: PM and Graphing in Excel

1. Open Microsoft Excel and save a file as a class name like "reading" or name it by year. Then use the tabs for individual student names. Change "sheet 1" to a student name, such as "Denise."

42	
43	
44	
45	
46	

Denise / Lauren / Sheet3

Ready

2. Enter dates across the top row.

	A	B	C	D	E	F	G	H
1	RECESS		19-May	20-May	21-May	22-Feb	23-May	
2								
3								

3. Enter data in a row.

	A	B	C	D	E	F	G
1			19-May	20-May	21-May	22-Feb	23-May
2							
3	Recess		C	D	C	B	A
4							

4. To graph the data, highlight across all the relevant rows. Anything you highlight will show up in the graph. Go to the "insert tab" and you will have options for a variety of charts. Select "Line."

If you were progress monitoring more than one behavior, your graph would show them all as different colored lines. Notice that we changed the letter grades to number values: A = 4, B = 3, C = 2 and so on.

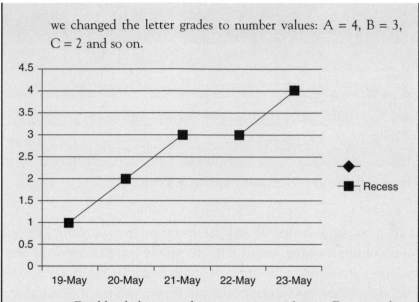

Double-click on anything you want to change. For example, if you want to change the X-axis to show that 1 is the lowest value and 4 is the highest value, you need to change the default axis, which will always give you values below and above your range. Double-click it to go to a screen to enter your own values. Here we did 1 and 4. If you want to change the lines or anything else, just double-click there as well.

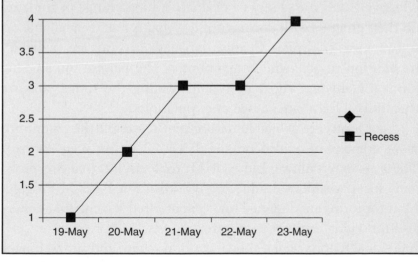

JOHN–HOMEWORK TRACKER				
	Monday	Tuesday	Wednesday	Thursday	Friday
Science	DAS	DAS	DAS	DAS	
Orchestra	Bob	Bob	Bob	Bob	
Social Studies	CRD	CRD		CRD	
Math		Payne	Payne	Payne	
Specials		Ja	Ja	Ja	
Language Arts	LV	LV	LV	LV	

Figure A.6. Sample 3 Progress-Monitoring Form

data provide a strong visual presentation for viewing current levels of functioning, making it easy to see improvement or degradation in skills. This type of data is useful for determining effects of medicine or classroom practices, and even home management and parenting practices.

Nationally normed and standardized progress monitoring also has much to offer in the context of PBIS or multitier service delivery models. For example, the BASC-2 PM is a way to easily monitor student progress after interventions have been implemented. Benefits include the simplicity to track progress effectively and the ability to evaluate a broad range of students on their progress with documentation that is readily available on software report systems. Spanish-language versions are available, in addition to an audio component of the parent and student forms for anyone who has trouble reading the forms, making them useful for a large range of populations.

Four forms are available for use that represent the composite score domains provided on the BASC-2 rating scale forms.[10] These are externalizing and ADHD problems, internalizing problems, social withdrawal, and adaptive skills. The BASC-2 Progress Monitor forms are designed for computerized scoring that generates individual reports, multirater reports, and progress reports. Individual reports offer a choice of norm groups and allow choices of which norms should be plotted. Areas for examiner and rater comments are provided on this form. Multirater reports allow comparison of parent and teacher ratings, whereas progress reports can be generated individually, representing how scores have changed over time.

Decision Making   Progress monitoring data lends itself to making decisions about the effectiveness of intervention (such as classroom instruction or behavior modification or pharmacology approaches) and these decisions have different levels of consequences. There are low stakes decisions such as "which group goes first for using the computer." Low stakes decisions are frequent, reversible, and have a minimal impact. High stakes decisions are typically less frequent, less reversible (if at all), and have a big impact. Whether or not to retain a student in a grade level has a high impact. These low, medium, or high stakes decisions happen all the time in schools but only recently with an emphasis on data that is objective and reliable. In a PBIS or three-tier model, the decision making may be about how a student responds to instruction (academic or behavioral) and the determination of responsiveness may be part of a decision to provide special education services and identify disability. This is a high stakes decision. It is not often made (maybe only once or once every three years), it is difficult to "reverse," and it has tremendous impact (that is, on the type of educational services provided to a child).

If and when progress-monitoring data are used in decision making, be sure that you are aware of the level of the decision and check the quality of the data (see Exhibit A.2). Let's talk about our examples again and assume that the decisions are in relationship to data from progress monitoring. Let's say that Lauren's attention is improving during one of the instructional times when the teacher added the use of guided notes where Lauren has more to "do" during the lesson than to just listen. If the teacher determines to try guided notes in other

Exhibit A.2: Examples of Acceptable Data for High, Medium, and Low Stakes Decisions

	Examples of Decision Making	Checking for Acceptable Data Sources
High Stakes	Special education placement changes, admission, or dismissal	Validity and reliability must be known and reported.
Medium Stakes	Instructional level, tutoring, small-group instruction	Validity and reliability are ideal but may be foregone given resource barriers.
Low Stakes	Opportunity to earn reinforcement, line leader, class privilege	Objectivity and accuracy are assumed but not checked.

classes, there is little risk to Lauren and the decision is easily reversed, so the teacher data meets the threshold for quality requirements. Denise's impulsivity is not better at recess after starting medication. So, based on the recess data, should parents determine to continue treatment? Probably this data is good but not good enough to make this determination. There are other areas of life to be assessed than just recess and a playground rating might not always be accurate because a teacher on duty is not watching only Denise and could easily miss something that is going on. Is the data useful for Denise and her teacher? Sure it is, but this data does not meet the quality criteria (objective and reliable) for a decision of higher order. John is turning in homework much more frequently now that he records his data in an effort to access the Xbox and the school wants to defer changing his class schedule to special education resource rooms now that he has improved his grades. This is a higher stakes decision also (like the medication issue), but the data in this case are more reliable and more objective. Turning in homework is easy to verify and the judgment of turning it in is objective. Unlike estimating impulsivity on a playground or evaluating the time paying attention during lecture, yes/no for turning in homework should be accurate and free from rater bias. This high stakes decision has data that meets the threshold.

The guidelines here about levels of decisions and quality of data are just that—guidelines. These are not "rules" but points to consider for your own information.

Team Meeting   Every school has some type of "student assistance team" or SAT. SATs may also go by the name of PBIS team, PST (problem-solving team), or RtI (response to intervention) team. This team usually meets as needed or periodically (let's say monthly, for example). Meetings occur for the purpose of addressing student problems in academics or behavior, or both. In addition, the meetings follow an agenda, report input from the staff and students, review campuswide and individual student behavior data to determine areas of strengths and weaknesses, and monitor school and student progress. The team generally is comprised of skilled teachers (perhaps representing each grade or content area) and some administrators. Sometimes personnel such as a behavior coach, special education teacher, or a special services coordinator may also be on the team. The team typically includes individuals in the roles of chairperson, secretary, database manager, communication coordinator, and timekeeper.

PBIS is a data-driven problem-solving process. At a school-wide level, team members review student discipline data to determine specific behaviors and areas of the school that are problematic. For example, at Lumber City Elementary, the PBIS team noticed that a majority of office discipline referrals originated in the cafeteria. The team decided to target the cafeteria for intervention. Expectations were posted, the students were taught and practiced the expectations, and students were allowed to enter a drawing for a bicycle when a teacher noticed that the student was following expectations in the cafeteria.

Student discipline data are reviewed by the team at the individual level also. If your child is receiving multiple office discipline referrals or one of his teachers asks the PBIS team for assistance, your child's data can be reviewed by the PBIS team and a plan can be written. The team will analyze the data from your child's behavior reports, in addition to any documentation about academic and behavioral progress or problems with your child, as well as the techniques and strategies of the teacher, and then determine what the next "best course of action" will be. They will note when and where your child is having the most problems and develop a plan to improve his behavior. This may range from additional management or instructional suggestions for the classroom teacher or additional time, tutoring, or programming. Some schools have "push-in" programs where a specialist or a volunteer will work individually or with small groups of students in the classroom; other schools have "pull-out" programs where children leave their classroom for a short period of time for some extra help. Examples of pull-out programs might include a small counseling group or a social skills instruction. Push-in programs can include the entire class, even if just one student is the target recipient. For example, a lesson on "waiting for a turn" could be appropriate for everyone in class.

The team may also select individual interventions. For example, Campbell, a 5-year-old with ADHD, was having prob-

From the Teacher

I believe it is important to clarify that although behaviors are sometimes a problem, children are not. Characteristics that make a child special and unique may or may not fit well within the structure of a public school. Neither the school nor the child is really "wrong," but the poor fit can create stress for both.

Figure A.7. Campbell's Bobcat Buck

lems during circle time in kindergarten. The team determined that he was having a difficult time sitting still throughout the lesson. As Campbell's data indicated that he was able to follow directions and routines in circle time for 10 minutes, but demonstrated problem behavior after that, the team decided to ask the teacher to include some type of activity requiring the students to move every 10 minutes. In addition, the teacher gave Campbell a "Bobcat Buck" (the school mascot was a bobcat) at the end of 10 minutes if he continued to follow directions (see Figure A.7). Campbell was allowed to trade his Bobcat Bucks for extra time in his favorite classroom center.

Tertiary: Tier 3   In most PBIS structures, interventions appropriate for tier 3 are considered special education interventions, or at least tier 3 is where a referral to special education is initiated. When a student has chronic or nonimproving problems, school personnel may suspect a disability and want to know more about the problem in order to make corrections in educational programming. This usually involves a team meeting of teachers and administrators to confirm the need for more information, followed by permission from a parent or guardian to complete a comprehensive assessment.

If the team determines that the teacher has exhausted the options of best practice and the child is still struggling, then typically a comprehensive assessment would be suggested and then requested. In this instance, you the parent or caregiver

From the Parent

When my child is complimented, I receive part of the credit. When my child runs the fastest or jumps the highest, I feel pride. These are only natural reactions. So what happens when my child demonstrates behavior that draws negative attention from the school? I feel shame, guilt, and responsibility. In the same way that I naturally take credit for the good, I take blame for the bad—whether or not the blame is there. With time I have realized that the school did not blame me. They wanted to help my child be successful. When I began to focus on what to do next rather than what I had or had not done in the past I was able to partner with the school better. I did not agree with everything, but I did not feel defensive or emotional anymore and I had a stronger voice to advocate for my child.

would receive a request for testing. The school cannot evaluate your child without your informed consent (for more on this see Chapter Ten). If the results of the assessment identify the presence of a disability and your child qualifies for special education services, then you and a special education team will build an individualized education plan (IEP) together.

Students in tier 3 (if considered special education within the model) have rights protected by state and federal law. They are entitled to a free appropriate public education in the least restrictive environment (see Chapter Ten for more information). IEPs are evaluated at least every year and the student is reevaluated every three years to determine whether he continues to need special education services as the disability continues to interfere with his education.

Request for Comprehensive Assessment In addition to a team generated request for assessment, a parent may also request evaluation for special education services. We have more information on this process in Chapter Ten. But know that this third level of support and services is available for students who qualify and that parents have the right to make this request. Do so in writing, keep your records, and date everything, as there are strict procedural compliance issues that must be adhered to in the school setting. Keep a calendar or log of any and all correspondence or communication both formal and informal. Because special education is not provided specifically for ADHD, you would be asking for evaluation for services as "other health impaired" or if applicable, "learning disability," or perhaps, "severe emotional disturbance." See Chapter Ten for further information on special education.

TO SUM UP

Positive behavioral support is a multitier service delivery model designed to sustain students in general education environments in order to maximize access to the curriculum. PBIS does not operate in all schools but when a good PBIS program is in place, schools see fewer office discipline referrals and more positive student-teacher interactions. Teachers in PBIS schools tend to demonstrate classroom management skills that are consistent with other teachers in the building. Students are explicitly taught the expectations for behavior and encouraged to demonstrate those behaviors. PBIS schools take time to develop; school reform is not an overnight process. For more information on PBIS, check out the national center, supported by the U.S. Department of Education.

Glossary

With Lauren E. Williams

ABC EVENT CHAIN An acronym used to determine the origin of a behavior or what helps maintain the behavior; "A" refers to the *antecedent* (the event occurring prior to seeing the behavior), "B" asks for you to talk about the *behavior* you observed, and "C" refers to the *consequence* (this happens right after the event).

ACCOMMODATION(S) Changes to the timing or scheduling of assignments or tests, the manner in which the student responds, the setting, or the method of presentation of instruction or tests to "level the playing field" for students with disabilities (not to provide a benefit above that given to other students). Accommodations are not changes to the skills or knowledge taught; rather, accommodations are changes that allow the child to access the same skills and knowledge as typically developing peers.

ACTIVITY REINFORCER Allowing an individual to participate in activities that are personally enjoyable (playing games, watching television, driving a car) to increase the likelihood that a behavior will occur.

ADHD-COMBINED TYPE (ADHD-C) A DSM-IV diagnostic subcategory of ADHD; an individual meets the diagnostic criteria if he or she demonstrates symptoms of hyperactivity, impulsivity, and inattention for the past six months that are maladaptive and inconsistent with the developmental level.

ADHD-NOT OTHERWISE SPECIFIED (ADHD-NOS) A DSM-IV diagnostic subcategory of ADHD given to individuals when symptoms of inattention, hyperactivity, or impulsivity are evidenced but the symptoms do not clearly meet the DSM-IV diagnostic criteria for either of the other ADHD diagnostic criteria.

ADHD-PREDOMINANTLY HYPERACTIVE-IMPULSIVE (ADHD PH-I) A DSM-IV diagnostic subcategory of ADHD given to individuals when the criteria for hyperactivity and impulsivity are met for the past six months that are maladaptive and inconsistent with the developmental level of the individual are met for the past six months, but the criteria for inattention are not met.

ADHD-PREDOMINANTLY INATTENTIVE (ADHD-PI) A DSM-IV diagnostic subcategory of ADHD given to individuals when the criteria for inattention that are maladaptive and inconsistent with the developmental level of the individual are met for the past six months, but the criteria for hyperactivity and impulsivity are not met.

ADMINISTRATIVE CHAIN OF COMMAND The order of individuals who are responsible for providing supervision and decision making, including responding to complaints about placement and programming (for example, director of special education, principal, assistant superintendent, superintendent, school board).

AMERICAN ACADEMY OF CHILD AND ADOLESCENT PSYCHIATRY (AACAP) A national professional medical association whose goal is to improve the quality of life and treat youth and families who have a mental, behavioral, or developmental disorder or who have a family member who does.

AMERICAN ACADEMY OF PEDIATRICS (AAP) A professional pediatrician organization that strives to achieve the most advantageous health and well-being for infants, children, adolescents, and young adults.

AMERICAN COUNCIL FOR EDUCATION (ACE) The higher education organization that represents presidents and chancellors and all types of U.S. colleges and universities.

AMERICAN MEDICAL ASSOCIATION (AMA) A professional organization providing a means for physicians to work as a group; accredits medical schools, provides continuing education to physicians, and can discipline physician members for inappropriate conduct.

AMERICAN PSYCHIATRIC ASSOCIATION'S DIAGNOSTIC AND STATISTICAL MANUAL OF MENTAL DISORDERS (DSM-IV-TR) The standard classification of mental disorders used by mental health professionals in the United States; it is used in many different settings (inpatient and outpatient clinics, consultation, private practice, primary care) by individuals with many different approaches to treatment and by many different professionals (psychiatrists and other physicians, psychologists, social workers, nurses, occupational and rehabilitation therapists, and counselors).

AMERICAN PSYCHOLOGICAL ASSOCIATION (APA) A scientific professional organization that represents psychology with the aim of advancing the development, dissemination, and application of psychological information to benefit society and improve people's lives.

AMERICANS WITH DISABILITIES ACT (ADA) A civil rights law that prohibits discrimination based on disability status.

AMERICANS WITH DISABILITIES ACT, AMENDMENTS OF 2008 A revision of the original ADA civil rights law; revisions were made to the definition of "disability" to extend the definition of "substantially limit a major life activity" to clarify that mitigating measures, including medication, assistive devices, auxiliary aids, accommodations, medical therapies, and supplies, do not exclude the rights of individuals, and to clarify that impairments that are episodic or in remission that substantially limit a major life activity, when active, continue to meet the definition of disability.

ANTECEDENT A situation, event, or other incident that occurs before a behavior.

ANXIETY An atypical and overwhelming sense of apprehension, excessive worry, and fear.

ASSISTIVE TECHNOLOGY Any item or piece of equipment that is used to increase, maintain, or improve the functioning of a child with a disability.

AT (ASSISTIVE TECHNOLOGY) EVALUATION The process of evaluating the needs of an individual to determine what, if any, assistive technology devices will be beneficial to the individual.

ATTENTION The act of concentrating or focusing on a single object or thought and maintaining selective or sustained concentration or focus.

ATTENTIONAL BIAS The preference of an individual to attend to specific items, thoughts, sounds, or activities.

AVERSIVE STIMULUS A punishment or action a person will avoid and that is usually intended to reduce the frequency of a behavior immediately; this is not a reinforcing stimulus, but rather something you might find unpleasant or painful; behavior followed by an aversive stimulus results in a decreased probability of the behavior occurring in the future.

AXON An arm of a neuron that carries electrical impulses away from the cell body toward the next neuron.

AXON TERMINAL The club-shaped ending an axon uses to make contact with other nerve cells.

BASAL GANGLIA A group of neurons in the brain that connect with the cerebral cortex, especially the frontal and pre-frontal regions, thalamus, and related brain areas, that acts as a cohesive functional unit as well as a neural pathway; associated with a variety of functions, including voluntary motor control most prominently, routinized learning or "habits" such as eye movements, as well as some cognitive and emotional functions. The basal ganglia are especially rich in dopamine and dopamine receptor sites.

BEHAVIOR ASSESSMENT SYSTEM FOR CHILDREN, 2ND EDITION (BASC-2) The most widely used behavioral assessment system in the U.S. public schools, the BASC-2 is used for diagnosis of all major forms of behavioral and emotional disorders in the 2- to 21-year-old population. It consists of a series of developmentally appropriate omnibus behavior rating scales completed by parents and by teachers, self-report scales, standardized observational procedures, and a structured developmental history. The BASC-2 is normed on a large nationally representative population of children from the United States, but is also available in local versions for many other countries and languages.

BEHAVIOR MANAGEMENT   Strategies or techniques used to maintain order in an environment such as a classroom; usually applied at the group level by a classroom teacher to produce high rates of appropriate behavior and learning and to minimize classroom disruption.

BEHAVIORAL CONTRACT   An agreement, usually in the form of a document, between a child or adolescent and an adult that specifies the target behavior to be increased, and the reinforcer that will be provided when the individual demonstrates the appropriate behavior; it may also list inappropriate behaviors and punishments that may occur with these undesired behaviors.

BEHAVIORAL DISINHIBITION   A lack of restraint in one's overt actions.

BEHAVIORAL AND EMOTIONAL SCREENING SYSTEM (BESS)   A derivative scale of the BASC-2, the BESS is a set of very rapid, brief screening scales, both rating scales and self-report scales, that take less than 5 minutes to complete and determine whether an individual is at increased risk of having or developing an emotional or behavioral disorder and whether more intensive follow-up assessments are necessary.

BEHAVIORAL THERAPY   A form of therapy characterized by reinforcing desired behaviors and punishing undesired behaviors.

BENADRYL   See diphenhydramine.

BIOLOGICAL CONDITION   The state of your physiological condition, including the structure and function of all physical parts of the body.

BRAIN ELECTRICAL ACTIVITY MAPS (BEAM)   A specialized measure of brain electrical activity; brainwave functions measured include speed, power, rhythm, and symmetry. A BEAM is based on the electroencephalograph (EEG), but it samples on many more points for longer durations than the standard EEG and reports on patterns of altered brainwave functions.

BRAIN IMAGING   Viewing the structure and/or function of the physical brain in process via pictures of various brain structures in vivo as well as creating pictures from various measures of brain metabolism; this can be done with multiple approaches such as positron emission tomography (PET), single photon emission computed tomography (SPECT), magnetic resonance imaging (MRI), and/or an electro-encephalography (EEG).

BRAIN VOLUME   The mass of the brain including it structure, chemistry, and connections.

BROWN V. BOARD OF EDUCATION   A decision of the United States Supreme Court declaring segregated schools (all-black and all-white schools) unconstitutional; the decision overturned the Plessy v. Ferguson case of 1896 which allowed state-sponsored segregation.

BROWN V. COX MEDICAL CENTERS (8TH CIR 2002) An ADA action case; Coralyn Anne Brown, registered nurse, was transferred to a nonnursing clerk position after the director of surgical services found out she had multiple sclerosis. The Court decided: (1) "cognitive thinking" is a major life activity; (2) there was evidence to support the fact that the employer regarded her as a disabled person with a disability; and (3) the transfer to a nonnursing position was an adverse action as Brown was told it was temporary, the transfer hurt her career opportunities, and it also prevented her from applying her nursing skills; it was decided that this was a status demotion.

CELIAC DISEASE A medical condition in which the lining of the small intestine is damaged preventing it from absorbing parts of food that are essential in staying healthy; the damage is due to a reaction to eating gluten (found in wheat, barley, and rye).

CELLULAR NEUROBIOLOGY A study of the properties of cells in the brain, and how cells interact and communicate with each other.

CENTERS FOR DISEASE CONTROL (CDC) A U.S. government–sponsored center that protects health and promotes quality of life through the prevention and control of disease, injury, and disabilities, and maintenance of a statistical database on disease.

CEREBELLUM A region of the brain located at the base of the cortex below the occipital lobes that plays an important role in motor control, particularly inhibition of unwanted movement; the cerebellum has more recently been discovered to have involvement in cognitive functions such as attention and language, and in certain emotional functions.

CHALLENGING HORIZONS PROGRAM (CHP) A school-based set of interventions for adolescents with ADHD focused on improving common areas of impairment such as organization, homework management, studying, note taking, socialization, goal setting, and behavior regulation combined with recreational activities.

CHILD BEHAVIOR CHECKLIST (CBCL) A set of behavior ratings used to assess the behavioral problems and social competencies of children reported by parents and teachers in a standardized format.

CHILDHOOD PSYCHOPATHOLOGY The demonstration of psychological disorders during childhood and adolescence (such as oppositional defiant disorder, attention-deficit hyperactivity disorder, and pervasive developmental disorder).

CHILDREN AND ADULTS WITH ATTENTION-DEFICIT HYPERACTIVITY DISORDER (CHADD) A nonprofit organization helping individuals with ADHD and their families; CHADD was founded in response to the frustration and sense of isolation experienced by parents and their children with ADHD.

CINGULATE GYRUS A part of the brain situated in the medial aspect of the cortex and usually considered part of the brain's limbic system and a key communication pathway, carrying messages from the frontal and especially the prefrontal region to the internal and posterior regions of the brain.

CLASSROOM MANAGEMENT Methods and strategies used by professionals to maintain a classroom environment that is conducive to student success and learning.

CLINICAL INTERVIEW   An interview conducted by a clinician (such as a psychologist or therapist) to uncover evidence that will assist with diagnosis and treatment planning.

CODE OF CONDUCT   Principles and expectations that are considered binding to members of a particular group (such as students at a school or members of a professional organization).

COGNITIVE IMPAIRMENT   A reduction in mental functioning that may be present at birth or acquired at any point in a person's life; it can include loss of higher reasoning, forgetfulness, learning disabilities, concentration difficulties, or decreased intelligence.

COGNITIVE RESTRUCTURING   A process of changing negative thinking caused by past experiences.

COLLEGE ENTRANCE EXAMINATION BOARD (CEEB)   An organization that governs and structures college admissions testing.

COMORBIDITY   The existence of two or more disorders in the same person.

COMPLEX SYNDROME   A specified combination of problems that co-occur in predictable ways.

COMPREHENSIVE ASSESSMENT   An assessment process that evaluates a student's full range of abilities, behaviors, skills, and emotions; also known as a full and individual evaluation.

COMPUTED TOMOGRAPHY/COMPUTERIZED AXIAL TOMOGRAPHY (CT)/(CAT)   A scanning process combining special x-ray equipment with computers to produce multiple images or pictures of the inside of the body, including scans of internal organs, bones, soft tissue, and blood vessels, that provide greater clarity and reveal more details than regular x-ray exams; this helps radiologists more easily diagnose problems in the body (such as bleeding into the brain, cancers, cardiovascular disease, infectious diseases, appendicitis, trauma, and musculoskeletal disorders).

CONCENTRATION Focusing one's attention or mental effort on a specific task or thought.

CONDUCT DISORDER (CD) A behavior disorder of child-hood defined by the DSM-IV-TR characterized by antisocial behaviors violating the rights of others, social standards, and rules, including aggression toward people and animals, destruction of property, deceitfulness or theft, and serious rule violations.

CONTINGENCY PLAN A technique to provide reinforcement for specific behaviors; the individual will know what behavior is expected of him or her and what reinforcement will be provided or earned when that behavior is demonstrated.

CONTINUOUS PERFORMANCE TEST (CPT) A psychological test measuring a person's sustained and selective attention and impulsivity; typically, examinees are presented with a repetitive, "boring" task and must maintain their focus over a period of time in order to respond to some targets and inhibit responding to others; tests may use numbers, symbols, or even sounds, but each basic task has the same concept.

COTEACHING Two or more people sharing responsibility for teaching some or all of the students assigned to a classroom;

teacher responsibilities are distributed among both teachers for planning, instruction, and evaluation for the classroom.

COUNCIL FOR EXCEPTIONAL CHILDREN (CEC)   An organization for educators, parents, and others with interests in youth with disabilities that aims to improve the education of people with disabilities and/or gifts and talents, advocates for governmental policies and for individuals with disabilities, sets professional standards, provides professional development, and assists professionals in securing resources for effective professional practice.

DAILY BEHAVIOR REPORT CARD (DBRC)   A method of teacher communication of behaviors demonstrated by a child or adolescent at school to a parent on a daily basis. It has various forms and formats. It can help parents create realistic behavior goals, stay on top of their child's progress, establish consequences, and decide whether the teacher's approach is working to improve their child's behavior.

DENDRITE   The branching projections of a neuron that act to conduct the electrochemical stimulation received from the axon terminals of the communicating neuron to the cell body of the receiving neuron.

DEOXYRIBONUCLEIC ACID (DNA)   A nucleic acid containing the genetic instructions used in the development and functioning of all known living organisms and immortalized in the shape of the double helix.

DEPRESSION   A mood disorder defined by the DSM-IV-TR marked by feelings of sadness, loss, anger, or frustration to a significant degree that create impairment in everyday life activities for an extended period of time.

DEVELOPMENTAL DELAY When a child does not reach his or her developmental milestones at the expected times in areas such as motor, intelligence, and even social skills to the extent that the degree of delay interferes with one or more major life functions; most often a diagnosis made by a doctor.

DIFFERENTIAL REINFORCEMENT The reinforcement of a specific behavior and not another.

DIPHENHYDRAMINE One of the most commonly used medications with children used to relieve red, irritated, itchy, watery eyes; sneezing; and runny nose caused by hay fever, allergies, or the common cold; side effects can include sedation but also adverse reactions such as increased activity levels and attention problems that may mimic ADHD; also well known by its trademark name, Benadryl.

DISTRACTIBILITY When attention wavers or wanders and cannot remain focused on any one subject; an inability to resist moving attention from one object or event to another too rapidly and inappropriately and that disrupts concentration; being constantly drawn to attend to many different competing objects or events in the immediate vicinity and experiencing difficulty discerning which are the most important.

DOPAMINE A common neurotransmitter, dopamine assists in regulating movement and emotional responses (as well as physiological responses such as blood pressure) and is heavily involved in the pleasure and reward systems of the brain; dopamine deficiencies have been implicated in many mood disorders, especially depression, but also in ADHD.

DRUG ENFORCEMENT ADMINISTRATION (DEA) A federal law enforcement agency under the U.S. Department of Justice whose main focus is stopping drug smuggling and drug use.

DUE PROCESS A series of steps that must be followed to challenge a legally contested issue or to deprive a person of any legal right.

DYSLEXIA A specific learning disability which is an unexpected difficulty in reading resulting from a fundamental problem in getting to the sounds of spoken words which impacts both spoken and written language. Characteristics include difficulties with word retrieval of spoken words, lack of fluency so that reading is slow and effortful, and difficulties with spelling.

EDUCATION FOR ALL HANDICAPPED CHILDREN ACT (PL 94–142) A federal law signed by President Gerald Ford in 1975 that created the right to a free appropriate education (FAPE) for children with disabilities.

EDUCATIONAL TESTING SERVICE (ETS) A nonprofit corporation focused on developing, administering, and scoring more than 50 million tests annually (TOEFL, TOEIC tests, the GRE General and Subject Tests, and The Praxis Series assessments); ETS also conducts educational research, data analysis, and conducting policy studies as well as developing individualized services and products for teacher certification, English language learning, and elementary, secondary, and postsecondary education.

ELECTROENCEPHALOGRAM (EEG) The recording of electrical activity along the scalp measuring voltage fluctuations resulting from electrical current flows within the neurons of the brain.

EMOTIONAL DISTURBANCE (ED) An educational disability defined by IDEIA as being "characterized by one or more of the following over a long period of time and to a marked degree, which adversely affects educational performance: an inability to learn which cannot be explained by intellectual, sensory, or health factors; an inability to build or maintain satisfactory interpersonal relationships with peers and teachers. Inappropriate types of behavior or feelings under normal circumstances; a general pervasive mood of unhappiness or depression; a tendency to develop physical symptoms or fears associated with personal or school problems. This includes children or adolescents with schizophrenia, but not socially maladjusted (unless it is determined that he/she has an emotional disturbance)."

EXPULSION FROM SCHOOL The act of removing a student from school for more than 10 days.

FOOD AND DRUG ADMINISTRATION (FDA) This government agency ensures the safety, efficacy, and security of human and veterinary drugs, biological products, medical devices, our nation's food supply, cosmetics, and products that emit radiation, and protects health of the public; the FDA is responsible for advancing the public health by helping to speed innovations that make medicines and foods more effective, safer, and more affordable.

FREE APPROPRIATE PUBLIC EDUCATION (FAPE) An educational right of children with disabilities in the United States implemented as a result of the Rehabilitation Act of 1973 and the Individuals with Disabilities Education Improvement Act (IDEIA). Under Section 504 it is defined as "the provision of regular or special education and related aids and services that are designed to meet individual needs of handicapped persons as well as the needs of non-handicapped persons are met, and based on adherence to procedural safeguards outlined in the law." All children have the right to a free appropriate public education.

FRONTAL LOBE   The executive control center of the brain; the area that is home to one's personality; this lobe is involved in coordination of the brain's higher cortical functions but also plays a key primary role in motor function, problem solving, decision making, spontaneity, memory, language, and behavioral initiation, as well as inhibition, judgment, impulse control, and social and sexual behavior.

FUNCTION OF A BEHAVIOR   The purpose served by a behavior.

FUNCTIONAL IMPAIRMENT   A condition that substantially interferes with or limits the person's functioning in the family, school, workplace, or the community; functional impairment can be in the areas of (but not limited to) learning, family or peer relations, safety, social skills, relations, bathing, dressing, preparing meals, feeding, grooming, and taking medications.

FUNCTIONAL NEUROIMAGING   The use of any of a class of neuroimaging technology (for example, PET, fMRI, SPECT, MEG, BEAM) to measure brain function or actions of the brain that involves creating a visual image based upon the metabolism or electrical output of the brain, often with a view to understanding the relationship between activity in certain brain areas and specific mental functions; neuroimaging is a fast-growing field used not only for diagnosis but broadly as a research tool in cognitive neuroscience, cognitive psychology, neuropsychology, and social neuroscience.

GABAMINOBUTYRIC ACID (GABA) The primary inhibitory neurotransmitter in the mammalian central nervous system, GABA plays a major role in regulating neuronal excitability and "soothes" neurons throughout the nervous system of the entire body; in humans, it is also directly responsible for the regulation of muscle tone.

GAGLIARDO V. CONNAUGHT LABORATORIES, INC. (3D CIR. 2002) An ADA and Pennsylvania Human Relations Act (PHRA) action. Jane Gagliardo suffered from multiple sclerosis (MS) and sought accommodations on her job, but none were provided, and she was terminated. The courts ruled in her favor and noted that (1) concentrating and remembering are major life activities; (2) Gagliardo was substantially limited in these major life activities due to her MS; (3) the federal damages cap does not limit recovery under state law; (4) district court was not required to charge jury that plaintiff was an employee at will; (5) there was sufficient evidence to support award of punitive damages; and (6) upheld a monetary award for emotional distress.

GENERALIZED ANXIETY DISORDERS (GAD) An anxiety disorder characterized by chronic anxiety, exaggerated worry, and tension, and often accompanied by physical symptoms.

GENETIC CODE The set of rules by which information encoded in genetic material is translated into proteins by living cells.

GENETIC DISORDER A condition caused by abnormalities in genes or chromosomes.

GLUCOSE A simple sugar (monosaccharide); an important carbohydrate in biology that cells use as their primary source of energy.

GLUTEN INTOLERANCE   See Celiac disease.

GRADUATE RECORD EXAM (GRE)   A standardized exam used to measure one's aptitude; commonly used by graduate schools to determine program admissions.

GROUP CONTINGENCY   The process of providing rein- forcement dependent upon the behavior of an individual member of a group, a part of the group, or everyone in the group.

HEMISPHERE   Either half of the cerebrum or neocortex of the brain.

HETEROGENEOUS DISORDER   A disorder that may manifest itself in slightly different ways from person to person, including the degree to which symptoms are manifested and the presence of secondary characteristics.

HETEROGENEOUS GROUP   A group that includes stu- dents with a wide variety of instructional levels.

HIGH STAKES TESTING   An important test that deter- mines future educational decisions for examinees and benefits for the examinees (license to practice a certain skill).

HOME BEHAVIOR CHART   A chart or graph used to record, monitor, and reinforce expectations at home.

HYPERACTIVITY   A physical state in which a person is abnormally active relative to the expectations of the circum- stances; excessive restlessness and movement (for example, having too many ideas too quickly).

HYPERFOCUS   An intense form of mental concentration or visualization from which one is not easily drawn away.

IMPAIRMENT   A function that is below normal expectation in its performance.

IMPULSIVITY   The initiation of behavior without adequate forethought as to the consequences of actions; acting on the spur of the moment; acting (including speaking) without thinking.

INATTENTION   The difficulty or absence of the ability to direct attention or regard to a desired object or event in the immediate environment and difficulty determining that attention is required or best directed to a particular object or event.

INCLUSION (EDUCATIONAL)   A process in which students with special needs receive some or all of their time with nondisabled students in a general education classroom setting.

INDEPENDENT EDUCATIONAL EVALUATION (IEE) An evaluation given to students by a person who is not employed by the school district (also cannot be part of the educational decision-making process for the student); parents have the right to this type of evaluation at public expense if the parent disagrees with an evaluation obtained by the public agency.

INDIVIDUAL CONTINGENCY A reinforcement that depends on the behavior of an individual child (as opposed to group contingency when reinforcement is provided to an entire group).

INDIVIDUAL EDUCATION PROGRAM (IEP)   An education program required for all students in special education programs that is designed to meet the unique educational needs of the child; includes educational goals and objectives based on strengths and weaknesses uncovered through evaluation processes.

INDIVIDUALS WITH DISABILITIES EDUCATION IMPROVEMENT ACT (IDEIA)   The United States' current special education law, this act requires states to provide a free appropriate public education (FAPE) in the least restrictive environment (LRE) to students with disabilities.

INSTRUCTIONAL STRATEGY   A technique used by teachers when teaching content to students to increase the likelihood that the student will learn the material.

INTERPERSONAL COMMUNICATION   A way of communicating ideas, thoughts, and feelings to another person; behaviors are learned for this skill and there are strategies to help a person improve their communication skills, such as improved knowledge, practice, feedback, and personal reflection.

INTERVENTION   A technique implemented through a systematic process to teach new knowledge, skills, or behaviors or to increase the use of appropriate behaviors; planned methods used to create change.

JOB COACH   A person who trains and works directly with an employee with a disability to perform job tasks as required by the employer and to learn the interpersonal skills needed for the job site.

KINETIC ACTIVITY   A dynamic movement activity that works towards functional performance such as lifting, bending, pushing, pulling, jumping, and reaching.

LAW SCHOOL ADMISSIONS TEST (LSAT) A test designed to measure skills that are considered essential for success in law school and used, in part, to determine acceptance into law school.

LEAST RESTRICTIVE ENVIRONMENT (LRE) The educational circumstance dictating that students with disabilities must be educated alongside nondisabled peers, to the greatest extent appropriate, and have the same access to educational activities as other students as well as social school events; implementation and the need for pullout or separatist programs are determined on an individual basis.

LOCKE-WALLACE MARITAL ADJUSTMENT SCALE A marriage questionnaire consisting of 15 items where partners rate certain aspects of their relationship.

MAGNESIUM The eleventh most abundant element by mass in the human body; essential to all living cells.

MAGNETIC RESONANCE IMAGING (MRI) A neuro-imaging procedure that uses a magnetic field and pulses of radiowave energy to assess the relative density of organs and structures inside the body allowing images or pictures to be developed; in many cases these pictures give different information about structures in the body than can be seen with an X-ray, ultrasound, or computed tomography (CT) scan; the MRI may detect problems that cannot be seen with other imaging methods as MRI achieves great clarity of detail and focus with a resolution of less than one square millimeter.

MAJOR LIFE ACTIVITY An activity that includes but is not limited to learning, caring for oneself, performing manual tasks, seeing, hearing, eating, sleeping, walking, standing, lifting, bending, speaking, breathing, learning, reading, concentrating, thinking, communicating, and working.

MALADAPTIVE BEHAVIOR   A behavior that has a negative impact on the person displaying the behavior; also known as inappropriate behavior or misbehaving.

MEDICAL COLLEGE ADMISSIONS TEST (MCAT)   A standardized, multiple-choice examination to measure prerequisites to the study of medicine.

METABOLISM, CELLULAR   The chemical processes occurring within a living cell that are necessary for the maintenance of the life of the individual cell and that may lead to the production of chemicals useful to other cells as well. In metabolism, some substances are broken down (for example, glucose and oxygen) to yield energy for vital processes while other substances, necessary for life, are created. In the brain, this includes the manufacturing of neurotransmitters for communication among neurons.

METABOLISM, GENERAL   The sum of the physical and chemical processes in the body that develop or use energy.

MINIMAL BRAIN DYSFUNCTION (MBD)   Minimal brain damage; brain functions that appear on a subjective basis to be disrupted but for which there are no physical findings of brain injury or physical malfunction; this term was important historically in ADHD and in learning disabilities but is now considered archaic.

MIXED RATE OF INSTRUCTION   The method of presenting the material to the students at a brisk rate when the students appear to understand and then slowing the rate when the students are struggling to grasp the content.

MODIFICATION   A change to the general education curriculum (skills and knowledge taught) in order to meet the needs of the student; made when the expectations are beyond the student's level of ability; may be minimal or very complex depending on the student performance; must be clearly acknowledged in the individual education program (IEP).

MOOD DISORDER   A group of diagnoses in the *Diagnostic and Statistical Manual of Mental Disorders* (DSM IV-TR) classification system where a disturbance in the person's mood is hypothesized to be the main underlying feature.

MOTOR CONTROL   The internal process that executes complex motor sequences and responses or behavior which, chained together, make up goal directions, motivation, and persistence.

MULTIDISCIPLINARY TEAM   A team, made up of professionals from different positions within the school, required by federal law to make disability decisions for special education; the team brings many ideas to the table when making decisions regarding a student identified to receive special education services; identifies student's academic, social, and vocational needs when developing an individualized educational program (IEP) for the student; functions to support students needing special education and related services, and to help keep students in the regular educational settings.

MULTIMODAL INTERVENTION OR TREATMENT PROGRAMS   An intervention or treatment program with multiple interventions implemented simultaneously based on the needs of the individual child; also known as multicomponent intervention.

MULTIPLE DISABILITIES   The presence of more than one significant disability (movement difficulties, sensory loss, and/or a behavior or emotional disorder).

MYELIN SHEATH   The insulating shield of myelin that surrounds nerve fibers or axons and facilitates the transmission of nerve impulses, acting as insulation—much as electrical wiring in the physical environment acts better when insulated.

NARROWBAND BEHAVIOR RATING SCALE   Assessment that focuses only on characteristics of one individual's mental health disorders.

NATIONAL INSTITUTES OF HEALTH (NIH)   The federal government's medical research agency.

NATURAL REINFORCER   A stimulus that maintains or strengthens a desired response and that occurs in the environment without prior planning.

NEGATIVE SELF-TALK   A mixture of thoughts that include partial truths, illogical concepts, and distortions of reality that perpetuates negative emotions (pessimism, guilt, fear, anxiety, and self-sabotaging behaviors); sometimes occurs in times of emotional turmoil, or in times of extreme stress or a personal transition; part of a daily inner dialogue.

NEURAL PATHWAY   Connection from one part of the nervous system to another and usually consists of bundles of elongated, myelin-insulated neurons; serves to connect relatively distant areas of the brain or nervous system and facilitates patterns of neural communication.

NEURAL SYNAPSE   A junction between two neurons across which neurotransmitters are passed (from the axon terminal of one neuron to the receptor site of the receiving neuron) as a means of inter-cellular communication; there is a microscopic gap at this junction known as the synaptic cleft, across which neurotransmitters must travel to communicate.

NEUROBIOLOGICAL DISORDER   An illness of the nervous system caused by genetic, metabolic, or other biological factors (for example, autism, bipolar disorder, obsessive-compulsive disorder, schizophrenia, and Tourette's syndrome).

NEUROCHEMISTRY   The study of the chemical composition and processes of the nervous system and the effects of chemicals on it.

NEURONS   A type of cell in the brain which can hold and transmit electrical signals.

NEUROSCIENTIST   An individual who studies the brain or any aspect of the central nervous system or other neuronal bodies via applications of the scientific method.

NEUROTRANSMITTERS   Chemicals manufactured in various neurons that transmit signals from a neuron to a target cell across the synaptic cleft, they are stored into synaptic vesicles located just beneath the membrane of the axon terminal on the presynaptic side of a synapse, and are released into the synaptic cleft, where they attempt to bind to receptor sites in the membrane on the postsynaptic side of the synapse, thus transmitting their message. They are then released and may be reabsorbed (taken back) by the secreting neuron via a reuptake pump.

NONDISCRIMINATORY EVALUATION AND IDENTIFICATION FOR SPECIAL EDUCATION   An evaluation that determines whether a child has a disability and, if so, whether special education services are needed; this evaluation tests specific areas of educational need rather than only general intelligence, places students in an appropriate educational setting on the basis of two or more tests, considers other information (that is, physical development, race, culture, language, and adaptive behavior) in conjunction with test scores, and sets up a team to evaluate and appropriately place a student.

NORADRENALIN FACILITATORS   Medicines that enhance the manufacture or use of noradrenaline in the body (for example, Ritalin and Strattera).

NORADRENALINE   Also called norepinephrine and a member of the catecholamine group, noradrenalin is manufactured as a drug and produced naturally in the human body; it has two roles and acts as a hormone, but also is a potent neurotransmitter. As a hormone it helps regulate the body's response to stress and the flight or fight mechanisms of the limbic system and also is involved in the attentional system; noradrenaline is derived from dopamine as well and its primary pathways in the brain are significantly correlated with those of dopamine; as a drug it is commonly used to treat low blood pressure and chronic depression; deficiencies of noradrenalin are also implicated in the origin of ADHD and noradrenaline reuptake inhibitors show benefit in treatment of ADHD.

NOREPINEPHRINE   See noradrenaline.

NUCLEUS The center of the cell body of a neuron in which the cell consumes oxygen and glucose and manufactures other chemical needs conducting the primary metabolism of the cell.

OCCIPITAL LOBE The region in the back of the brain that processes visual information and helps in the visual recognition of shapes and colors; damage to this lobe can cause visual deficits.

OFFICE OF DISABILITY SUPPORT SERVICES A university office responsible for managing the support of students who have a documented disability.

OFFICE DISCIPLINE REFERRAL (ODR) A written document recording student noncompliance with expectations and/ or the student code of conduct in schools designed to inform a principal of the behavior for disciplinary action; typically result in a negative consequence.

OFFICE OF SPECIAL EDUCATION AND REHABILITATIVE SERVICES (OSERS) A program within the United States Department of Education committed to improving results and outcomes for people with disabilities of all ages by providing a wide array of supports to parents and individuals, school districts, and states in three main areas: special education, vocational rehabilitation, and research.

ORTHOPEDIC IMPAIRMENT A structural physical impairment associated with the musculoskeletal system that adversely affects a child's educational performance; includes impairments caused by a congenital anomaly, impairments caused by disease (poliomyelitis, bone tuberculosis), and impairments from other causes (cerebral palsy, amputations, and fractures or burns that cause contractures).

OTHER HEALTH IMPAIRMENT An educational disability category characterized by limited strength or alertness which is due to chronic or acute health problems such as asthma, attention-deficit hyperactivity disorder, diabetes, epilepsy, a heart condition, hemophilia, lead poisoning, leukemia, nephritis, rheumatic fever, sickle cell anemia, and Tourette's syndrome; and also adversely affects a child's educational performance.

PARENT TRAINING Providing instruction to families to teach strategies and techniques to prevent and remediate problem behaviors at home and at school; can be done with a group or individually.

PARENTING RELATIONSHIP QUESTIONNAIRE (PRQ) An assessment instrument published by Pearson Clinical Assessments that provides a thorough look at how you relate to your child and how you see your child relating to you; provides information on how your relationship compares to similar factors among other parents of similarly aged children; this questionnaire also looks at parent-child attachment, communications, involvement, parenting confidence, disciplinary practices, relational frustration, and satisfaction with school.

PARIETAL LOBES The lobes of the neocortex located behind the frontal lobe at the top of the brain in both the right and left hemispheres and containing the primary sensory cortex which controls sensation (touch, pressure); damage to this area can cause visuospatial deficits (for example, may have difficulty finding their way around new, or even familiar, places), difficulty recognizing body language, and difficulties with prosody and recognition of emotions.

PEER REJECTION   Occurs when someone is excluded from a social relationship or social interaction by a peer group.

PERSONAL DIGITAL ASSISTANT (PDA)   A handheld device that combines computing, telephone, Internet, and networking features.

PLANNED IGNORING   The process of providing absolutely no attention to maladaptive or other behavior with the intention of reducing its frequency of occurrence.

POLYGENIC   Pertaining to two or more genes.

POSITIVE AFFIRMATION   Positive statements validating and providing verbal reinforcement for the behavior of others or self.

POSITIVE BEHAVIORAL INTERVENTION AND SUPPORT (PBIS)   A three-tier process that teaches and reinforces positive behaviors demonstrated by students in elementary and secondary schools; includes behavior management strategies appropriate for the classroom and other educational environments, such as the playground, cafeteria, gym, restrooms, and hallways; also known as PBS.

POSITIVE CONSEQUENCE   A natural or planned incentive or reward that occurs after appropriate behavior to increase the likelihood that the behavior will reoccur.

POSITIVE REINFORCEMENT   An action or item that increases the likelihood of the desired behavior or a new skill.

POSITRON EMISSION TOMOGRAPHY (PET)   A test that uses a special type of camera and a tracer (radioactive chemical) to look at organs in the body; during this test the tracer liquid is put into a vein (intravenous, or IV) in the arm. The tracer gives off tiny positively charged particles. The camera records the particles and turns the recording into pictures on a computer. This scan is used to evaluate cancer, check blood flow, or see how an organ is working. It is sometimes used to assess the metabolic rate of different parts of the brain.

PRECORRECTION   The use of reminders of expectations prior to situations in which you think problem behaviors are likely to occur.

PREREFERRAL INTERVENTION The provision of evidence-based alternative academic or behavioral strategies identified, developed, and implemented before a referral for special education.

PROCEDURAL SAFEGUARDS   A list of requirements that ensure children with disabilities are provided a free appropriate public education (FAPE). Under Section 504 the following procedural safeguards are listed: parents or caregivers must receive notice (1) when your child is being considered for identification as a child with a disability under Section 504, and (2) when the school will review all pertinent information and/or conduct an assessment.

PROGRESS MONITORING (PM)   A process where teachers or other professionals keep track of how a student is doing behaviorally, record student level data, and transfer the data to a graph.

PROMPT   An action that occurs prior to a behavior to remind or help students to elicit the correct response (for example, hinting or suggesting) or demonstrate the appropriate behavior; also see cue.

PROPOFOL   An anesthetic drug believed to be a GABA mimic that reduces anxiety and tension, and promotes relaxation and sleep or loss of consciousness; provides loss of awareness and prevents memory formation for short diagnostic tests and surgical procedures, and supplements other types of general anesthetics; due to its white cloudy color, it is often referred to informally as "milk of amnesia."

PROSOCIAL BEHAVIOR   An act that demonstrates a sense of empathy, caring, and ethics.

PSYCHIATRIST   A physician who specializes in the prevention, diagnosis, and treatment of mental health disorders.

PSYCHOEDUCATIONAL TESTING The assessment process that aids in the identification of cognitive strengths and weaknesses of students and in the development of academic interventions; this assessment can also yield information to help confirm or disconfirm mental health diagnoses, such as developmental delay or attention disorders.

PSYCHOLOGIST   A person who studies the human mind and human behavior or who practices psychology clinically, applying knowledge of the science of psychology to the problems of the human condition.

PSYCHOSTIMULANTS   A class of drugs that induce temporary improvements in brain function, motor skills, attention, and have other temporary benefits to mood and behavioral control when used as prescribed.

PSYCHOTROPIC MEDICATION Any medication capable of affecting the mind, emotions, and behavior.

PUNISHMENT An undesirable consequence for an undesired behavior that decreases the probability that the behavior will occur again; this can include taking away a desired activity or object (negative punishment) or giving something undesirable (positive punishment).

REPLACEMENT BEHAVIOR OR SKILL A behavior intended to replace a target, or problem behavior.

RESOURCE CLASSROOM An educational setting in which a special education program can be delivered to a student with a disability who needs more specialized individual instruction in a small-group setting than can be delivered in a general education setting.

RESPONSE COST A negative consequence, similar to a "fine," often included in effective behavior management plans when combined with positive consequences; the loss of a reward or reinforcing activity that occurs when the student displays an inappropriate behavior.

RESPONSE TO INTERVENTION (RTI) A multitier prevention process that combines assessment and intervention to maximize student achievement and to decrease behavioral problems; a process of data-driven decisions to (1) identify students at risk, (2) monitor progress, and (3) select and implement interventions with research support and adjust the interventions as needed.

REUPTAKE INHIBITOR A molecule that partially blocks or inhibits the transportation of a neurotransmitter back into the secreting neuron (the presynaptic neuron) before it has the opportunity to act on the receiving neuron, and is also known as a transporter blocker; as medicines, these act to increase the amount of a specific neurotransmitter in the synaptic cleft, thereby enabling more neurotransmission to occur and thus enhancing communication in the brain.

REUPTAKE PUMP The large molecule that transports neurotransmitter molecules back into the axon terminals that released them.

SCHOLASTIC ASSESSMENT TEST (SAT) A globally recognized college admission test that lets students show colleges what they know and how well they can apply that knowledge; tests knowledge of reading, writing, and math; typically, students take this test during their junior or senior year of high school, and almost all colleges and universities use the test to make admission decisions.

SCHOOL CLIMATE The culture of a school including the values, safety, relationships, organization, norms, and goals of the school.

SCHOOLWIDE EXPECTATIONS (SWE) A list of broad, positively stated behaviors that are desired by all faculty and students and is aligned with the school's mission statement; these expectations are taught to all faculty, students, and families.

SEDENTARY ACTIVITY A medical term used to denote a type of lifestyle with no or irregular physical activity; a person who lives this type of lifestyle may be known as a "couch potato" (for example, sitting, reading, watching television, and computer use for much of the day with little or no vigorous physical exercise).

SELECTIVE SEROTONIN REUPTAKE INHIBITOR (SSRI)   The name given to a group of antidepressant medicines that block the reuptake of the neurotransmitter serotonin (see reuptake inhibitor).

SELF-ADVOCATE   The process of speaking or arguing on our own behalf for our needs and desires.

SELF-MANAGEMENT   The process of monitoring, recording, and reinforcing our own behavior.

SELF-REGULATION   The exercise of control over voluntary actions and behavior including impulse control, directing attention, delaying gratification, and raising and lowering levels of voluntary arousal and controlling mood; the executive system of the brain mediates our thoughts and actions and decides which should be expressed to the outside world.

SENSORY INTEGRATION DISORDER (SID)   A controversial neurological disability in which the brain is hypothesized to be unable to accurately process and integrate information coming in from the senses and believed by its advocates to produce learning and behavior problems.

SEROTONIN   A key neurotransmitter in the brain, thought of as a class of neuromodulator, that assists in regulating mood and affect in addition to its hormonal role in regulating several physiological actions such as blood pressure and vessel dilation. Serotonin deficiencies are commonly related to depression as well as several other mood disturbances and are treated with SSRIs (selective serotonin reuptake inhibitors) such as Prozac.

SHIFTING ATTENTION   The ability to transfer focus or concentration from one activity or object to another.

SINGLE PHOTON EMISSION COMPUTED TOMOGRA-PHY (SPECT)   A scan primarily used to view how blood flows through arteries and veins in the brain and, when applied to the brain, a method of neuroimaging used to observe brain metabolism in various regions.

SKILL DEFICIT   The lack of or below expected performance of a skill.

SMARTBOARD   An interactive whiteboard to help improve learning outcomes; a combination of a whiteboard and a computer.

SOCIAL REINFORCER   An expression of praise from another (a pat on the back, a smile, clapping, nodding, positive comments).

SOMATOSENSORY STRIP   The region of the brain immediately posterior to the central sulcus and at the beginning of the superior portion of the parietal lobe that receives all tactile sensory input from the body.

SPATIAL ABILITY   The ability to judge and manipulate space, distance, and objects mentally.

SPECIFIC LEARNING DISABILITY (SLD/LD)   A disability category used by the federal government to define a complex cluster of lifelong neurobiological disorders that can severely interfere with a person's ability to acquire competency in one or more of the following areas: oral language, reading, written language, mathematics, executive functioning, and socialization.

SPEECH OR LANGUAGE IMPAIRMENT   A communication disorder, such as stuttering, impaired articulation, a language impairment, or a voice impairment, that adversely affects a child's educational performance.

STIMULANT MEDICATION   A class of medications used most often to treat ADHD.

STRUCTURAL IMAGING   The construction of pictures of the physical structure of an organ in the body not readily visible with the naked eye and requiring specialized technology such as an x-ray, MRI, PET, and the like.

SUSPENSION   A temporary placement outside of school or a place that a student receives instruction that varies from the student's normal instructional environment for less than 10 days.

SYNAPTIC CLEFT   The microscopic space between two nerve cells across which neurotransmitters cross to communicate impulses from one nerve cell to another.

TANGIBLE REINFORCER   The physical item that increases or maintains behavior and thus is reinforcing (a new book or toy, a favorite food, and so forth).

TARGET BEHAVIOR   A specific behavior chosen for immediate change in order to increase (if a positive behavior) or decrease (if a negative behavior).

TEMPORAL LOBE   The right and left temporal lobes of the brain are part of the neocortex and are located just below the parietal lobes and behind the frontal lobes, beneath the central fissure. They are heavily involved in information processing and in establishing long-term memory, regulating attention, and in the comprehension of language and nonlanguage sounds, and important to the reading process as well.

THALAMUS A centrally located brain structure that controls the flow of information to the cortex.

TOKEN An item that can be exchanged for other reinforcers.

TOKEN ECONOMY SYSTEM A systematic program in which an individual receives a token when a desirable target behavior is demonstrated; tokens are exchanged at a later time for a primary reinforcer (usually student selected).

TRAUMATIC BRAIN INJURY (TBI) An acquired injury to the brain caused by an external physical force, resulting in total or partial functional disability or psychosocial impairment, or both.

U.S. OFFICE OF CIVIL RIGHTS (OCR) A federal agency designated to ensure equal access in many areas of life but especially in education and promotes educational excellence throughout the nation through vigorous enforcement of civil rights laws including the ADA, Section 504, and IDEIA.

VISUAL IMPAIRMENT A deficiency in vision that, even with correction, adversely affects the performance of any major life function; the term includes both partial sight and blindness.

WORKING MEMORY A system for temporarily storing and managing the information required to carry out complex cognitive tasks such as learning, reasoning, and comprehension.

YOUTH EXPERIENCING SUCCESS IN SCHOOLS (YESS) A collaborative school-based program designed to increase access to evidence-based support services for children who struggle with inattention and disruptive behavior problems.

ZERO REJECT   A rule of providing a free appropriate public education to all students with disabilities regardless of the severity of the disability and impairment; exclusion is not an option.

ZERO TOLERANCE POLICY   A policy of punishing any infraction of a rule, regardless of accidental mistakes, ignorance, or extenuating circumstances, and providing a common punishment regardless of circumstances or intent.

NOTES

CHAPTER ONE

1. Barkley, R. A., et al. (2002). International consensus statement on ADHD, January 2002, signed by over 70 leading scientists. *Clinical Child Family Psychology Review, 22,* 89–111.
2. Barkley, R. A. (2006). *Attention-deficit hyperactivity disorder: A handbook for diagnosis and treatment* (3rd ed.). New York: Guilford Press.
3. American Psychiatric Association. (2000). *Diagnostic and statistical manual of mental disorders: Text revisions* (4th ed.). Washington, DC: Author, 93.
4. American Psychiatric Association, *Diagnostic and statistical manual of mental disorder: Text revisions* (4th ed.).
5. *Journal of Attention Disorders,* May 2008, *11*(6).
6. American Psychiatric Association, *Diagnostic and statistical manual of mental disorders: Text revisions* (4th ed.).
7. *Journal of Attention Disorders.*
8. Barkley, R. A. (2006). *Attention-deficit hyperactivity disorder: A handbook for diagnosis and treatment* (3rd ed.). New York: Guilford Press.
9. American Psychiatric Association. (1980). *Diagnostic and statistical manual of mental disorders* (3rd ed.). Washington, DC: Author.
10. American Psychiatric Association. (1987). *Diagnostic and statistical manual of mental disorders* (3rd ed., Revised). Washington, DC: Author.

CHAPTER TWO

1. Harrison, J. R., Vannest, K. J., & Reynolds, C. R. (2010). Behaviors that discriminate ADHD: Primary symptoms, symptoms of comorbid conditions, or functional impairment? *Journal of Attention Disorders*, 15(2), 147–160.
2. Beck, G. (Interviewer) & Pennington, T. (Interviewee). (2008). *Glenn interviews Ty Pennington*. Retrieved from http://www.glennbeck .com/content/articles/article/196/12741/
3. Lewis, M. (n.d.). The Upside of ADHD: Enthusiasm, empathy and high energy among traits the disorder carries. *MSN*. Retrieved from http://health.msn.com/health-topics/adhd/articlepage.aspx?cp-documentid=100109339.
4. Beck & Pennington, *Glenn interviews Ty Pennington*.
5. Riccio, C. R., Reynolds, C. R., Lowe, P. A., & Moore, J. J. 2002 continuous performance test: A window on the neural substrates for attention? *Archives of Clinical Neuropsychology*, 17, 235–272.
6. American Psychiatric Association. (2000). *Diagnostic and statistical manual of mental disorders: Text revisions* (4th ed.). Washington DC: Author.
7. Ibid.
8. Angold, A., Costello, E. J., & Erkanli, A. (1999). Comorbidity. *Journal of Child Psychology and Psychiatry*, 40, 57–87.
9. *Individuals with Disabilities Education Improvement Act* (2004); *Individuals with Disabilities Education Act*, 20 U.S.C. §1401 et seq.
10. Harrison et al., Behaviors that discriminate ADHD.
11. Riccio, Reynolds, Lowe, & Moore, 2002.
12. Biederman J., et al. (1998). Does attention-deficit hyperactivity disorder impact the developmental course of drug and alcohol abuse and dependence? *Biological Psychiatry*, 44, 269–273.
13. Schubiner et al. (2002). Double-blind placebo-controlled trial of methylphenidate in the treatment of adult ADHD patients with comorbid cocaine dependence. *Experimental and Clinical Psychopharmacology*, 10, 286–294.
14. Biederman, Does attention-deficit hyperactivity disorder impact the developmental course of drug and alcohol abuse and dependence?
15. Ibid.
16. Reynolds, C. R., & Kamphaus, R. W. (2004). *Behavior assessment for children* (2nd ed.). Circle Pines, MN: AGS.

17. DuPaul, G. J., & Power, T. J. (2000). Educational interventions for students with attention-deficit disorders. In T. E. Brown (Ed.), *Attention-deficit disorders and comorbidities in children, adolescents, and adults* (pp. 607–635). Washington, DC: American Psychiatric Press.

18. DuPaul, G. J., et al. (2001). Self-report of ADHD symptoms in university students: Cross-gender and cross-national prevalence. *Journal of Learning Disabilities, 34*(4), 370–379.

19. Walcott, C. M., & Landau, S. (2004). The relationship between disinhibition and emotional regulation in boys with attention-deficit hyperactivity disorder. *Journal of Clinical Child and Adolescent Psychology, 33,* 772–782.

CHAPTER THREE

1. Kamphaus, R., & Reynolds, C. R. (2006). *Parenting relationship questionnaire.* Bloomington, MN: Pearson Assessments.

2. Dubey, D. R., O'Leary, S. G., & Kaufman, K. F. (1983). Training parents of hyperactive children in child management: A comparative outcome study. *Journal of Abnormal Child Psychology, 11,* 229–246.

   Gittelman, R., Abikoff, H., Pollack, E., Klein, D., Katz, S., & Mattes, J. (1980). A controlled trial of behavior modification and methylphenidate in hyperactive children. In C. Whalen & B. Henker (Eds.), *Hyperactive children: The social ecology of identification and treatment* (pp. 221–246). New York: Academic Press.

3. Barkley, R. A. (2000). *Taking charge of ADHD (Rev. ed.):The complete, authoritative guide for parents.* New York: Guilford Press.

4. MTA Cooperative Group (1999). A 14-month randomized clinical trial of treatment strategies for attention-deficit/hyperactivity disorder. *Archives of General Psychiatry, 56,* 1073–1086.

   MTA Cooperative Group (1999). Moderators & mediators of treatment response for children with attention-deficit/hyperactivity disorder: The multimodal treatment study of children with attention-deficit/hyperactivity disorder. *Archives of General Psychiatry, 56,* 1088–1096.

   Coie, J. D., Dodge, K. A., & Coppotelli, H. (1982). Dimension and types of social status: A cross-age perspective. *Development Psychology, 18,* 557–570.

5. Hoza, B. (2007). Peer functioning in children with ADHD, *Journal of Pediatric Psychology, 32*(6) 719–727.
   Coie, et al., Dimension and types of social status.
6. Coie, et al., Dimension and types of social status.
7. Chronis, A. M., Chacko, A., Fabiano, G. A., Wymbs, B. T., & Pelham, W. E. (2004). Enhancements to the standard behavioral parent training paradigm for families of children with ADHD: Review and future directions. *Clinical Child and Family Psychology Review, 7,* 1–27.
8. Alberts-Corush, J., Firestone, P., & Goodman, J. T. (1986). Attention and impulsivity characteristics of the biological and adoptive parents of hyperactive and normal control children. *American Journal of Orthopsychiatry, 56,* 413–423.
   Chronis, A. M., Lahey, B. B., Pelham, W. E., Kipp, H., Baumann, B., & Lee, S. S. (2003). Psychopathology and substance abuse in parents of young children with ADHD. *Journal of the American Academy of Child and Adolescent Psychiatry, 42,* 1424–1432.
9. Pelham, W. E., et al. (1997). Effects of deviant child behavior on parental distress and alcohol consumption in laboratory interactions. *Journal of Abnormal Child Psychology, 25,* 413–424.
   Pelham, W. E., Wheeler, T., & Chronis, A. (1998). Empirically supported psychosocial treatments for attention-deficit hyperactivity disorder. *Journal of Clinical Child Psychology, 27,* 190–205.
10. Lang, A. R., Pelham, W. E., & Atkeson, B. M. (1999). Effects of alcohol intoxication on parenting behavior in interactions with child confederates exhibiting normal or deviant behaviors. *Journal of Abnormal Child Psychology, 27,* 177–189.
11. Befera, M. S., & Barkley, R. A. (1985). Hyperactive and normal girls and boys: Mother-child interactions, parent psychiatric status and child psychopathology. *Journal of Child Psychology and Psychiatry, 26,* 439–452.
    Murphy, K. R., & Barkley, R. A. (1996). ADHD adults: Comorbidities and adaptive impairments. *Comprehensive Psychiatry, 37,* 393–401.
12. Pfiffner, L. J., McBurnett, K., & Rathouz, P. J. (2001). Father absence and familial antisocial characteristics. *Journal of Abnormal Child Psychology, 29*(5), 357–367.
13. Dubey et al., Training parents of hyperactive children in child management.
    Whalen & Henker, *Hyperactive children.*

Pisterman, S., McGrath, P., Firestone, P., & Goodman, J. T. (1989), Outcome of parent-mediated treatment of preschoolers with attention-deficit disorder with hyperactivity. *Journal of Consulting and Clinical Psychology, 57,* 636–643.

Pollard, S., Ward, E. M., & Barkley, R. A. (1983).The effects of parent training and Ritalin on the parent-child interactions of hyperactive boys. *Child & Family Behavior Therapy, 5,* 51–69.

14. Pisterman, S., et al. (1992). The effects of parent training on parenting stress and sense of competency. *Canadian Journal of Behavioral Science, 24,* 41–58.

Anastopouos, A. D., Shelton, T. L., Du Paul, G. J., & Guevremont, D. C. (1993). Parent training for attention-deficit hyperactivity disorder: Its impact on parent functioning. *Journal of Abnormal Child Psychology, 21,* 581–596.

15. Dadds, M. R., & Powell, M. B. (1991). The relationship of interparental conflict and global marital adjustment to aggression, anxiety and immaturity in aggressive and nonclinic children. *Journal of Abnormal Child Psychology, 19,* 553–567.

Johnston, C., & Behrenz, K. (1993). Childrearing discussions in families of nonproblem children and ADHD children with higher and lower levels of aggressive-defiant behavior. *Canadian Journal of School Psychology, 9,* 53–65.

Mahoney, A., Jouriles, E. N., & Scavone, J. (1997). Marital adjustment, marital discord over childrearing, and child behavior problems: Moderating effects of child age. *Journal of Clinical Child Psychology, 26,* 415–423.

16. Finchman, F. D., Grych, J. H., & Osborne, L. N. (1994). Does marital conflict cause child maladjustment: Directions and challenges for longitudinal research. *Journal of Family Psychology, 8,* 128–140.

Davies, P. T., & Cummings, E. M. (1994). Marital conflict and child adjustment: An emotional security hypothesis. *Psychological Bulletin, 116,* 387–411.

Webster-Stratton, C., & Hammond, M. (1999). Marital conflict management skills, parenting style, and early-onset conduct problems: Processes and pathways. *Journal of Child Psychology and Psychiatry, 40,* 917–927.

17. Dadds, M., Sanders, M., Behrens, B., & James, J. (1987). Marital discord and child behavior problems: A description of family

interactions during treatment. *Journal of Clinical Child Psychology, 16,* 192–203.

18. Abidin, R. (1986). *Parenting Stress Index* (2nd ed.). Charlottesville, VA: Pediatric Psychology Press.

19. Johnston, C., & Marsh, E. J. (1989). A measure of parenting satisfaction and efficacy. *Journal of Clinical Child Psychology, 18,* 167–175.

20. Locke, H. J., & Wallace, K. M. (1959). Short marital adjustment and prediction tests: Their reliability and validity. *Journal of Marriage and Family Living, 21,* 251–255.

21. Anastopouos, A. D., Shelton, T. L., Du Paul, G. J., & Guevremont, D. C. (1992). Test of ADHD Knowledge, Unpublished manuscript. As referenced in Anastopoulos, A. D., Shelton, T. DuPaul, G. J., & Guevremont, D. C. (1993). Parent training for Attention-Deficit Hyperactivity Disorder: Its impact on parent functioning. *Journal of Abnormal Child Psychology, 21,* 581–596.

22. Gibaud-Wallston, J., & Wandersman, L. P. (1978). Development and utility of the parenting sense of competency scale. Paper presented at the 86th Annual Convention of the American Psychological Association, Toronto, Ontario, Canada.

23. Kamphaus & Reynolds, *Parenting relationship questionnaire.*

24. Bor, W., Sanders, M. R., & Markie-Dadds, C. (2002). The effects of the triple P Positive Parenting program on preschool children with co-occurring disruptive behavior and attentional/hyperactive difficulties. *Journal of Abnormal Child Psychology, 30*(6), 571–578.

25. Campbell, S. B. (1995). Behavior problems in preschool children: A review of recent research. *Journal of Child Psychology and Psychiatry, 36,* 113–149.

26. Bor, et al., The effects of the triple P Positive Parenting program. Kazdin A. E. (2000). *Psychotherapy for children and adolescents: Directions for research and practice.* New York: Oxford University Press. Sanders, M. R., & Dadds, M. R. (1993). *Behavioral family intervention.* Needham Heights, MA: Allyn & Bacon.

27. Harpin, V. (2005). The effect of ADHD on the life of an individual, their family and community from preschool to adult life. *Archives of Diseases in Childhood, 90,* i2–i7.

28. Barkley, R. A. (1998). *Attention-deficit hyperactivity disorder. A handbook for diagnosis and treatment* (2nd ed.). New York: Guilford Press.

CHAPTER FOUR

1. Reynolds, C. R., & Kamphaus, R. W. (2004). *Behavior Assessment System for Children-Second Edition*. Bloomington, MN: Pearson Clinical Assessments.
2. Vannest, K., Reynolds, C. R., & Kamphaus, R. W. (2008). *The intervention guide for behavioral and emotional issues*. Bloomington, MN: NCS Pearson.
3. American Academy of Pediatrics: Committee on Quality Improvement, Subcommittee on Attention-Deficit/Hyperactivity Disorder. (2000). Clinical practice guideline: Diagnosis and evaluation of the child with Attention-Deficit/Hyperactivity Disorder. *Pediatrics*, *105*(5), 1158–1170.
4. Reynolds & Kamphaus, *Behavior Assessment System for Children*. Goldstein, S. (2011). Attention-deficit/hyperactivity disorder. In S. Goldstein & C. R. Reynolds (Eds.), *Handbook of neurodevelopmental and genetic disorders in children*. New York: Guilford Press.
5. Reynolds, C. R., & Kamphaus, R. W. (1994). *Behavior assessment system for children*. Circle Pines, MN: American Guidance Service.
6. Reynolds & Kamphaus, *Behavior Assessment System for Children*.
7. Goldstein, Attention-deficit/hyperactivity disorder.
8. Reynolds & Kamphaus, *Behavior Assessment System for Children*.
9. Achenbach, T., & Rescorla, L. (2001). *Manual for ASEBA school-age forms and profiles*. Burlington: University of Vermont.

CHAPTER FIVE

1. Kesler, S. R., Wilde, E., Bruno, J., & Bigler, E. (2011). *Neuroimaging and genetic disorders*. (pp. 58–83). In S. Goldstein & C. R. Reynolds (Eds.), *Handbook of neurodevelopmental and genetic disorders in children* (2nd edition). New York: Guilford Press.
2. Zametkin, A. J., & Rapoport, J. L. (1987). Neurobiology of attention-deficit disorder with hyperactivity: Where have we come in 50 years? *Journal of the American Academy of Child and Adolescent Psychiatry, 26*, 676–686.
3. Goldstein, S. (2011). Attention-deficit/hyperactivity disorder. (pp. 131–150). In S. Goldstein & C. R. Reynolds (Eds.), *Handbook of neurodevelopmental and genetic disorders in children* (2nd ed.). New York: Guilford Press.

4. Goldstein, Attention-deficit/hyperactivity disorder.
5. Ibid.
6. Ibid.
7. Ibid.

CHAPTER SIX

1. American Academy of Pediatrics. (2000). Clinical practice guidelines: Diagnosis and evaluation of the child with attention-deficit/hyperactivity disorder. *Pediatrics, 105,* 1158–1170.
2. Cala, S., Crismon, M. L., & Baumgartner J. (2003). A survey of herbal use in children with attention-deficit-hyperactivity disorder or depression. *Pharmacotherapy, 23*(2), 222–230.
3. Wolraich, M., Milich, R., Stumbo, P., & Schultz, F. (1985). The effects of sucrose ingestion on the behavior of hyperactive boys. *Pediatrics, 106*(4), 657–682.
   Wolraich, M., Wilson, D. B., & White, J. W. (1995). The effect of sugar on behavior or cognition in children: A meta-analysis. *Journal of the American Medical Association, 274*(20), 1617–1621.
4. Wolraich et al., The effect of sugar on behavior or cognition in children.
5. Wolraich et al., The effects of sucrose ingestion on the behavior of hyperactive boys.
6. Milich, R., Wolraich, M., & Lindgren, S. (1986). Sugar and hyperactivity: A critical review of empirical findings. *Clinical Psychology Review, 6,* 493–513.
7. Hoover, D.W., & Milich, R. (1994). Effects of sugar ingestion expectations on mother-child interactions. *Journal of Abnormal Child Psychology, 22*(4), 501–505.
8. Haslma, R. H., Dalby, J. T., Rademaker, A. W. (1984). Effects of megavitamin therapy on children with attention-deficit disorders. *Pediatrics, 74*(1), 103–111.
9. DuPaul, G. J., & Stoner, G. (2003). *ADHD in the schools: Assessment and intervention strategies* (2nd ed.). New York: Guilford Press.
10. Skinner, B. F. (1953). *Science and human behavior.* New York: MacMillan.
11. Safren, S. A. (2006). Cognitive-behavioral approaches to ADHD in adulthood. *Journal of Clinical Psychiatry, 67,* 46–50.

CHAPTER SEVEN

1. Johnson, C., & Mash, E. J. (2001). Families with children with attention-deficit hyperactivity disorder: Review and recommendations for future research. *Clinical Child and Family Psychology Review*, 4(3), 183–207.

2. Chronis, A. M., Chacko, A., Fabiano, G. A., Wymbs, B. T., & Pelham, W. E. (2004). Enhancements to the behavioral parent training paradigm for families of children with ADHD: Review and future directions. *Clinical Child and Family Psychology Review*, 7(1), 1–27.

3. Wood, A. C., & Neale, M. C. (2010). Twin studies and their implications for molecular genetic studies: Endophenotypes Integrate Quantitative and Molecular Genetics in ADHD Research. *Journal of the American Academy of Child and Adolescent Psychiatry*, 49(9), 874–883.

4. Loeber, R., & Stouthamer-Loeber, M. (1986). Family factors as correlates and predictors of juvenile conduct problems and delinquency. In M. H. Tonry & N. Morris (Eds.), *Crime and justice: An annual review of research*, Vol. 7 (pp. 29–149). Chicago: University of Chicago Press.

5. Amen, D. (2000). *New skills for frazzled parents: The instruction manual that should have come with your child.* Newport Beach, CA: MindWorks Press.

6. Ibid.

7. Vannest, K. J., Davis, J. L., Davis, C. R., Mason, B. A., & Burke, M. D. (2010). Effective intervention for behavior with a daily behavior report card: A meta-analysis. *School Psychology Review*, 39(4), 564–672.

8. Vannest, K., Burke. M., & Adiguzel, T. (2006). Electronic Daily Behavior Report Card (e-DBRC): A web-based system for progress monitoring (Beta Version) [Web-based application]. College Station: Texas A&M University.

9. Pfiffner, L. J., & O'Leary, S. G. (1987). The efficacy of all positive management as a function of prior use of negative consequences. *Journal of Applied Behavior Analysis*, 20(3), 265–271.

10. Fabiano et al. (2004). An evaluation of three time-out procedures for children with attention-deficit/hyperactivity disorder. *Behavior Therapy*, 35(3), 449–469.

11. Milich, R., & Landau, S. (1982). Socialization and peer relations in hyperactive children. In K. D. Gadow & I. Bialer (Eds.), *Advances*

in learning and behavior disabilities (Vol. 1, pp. 283–339). Greenwich, CT: JAI.

12. Bagwell, C. L., Molina, B. S. G., Pelham, W. E., & Hoza, B. (2001). Attention-deficit hyperactivity disorder and problems in peer relations: Predictions from childhood to adolescence. *Journal of the American Academy of Child & Adolescent Psychiatry, 40,* 1285–1292.

13. Lorch, E. P., Milich, R., Astrin, C. C., & Berthiaume, K. S. (2006). Cognitive engagement and story comprehension in typically developing children and children with ADHD from preschool through elementary school. *Developmental Psychology, 42,* 1206–1219.

14. Greene, R. W., et al. (2001). Social impairment in girls with ADHD: Patterns, gender comparisons, and correlates. *Journal of the American Academy of Child and Adolescent Psychiatry, 40,* 704–710.

15. Marshal, M. P., Molina, B. S. G., & Pelham, W. E. (2003). Childhood ADHD and adolescent substance use: An examination of deviant peer group affiliation as a risk factor. *Psychology of Addictive Behaviors, 17,* 293–302.

16. Brendgen, M., et al. (2001). Reactive and proactive aggression: Predictions to physical violence in different contexts and moderating effects of parental monitoring and caregiving behavior. *Journal of Abnormal Child Psychology, 29*(4), 293–304.

Choquet, M., et al. (2008). Perceived parenting styles and tobacco, alcohol and cannabis use among French adolescents: Gender and family structure differentials. *Alcohol and Alcoholism, 43*(1), 73–80.

Cota-Robles, S., & Gamble, W. (2006). Parent-adolescent processes and reduced risk for delinquency: The effect of gender for Mexican American adolescents. *Youth & Society, 37*(4), 375–392.

Li, X., Feigelman, S., & Stanton, B. (2000). Perceived parental monitoring and health risk behaviors among urban low-income African-American children and adolescents. *Journal of Adolescent Health, 27*(1), 43–48.

Markham, C. M., et al. (2010). Connectedness as a predictor of sexual and reproductive health outcomes for youth. *Journal of Adolescent Health, 46*(3 Suppl 1), S23–S41.

CHAPTER EIGHT

1. DuPaul, G. J., & Stoner, G. (2003). *ADHD in the schools: Assessment and intervention strategies* (2nd ed.). New York: Guilford Press.

2. Hoza, B., et al. (2004). Self-perceptions of competence in children with ADHD and comparison children. *Journal of Consulting and Clinical Psychology, 72*(3), 382–391.

   Owens, J. S., Goldfine, M. E., Evangelista, N. M., Hoza, B., & Kaiser, N. M. (2007). A critical review of self-perceptions and the positive illusory bias in children with ADHD. *Clinical Child and Family Psychology Review, 10*, 335–351.

3. Chickering, A. W., & Reisser, L. (1993). *Education and Identity* (2nd ed.). San Francisco: Jossey-Bass.

4. Vannest, K. J., Harrison, J. R., Davis, J. L., & Reynolds, C. R. (in press). Common problem behaviors of children and adolescents in general education classrooms in the United States, *Journal of Emotional and Behavioral Disorders*.

5. Kaufman, J. S., et al. (2010). Patterns in office discipline referral data by grade, race/ethnicity, and gender. *Journal of Positive Behavior Interventions, 12*(1), 44–54.

   Spaulding, S. A., et al. (2010). Schoolwide social-behavioral climate, student problem behavior, and related administrative decisions: Empirical patterns from 1,510 schools nationwide. *Journal of Positive Behavior Interventions, 12*(2), 69–85.

6. Vannest et al., Common problem behaviors of children and adolescents.

7. Kaufman et al., Patterns in office discipline referral data.

   Spaulding et al., Schoolwide social-behavioral climate, student problem behavior, and related administrative decisions.

8. Brand, E., & van der Vlugt, H. (1989). Activation: Base-level and responsivity. A search for subtypes of ADDH children by means of electrocardiac dermal and respiratory measures. In T. Sagvolden & T. Archer (Eds.), *Attention deficit disorder: Clinical and basic research* (pp. 137–150). Hillsdale, NJ: Erlbaum.

   Lee, D. L., & Zentall, S. S. (2002). The effects of visual stimulation on the mathematics performance of children with attention-deficit/hyperactivity disorder. *Behavior Disorders, 27*, 272–288.

9. Meyer, M. J., & Zentall, S. S. (1995). Influence of loud behavioral consequences on attention-deficit hyperactivity disorder. *Behavior Therapy, 26*, 351–370.

10. Fabiano, G. A., Pelham, W. E., Karmazin, K., Kreher, J., Panahon, C. J., & Carlson, C. (2008). A group contingency program to improve the behavior of elementary school students in a cafeteria. *Behavior Modification, 32*(1), 121–132.

11. Copeland, A. P., & Wisniewski, N. M. (1981). Learning disability and hyperactivity: Deficits in selective attention. *Journal of Experimental Child Psychology, 32,* 88–101.
    Zentall, S. S. (1989). Attentional cuing in spelling tasks for hyperactive and comparison regular classroom children. *Journal of Special Education, 23,* 83–93.

12. Evans, S. W., Pelham, W., & Grudberg, M. V. (1995). The efficacy of notetaking to improve behavior and comprehension of adolescents with attention-deficit hyperactivity disorder. *Exceptionality, 5,* 1–17.

13. Evans, S. W., Serpell, Z. N., Schultz, B. K., & Pastor, D. A. (2007). Cumulative benefits of secondary school-based treatment of students with Attention-Deficit Hyperactivity Disorder. *School Psychology Review, 36*(2), 256–273.

14. Ibid.

15. Gureasko-Moore, S., DuPaul, G. J., & White, G. P. (2006). The effects of self-management in general education classrooms on the organizational skills of adolescent with ADHD. *Behavior Modification, 30,* 159–183.

16. DuPaul, G. J., & Eckert, T. L. (1997). The effects of school-based interventions for Attention-Deficit Hyperactivity Disorder: A meta-analysis. *School Psychology Review, 26,* 5–27.
    Zentall, S. S. (1989). Attentional cuing in spelling tasks for hyperactive and comparison regular classroom children. *Journal of Special Education, 23,* 83–93.

17. Fabiano et al. (2010). Enhancing the effectiveness of special education programming for children with Attention-Deficit Hyperactivity Disorder using a daily report card. *School Psychology Review, 39*(2), 219–239.
    Owens, J. S., Murphy, C. E., Richerson, L., Girio, E. L., & Himawan, L. K. (2008). Science to practice in underserved communities: The effectiveness of school mental health programming. *Journal of Clinical Child and Adolescent Psychology, 37,* 434–447.

18. Fabiano et al., Enhancing the effectiveness of special education programming.
    Owens et al., Science to practice in underserved communities.
    Burke, M. D., & Vannest, K. J. (2008). Behavioral progress monitoring using the Electronic Daily Behavior Report Card (e-DBRC) system. *Preventing School Failure, 52*(30), 51–59.

19. Separate and combined effects of methylphenidate and behavior modification on boys with attention-deficit hyperactivity disorder in the classroom. *Journal of Consulting and Clinical Psychology, 61,* 506–515.

    Reitman, D., Hupp, S. D. A., O'Callahan, P. M., Gulley, V., & Northup, J. (2001). The influence of token economy and methylphenidate on attentive and disruptive behavior during sports with ADHD-diagnosed children. *Behavior Modification, 25,* 302–323.
20. Evans, S. W., Langberg, J., Raggi, V., Allen, J., & Buvinger, E. (2005). Development of a school-based treatment program for middle school youth with ADHD. *Journal of Attention Disorders, 9,* 343–353.

    Evans, S. W., Axelrod, J., & Langberg, J. (2004). Efficacy of a school-based treatment program for middle school youth with ADHD. *Behavior Modification, 28*(4), 528–547.
21. Owens, J. S., Richerson, L., Beilstein, E. A., Crane, A., Murphy, C. E., & Vancouver, J. B. (2005). School-based mental health programming for children with inattentive and disruptive behavior problems: First-year treatment outcome. *Journal of Attention Disorders 9,* 261–274.

    Owens et al., School-based mental health programming for children with inattentive and disruptive behavior problems.

CHAPTER NINE

1. *Section 504 of the 1973 Rehabilitation Act,* Pub. L. No. 93-112, 87 Stat. 394 (Sept. 26, 1973), codified at 29 U.S.C. § 701.
2. *The Americans with Disabilities Act (1990),* 104 Stat. 328, 42 U. S. C. § 12101.
3. *Individuals with Disabilities Education Improvement Act (2004); Individuals with Disabilities Education Improvement Act, 20* U.S.C. § 1404 (a) (C) (2004).
4. Thomas, H. (2009, April). Discovering Lightner Witmer: A forgotten hero of psychology. *Journal of Scientific Psychology,* 3–13.
5. Council for Exceptional Children (2008). *CEC 2008 Annual Report.* Retrieved from http://www.cec.sped.org/Content/NavigationMenu /AboutCEC/GovernanceLeadership/2008AnnualReport/2008CECA nnualReport.pdf.
6. Weber, M. (1992). *Special education law and litigation treatise.* Horsham, PA: LRP.

7. *Brown v. Board of Education*, 347 US 483 (1954).
8. Fuchs, L. S., & Fuchs, D. (2001). Principals for the prevention and intervention of mathematics difficulties. *Learning Disabilities Research & Practice*, 16, 85–95.

   Fuchs, D., Fuchs, L., Thompson, A., Al Otaiba, S., Yen, L., & Braun, M. (2000). *Peer-assisted learning strategies for kindergarten: A teacher's manual*. Retrieved from www.peerassistedlearning strategies.net.

   Phillips, S. E. (1994). High-stakes testing accommodations: Validity versus disabled rights. *Applied Measurement in Education*, 7(2), 93–120.
9. Zentall, S. S. (1989). Attentional cuing in spelling tasks for hyperactive and comparison regular classroom children. *Journal of Special Education*, 23, 83–93.
10. Pariseau, M., Fabiano, G., Massetti, G., Hart, K., & Pelham, W. (2010). Extended time on academic assignments: Does increased time lead to improved performance with Attention-Deficit/Hyperactivity Disorder? *School Psychology Review*, 25, 236–248.
11. *Individuals with Disabilities Education Improvement Act* (2004); *Individuals with Disabilities Education Improvement Act*, 20 U.S.C. § 1404 (a) (C) (2004).
12. Ibid.
13. Reid, R., Maag, J. W., Vasa, S. F., & Wright, G. (1994). Who are the children with ADHD: A school-based survey. *Journal of Special Education*, 28, 117–137.
14. Martin, J. E., Marshall, L. H., Maxson, L. M., & Jerman, P. L. (1996). *The self-directed IEP*. Longmont, CO: Sopris West.

CHAPTER TEN

1. ADA Amendments Act of 2008 (ADAAA), Pub. L. No. 110-325, 122 Stat. 3553 (2008).
2. Ibid.
3. Kessler, R. C. et al., (2005). The prevalence and effects of adult attention-deficit/hyperactivity disorder on work performance in a nationally representative sample of workers. *Journal of Occupational and Environmental Medicine*, 47(6), 565–572.
4. Ibid.

5. Murphy, K. (2005). Psychosocial treatments for ADHD in teens and adults: A practice-friendly review. *Journal of Clinical Psychology, 61*(5), 607–619.
6. Dulcan, M., et al. (1997). Practice parameters for the assessment and treatment of children, adolescents, and adults with attention-deficit/ hyperactivity disorder. *Journal of the American Academy of Child and Adolescent Psychiatry, 36,* 85–120.
7. Biederman, J., Mick, E., & Faraone, S. V. (2005). Age-dependent decline of symptoms of attention-deficit hyperactivity disorder: Impact of remission definition and symptom type. *American Journal of Psychiatry, 157*(5), 816–818.
8. American Psychiatric Association. (2000). *Diagnostic and statistical manual of mental disorders: Text revisions* (4th ed.). Washington, DC: Author.
9. Murphy, Psychosocial treatments for ADHD in teens and adults.
10. Patton, E. (2009). When diagnosis does not always mean disability: The challenge of employees with attention deficit disorder (ADHD). *Journal of Workplace Behavioral Health, 24,* 326–343.
11. Weiss, M. D., & Weiss, J. R. (2004). A guide to the treatment of adults with ADHD. *Journal of Clinical Psychiatry, 65,* 27–37 (supp 3).
12. Ibid.
13. Patton, E. (2009). When diagnosis does not always mean disability.
14. Ibid.
15. Coralyn Anne Brown, Appellee, v. Lester E. Cox Medical Centers, d/b/a Cox Medical Centers South, Appellant. No. 01-1096, 01-1434, 01-2150. April 17, 2002.
16. Jane A. Gagliardo; John Gagliardo v. Connaught Laboratories, Inc., Appellant No. 01-4045. November 22, 2002.
17. Colloquy, from Congressional Record, Sept. 17, 2008. Comments from Rep. Peter Stark (D, CA) to George Miller (D, CA), Chairman of the Education and Labor Committee. Retrieved August 7, 2011, from http://dyslexia.yale.edu/Policy_StarkComments.html.
18. ADA Amendments Act of 2008.
19. Buginas, J. (2010). Life with ADHD: A mixed blessing. *MENSA Research Journal, 41*(3), 5–7.
20. Ramsay, J. R. (2010). *Nonmedication treatments for adult ADHD: Evaluating impact on daily functioning and well-being.* Washington, DC: American Psychological Association.

21. Zwart, L. M., & Kallemeyn, L. M. (2001). Peer-based coaching for college students with ADHD and learning disabilities. *Journal of Postsecondary Education and Disability, 15*(1), 1–15.

22. Sireci, S. G., Scarpati, S. E., & Li, S. (2005). Test accommodations for students with disabilities: An analysis of the interaction hypothesis. *Review of Educational Research, 75*(4), 457–490.

23. Elliott, H. W., Arnold, E. M., Brenes, G. A., Silvia, L., & Rosenquist, P. B. (2007). Attention-deficit hyperactivity disorder accommodations for psychiatry residents. *Academic Psychiatry, 31*(4), 290–296.

24. Lee, K. S., Osborne, R. E., Hayes, K. A., & Simoes, R. A. (2008). The effects of pacing on the academic testing performance of college students with ADHD: A mixed methods study. *Journal of Educational Computing Research, 39*, 123–141.

25. American Psychiatric Association. (2000). *Diagnostic and statistical manual of mental disorders: Text revisions* (4th ed.). Washington, DC: Author.

26. Lindstrom, J., & Gregg, N. (2007). The role of extended time on the SAT reasoning test for students with disabilities. *Journal of Learning Disabilities Research and Practice, 22*, 85–95.

27. Ibid.

APPENDIX A

1. Sugai, G., et al. (2010). *School-wide positive behavior support: Implementers' blueprint and self-assessment.* Eugene: University of Oregon.

2. American Psychological Association Zero Tolerance Task Force (2008). Are zero tolerance policies effective in schools? An evidentiary review and recommendations. *American Psychologist, 63*(9), 852–862.

3. Ibid.

4. Sailor, W., Dunlap, G., Sugai, G., & Horner, R. (Eds.). (2010). *Handbook of positive behavior support.* New York: Springer.

5. Ibid.

6. McIntosh, K., Campbell, A. L., Carter, D. R., & Dickey, C. R. (2009). Differential effects of a tier two behavior intervention based on function of problem behavior. *Journal of Positive Behavior Interventions, 11*(2), 82–93.

Horner, R. et al. (2009). A randomized, wait-list controlled effectiveness trial assessing school-wide positive behavior support in elementary schools. *Journal of Positive Behavior Interventions, 11,* 133–145.

7. Vannest, K. J., Reynolds, C. R., & Kamphaus, R. W. (2008). *Intervention guide for behavioral and emotional issues.* Minneapolis, MN: Pearson Publishing.

8. Crone, D. A., Hawken, L., & Horner, L. (2010). *Responding to problem behavior in schools: The Behavior Education Program* (2nd ed.). New York: Guilford Press.

9. Kamphaus, R. W., & Reynolds, C. R. (2009). *Behavior Assessment System for Children—Second Edition (BASC-2): Progress Monitor (PM).* Bloomington, MN: Pearson.

10. Kamphaus, R. W., & Reynolds, C. R. (2007). *Behavior Assessment System for Children—Second Edition (BASC-2): Behavioral and Emotional Screening System (BESS).* Bloomington, MN: Pearson.

INDEX

Page references followed by *fig* indicate an illustrated figure; followed by *t* indicate a table; followed by *e* indicate an exhibit.

A

A-B-C problem behavior chain: antecedent, behavior, and consequence, 62*fig*; learning to identify and manipulate, 61–62; precorrection strategy using, 181–182*fig*

Academic functioning: functional impairment impacting, 45–46; LRE (least restrictive environment) to facilitate, 232, 255, 259, 261–263, 265; unique challenges facing college students, 273–274. *See also* Special education

Accommodations: Americans with Disabilities Act (ADA) mandated, 279*fig*–297; classroom, 289; college assignments, studying, and housing, 289–292; college exams, 292–293; college high stakes testing, 293–297; courseloads and registration, 288–289; evaluation reports for testing, 294–297; helpful and beneficial, 177*fig*, 243*fig*; high school testing, 244; higher education, 286–297; postsecondary education environments and possible, 288*e*; potential testing, 297; questions used to select, 279*fig*; rationale and purpose of requested, 296–297; requesting and selecting, 279–280; sample websites for ADA information, 294*e*; Section 504 Plan on, 238, 240–245; workplace, 280–286. *See also* Equal access protections